CONNECTIONS

ideas for writing

CONNECTIONS

ideas for writing

SHEILA HANCOCK
ED HANCOCK
University of Nevada
Western Nevada Community College

HARCOURT BRACE JOVANOVICH, INC.
New York   Chicago   San Francisco   Atlanta

COPYRIGHTS AND ACKNOWLEDGMENTS

For permission to use the selections reprinted in this book, the authors are grateful to the following publishers and copyright holders:

BEACON PRESS   For "Stranger in the Village" from *Notes of a Native Son* by James Baldwin. Copyright © 1955 by James Baldwin. Reprinted by permission of Beacon Press.

THE BODLEY HEAD   For an excerpt from *Ulysses* by James Joyce. Reprinted by permission of The Bodley Head.

CORINTH BOOKS INC.   For "Preface to a Twenty Volume Suicide Note" from *Preface to a Twenty Volume Suicide Note* by LeRoi Jones. Copyright © 1961 by LeRoi Jones. Reprinted by permission of Corinth Books.

J. M. DENT & SONS LTD.   For "The force that through the green fuse drives the flower" from *Collected Poems* by Dylan Thomas. Reprinted by permission of J. M. Dent & Sons Ltd. and the Trustees for the Copyrights of the late Dylan Thomas.

DISSENT   For "Who Killed King Kong?" by X. J. Kennedy from *Dissent*, Vol. 7, No. 2 (Spring 1960). Reprinted by permission of *Dissent*.

DOUBLEDAY & COMPANY, INC.   For "Once More, the Round," copyright © 1962 by Beatrice Roethke as Administratrix of the Estate of Theodore Roethke, from *The Collected Poems of Theodore Roethke*. Reprinted by permission of Doubleday & Company, Inc.

EDITIONS JANUS, INC.   For "Meetings with Remarkable Men" by George Gurdjieff. Reprinted by permission of Editions Janus, Inc.

FABER AND FABER LTD.   For "The Unknown Citizen" from *Collected Shorter Poems 1927–1957* by W. H. Auden; for "The Love Song of J. Alfred Prufrock" from *Collected Poems 1909–1962* by T. S. Eliot; and for "Bustopher Jones" from *Old Possum's Book of Practical Cats* by T. S. Eliot. All reprinted by permission of Faber and Faber Ltd.

FARRAR, STRAUS & GIROUX, INC.   For an excerpt from *The Pump House Gang* by Tom Wolfe, copyright © 1968 by Tom Wolfe, copyright © 1966 by the World Journal Tribune Corporation. Copyright © 1964, 1965, 1966 by the New York Herald Tribune, Inc. Reprinted with the permission of Farrar, Straus & Giroux, Inc.

HARCOURT BRACE JOVANOVICH, INC.   For "The Love Song of J. Alfred Prufrock" from *Collected Poems 1909–1962* by T. S. Eliot, copyright, 1936, by Harcourt Brace Jovanovich, Inc.;

Pages 310–12 constitute a continuation of the copyright page.

PREFACE

In this book, which gives suggestions for both prewriting and writing, we have used the theme of opposites to stimulate thought and discussion. Each chapter presents—in pictures and quotations, in poetry, short stories, and expository selections—a different pair of opposed but complementary concepts. Each chapter also offers related discussion of a rhetorical mode and a writing strategy, revision hints, a student paper for analysis, and exercises. The exercises are of two kinds—those aimed at helping students conceptualize feelings and those suggesting ways in which students may relate what they see and read to their own experience of life.

Exposed to ideas embodied in the work of eminent artists and writers, students may begin to think and write with a more mature voice about relatively sophisticated aspects of self that they never articulated or even realized. And, using their experience of life to understand some of its inescapable dichotomies, they may write about their world without being carried off to that strange country where, losing touch with themselves, they begin to speak in awkward and pretentious language.

So that students may find matter appropriate to their interests and competence, we have provided material that deals with concepts ranging from the relatively simple to the complex. We have also tried to provide the instructor with latitude to alter, supplement, or make substitutions in the text.

For their help in the making of this book we thank Gordon Fairburn, Philip Ressner, Geri Davis, Arlene Kosarin, and Judith Aspinwall—all of Harcourt Brace Jovanovich. We also thank Maxwell King Redican, Robert Gorrell, and Winthrop Piper for their interest in this project and Darleen Stringer for her help in preparing the manuscript.

SHEILA HANCOCK
ED HANCOCK

TO THE STUDENT

This book offers a variety of materials—visual elements, discussion ideas, writing techniques, writing hints, prewriting and writing exercises, and examples of good writing. You may use them in these ways:

Visual elements (photographs, paintings, graphics, signs, symbols)

These are intended not as illustrations but as means of initiating thought. Look carefully at each visual element and ask yourself what it says to you, what connection it has with your life.

> 66 Thinking emerges from Seeing. Brains . . . could not have developed without the senses—particularly eyes—capable of providing advance information. 99
>
> R. L. GREGORY

Discussion ideas (short quotations embodying ideas from historians, psychologists, economists, philosophers, sociologists, journalists, scientists, novelists)

Other people's ideas can help you find your own. As a shoemaker needs good leather to make good shoes, you need good ideas to make good writing. When reading a quotation ask yourself: What is my experience of the idea? Do I agree with the statement? What evidence can I give to support my position? Discussion of ideas with others in your class can help clarify your thinking and can serve as a prewriting exercise. Should someone take a view different from yours, ask yourself whether they have understood something you have not. Consider what you might say to win them over and keep them in mind when you write your paper.

> 66 . . . I am still convinced that general ideas are not only a resource but also a duty that cannot be dodged just because it is a dangerous one. 99
>
> WAYNE C. BOOTH

Writing techniques (ways of passing on material to the reader clearly and forcefully)

Each chapter describes a different technique. Selection of the appropriate technique (or techniques) is the first step after you have discovered something that matters to you, something that you want to say.

> 66 To write well an author must be in full possession of his subject. . . . To write well—it is at once to think deeply, to feel vividly, and to express clearly. 99
>
> GEORGE LOUIS LECLERC DE BUFFON

Writing hints (suggestions that, when applied, can make the difference between strong writing and weak writing)

These hints are not, like the techniques of Egyptian embalming, secret and mysterious, but are quite obvious once stated. Using them in the right way, however, requires practice. Study the hint as it is illustrated, discuss it, look for examples of it in the student papers given in each chapter, and note its use by professional writers. Practice it in your writing. Read through your rough draft to see if using one or more of the writing hints would make the writing clearer.

Prewriting and writing exercises (ways of discovering your experience, understanding it, and writing about it)

Use these exercises to practice the laws of writing.

> 66 *Interviewer:* Are there devices one can use in improving one's [writing]?
> *Capote:* Work is the only device I know of. Writing has laws of perspective, of light and shade, just as

painting does, or music. If you are born knowing them, fine. If not, learn them. 99

Read through each of your papers or read them to a friend or to the class. If your writing does not please you, rewrite.

66 It has to please me, and if it doesn't . . . the only thing to improve it is to work on it some more. 99

WILLIAM FAULKNER

Examples of good writing (student papers, professional essays, poems, short stories, and portions of novels)

66 One learns to write by reading good [writing]. 99

F. L. LUCAS

Note, with particular attention to the techniques and devices used, how successful student writers and professional writers have treated their experience of the same aspect of life you are writing about. Look in their writing for parallels to your experience.

66 In the great fiction [students] will learn what it means to look at something with full attention, what it means to see beneath the surface of society's platitudes. 99

WAYNE C. BOOTH

We give the essentials that we believe will help you put together a piece of writing that can stand by itself. Throughout we suggest how you may use your writing to get a clearer, fuller view of the world around and within you. Make the effort to get your words to match your thoughts, and writing will never be a meaningless exercise. It is a little like magic: you write, and you pull a part of your understanding of life by the ears out of a hat. Of course, it is not that easy. Writing is work.

CHECKLIST

Ask yourself the following questions:

BEFORE YOU WRITE
What is my subject?
What do I know about it?

Do I have enough material?
Do I have more that I can deal with in a short paper?

What do I want to say?
How do I want to affect my reader?

What writing techniques shall I use to achieve my purpose?
What organization, what shape, shall I give my material?

WHILE YOU WRITE
Am I discovering more about the material in the process of writing about it?
Am I incorporating any discoveries into what I write?

BEFORE YOU REWRITE
Do my words do what I want them to?
Have I developed my ideas?

Do the details conform to my general purpose or abstract idea?
Do they support the idea?

Have I used personal experience, description, definition, example, narrative, or some other method?
Would simile or metaphor clarify my meaning?

Are any sentence structures confused?
Are there clearer or simpler ways to say what I said?

CONTENTS

OPPOSITION AND BALANCE 1

YOUTH AND AGE

ANXIETY AND TRANQUILLITY

PRIMITIVISM AND CIVILIZATION

CONSCIOUSNESS AND REVERIE

FEMALE AND MALE

INDIVIDUAL AND MASS

KNOWN AND UNKNOWN

REFERENCE CHART

CONNECTIONS

ideas for writing

OPPOSITION

1 AND

BALANCE

UNIT 1

PREWRITING

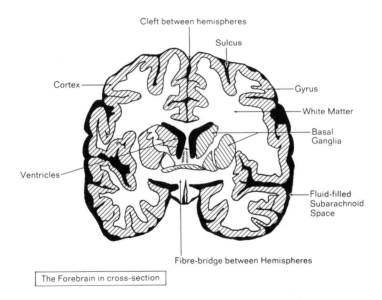

Cleft between hemispheres

Sulcus

Cortex

Gyrus

White Matter

Basal Ganglia

Ventricles

Fluid-filled Subarachnoid Space

Fibre-bridge between Hemispheres

The Forebrain in cross-section

The brain is divided into hemispheres, much like a walnut. Experiments in split-brain research reveal that the right hemisphere controls mainly spatial and visual abilities, the left, mainly speech and language. In this book we ask you to use both hemispheres of your brain; we ask you to see and think and to read and think.

We also ask you to discover your experience of a few inescapable features of life given in the form of opposing ideas. Face a pair of opposites and you will begin to look for your own place in relation to them. This first chapter introduces the ideas of opposition and balance. We think that as you work your way through this book you will find that you have used opposition and balance all your life and that the practice of thinking in this way comes quite naturally to you.

At some time you may have been told that you were a mass of contradictions. Human beings are often considered a bundle of opposing forces— probably because it is a human mind that does the considering. "There may be said to be two classes of people in the world," Robert Benchley observed, "those who constantly divide the people of the world into two classes, and those who do not." We see which of the two classes Benchley falls into. You probably find yourself making the same kinds of divisions.

Along with the impulse to split everything into two parts and pit one against the other, we have in us the desire for unity, the desire to harmonize opposites, to find our balance. We continually attempt to reconcile dualisms. We walk on two legs, a left and a right, and by means of this division keep ourselves balanced in an upright position.

DISCUSSION

Using the following pictures and quotations as a basis, start looking for both large and small oppositions in your life.

66 I have never learned to regard myself as "a member of society." For me there have always been two entities—myself and the world—and the normal relation between the two has been hostile. 99

GEORGE GISSING

Have you felt this way? In relation to what?

66 "I know what you're thinking about," said Tweedledum; "but it isn't so, no how."

"Contrariwise," continued Tweedledee, "if it was so, it might be; and if it were so, it would be; but as it isn't, it ain't." 99

LEWIS CARROLL

This is a basic pattern of most oppositions: Tweedledum tries to impose his will upon Tweedledee and Tweedledee tries to impose his on Tweedledum. Give an example of this kind of opposition in your life.

Day and night, light and dark grey fields rising to form birds, white and black birds, flying left and flying right into mirror landscapes—opposing formations set off in opposition.

M. C. Escher, *Day and Night.* Escher Foundation—Haags Gemeentemuseum—The Hague.

Look at the black birds. Now the white. Now try seeing <u>at one time</u> both black and white birds flying in both directions. Try describing what your mind must do to see both opposing formations at once.

66 "Corner" is found in a somewhat different form as a family game involving the children, where it resembles the "double bind." . . . Here the child is cornered, so that whatever he does is wrong. . . . The little boy or girl is urged to be more helpful around the house, but when he is, the parents find fault with what he does—a homely example of "damned if you do and damned if you don't." 99

ERIC BERNE

Find an example of a double bind in your life.

66 No two men . . . are likely to have the same ideas as to what they mean by such opposites as good and evil. Also there are no fixed criteria of judgment. According to one's experience of life, certain antagonisms seem fundamental, others of little moment. Moreover, they change. How I see opposites this year is not how I saw them last year, is not as I *may* see them tomorrow. 99

C. K. OGDEN

Give an example of a time when you took one position and later took another.

66 Yin is the principle of rest, the unchanging, the dark, the cool, the moist, the female, the side of the mountain in the shade. Yang is the principle of movement, of change, the bright, the hot, the dry, the male, the side of the mountain in the sun. Yin is continually going over to Yang, Yang continually going over to Yin. The two are combined . . . Yin has the seed of Yang in it, Yang has the seed of Yin; Yin is perpetually becoming Yang, Yang is perpetually becoming Yin; the whole harmoniously working together for the man, or the people, who can see the opposites in their deep consonance. 99

P. W. MARTIN

Name a few polarities that are important in your life, such as life/death, pleasure/pain, justice/injustice, growth/decay, studying/playing. Why are they important?

❝ It is one of the peculiar qualities of the human mind that, when confronted with a contradiction, it cannot remain passive. It is set in motion with the aim of resolving the contradiction. All human progress is due to this fact. ❞

ERIC FROMM

What human progress have you seen that has grown out of a desire to resolve a contradiction?

The Roman god, Janus, with one skull, one neck, two faces, and two pairs of eyes, looks both ways.

What meaning do you find in him?

CONNECTING EXERCISES

▶ A. Find an example of opposition or balance in some discipline you are now studying: biology, physics, mathematics, physical education, sociology, anthropology, history, political science.

▶ B. Look for an opposition in a TV show, advertisement, movie, or book you are reading.

▶ C. Every stick has two ends. Joy without sorrow doesn't exist any more than does a stick with one end. Find the two ends of an opposition that continually pops up in your thinking. Find something that pulls you two ways at one time, something that divides you. (The opposition you find need not be a major one in your life but may be as simple as the desire to go for a walk opposed by the feeling that you must study.) Or give opposing responses you have to two of your courses. The student paper at the end of this unit deals with the desire to stay in college and the desire to drop out.

Take notes on the opposition. Jot down in your writing notebook a few facts about the particular situation that has pulled you in opposing directions and any ideas you have about the facts. Give details.

After a day review your notes for points of interest to you. Focus on one central point and give more facts and ideas direc'y related to it.

UNIT GOOD WRITING 2

Most professional writers agree that *honesty* and *clarity* are essentials of good writing. This is not to say that they think a writer cannot invent a detail or two here or there or be sarcastic or ironic, but that a good writer does not fake. He knows his real feelings and attempts to communicate them clearly, either directly or ironically.

Write out of your own experience and understanding. Let what you write carry the stamp of your individual thoughts and emotions. One professional writer, F. L. Lucas, gives this advice: "First honesty. . . . As in life, one of the fundamentals is to find and be one's true self. . . . In writing in the long run, pretense does not work."

Get the material you write about out of your own living, reading, and understanding, and you will be started in the right direction. We live. That's basic.

66 We are liable to believe that the experience itself exists in letters and words. . . . The direct, genuine experience is basic, letters and verbal expressions of secondary importance. 99

MASTER RINZAI

The material for your composition lies close at hand within the compass of your experience. You see, hear, smell, taste, and touch. You listen, you read, you imagine. You receive and develop impressions of all kinds. The activity of uncovering this material is more like digging into the ground you stand on than flying off to a distant land. Start with this material, tell it as you see it, and you will begin to write honestly.

Find words that accurately express your thoughts and observations. Critic Arthur Quiller-Couch said: "The first aim of speech is to be understood. The more clearly you write the more easily and surely you will be understood [and] the more clearly you will understand yourself."

Without clarity you will fail to communicate in the way you want to. And without communication there can be no understanding. Without both communication and understanding we would all be something like the figures in this picture:

Jean-Michel Folon, *Grand Jeu.*

Good writing, then, is based on clear communication of experience.

Though you have been writing for years, you have probably come to realize that writing doesn't come as naturally to you as flying does to a bird—especially honest, clear writing. In the following pages of this book we suggest a number of techniques that will help you put together a successful piece of writing. One of these techniques is to become aware of jargon and to free yourself of it. Jargon is both dishonest and unclear. Like a mold it will arise in your writing if you don't take care to keep it out.

WRITING HINT:
FREE YOURSELF FROM JARGON

Clear and honest writing is free of jargon, a common kind of writing masquerading as sincere prose. Whenever a writer uses jargon, his personal thought and individual emotion disappear in a fog of borrowed feeling and artificial language. Ready-made phrases, vague strings of words, commonly accepted notions are pasted up in imitation of real thought and feeling.

You can find jargon almost everywhere. Scratch it whenever you find it in *your* writing.

"Modern writing at its worst does not consist in picking out words for the sake of their meaning and inventing images in order to make the meaning clearer. It consists in gumming together long strips of words which have already been set in order by someone else, and making the results presentable by sheer humbug. The attraction of this way of writing is that it is easy. It is easier—even quicker, once you have the habit—to say *In my opinion it is not an unjustifiable assumption that* than to say *I think.* **"**

GEORGE ORWELL

"So long as you prefer abstract words, which express other men's summarised concepts of things, to concrete ones which lie as near as can be reached to things themselves and are the firsthand material for your thoughts, you will remain, at the best, writers at second-hand. If your language be jargon, your intellect, if not your whole character, will almost certainly correspond. Where your mind should go straight, it will dodge: the difficulties it should approach with a fair front and grip with a firm hand it will be seeking to evade or circumvent.

ARTHUR QUILLER-COUCH

Make a habit of reading aloud the papers you write. Ask yourself: Does this sound right? How will it affect my reader? Is any of it artificial or unclear? What did I want to say? Do these words say it? Is this what I actually feel and think? Can I make what I have said clearer? Where was I emotionally and mentally when I wrote this? What kind of a person wrote this?

▶ A. Compare the quotes to the left with those to the right. Indicate which you prefer and why.

In proportion as the manners, customs, and amusements of a nation are cruel and barbarous, the regulations of their penal code will be severe.

In proportion as men delight in battles, bull-fights, and combats of gladiators, will they punish by hanging, burning, and the rack.

Objective consideration of contemporary phenomena compels the conclusion that success or failure in competitive activities exhibits no tendency to be commensurate with innate capacity, but that a considerable element of the unpredictable must inevitably be taken into account.

I returned, and saw under the sun, that the race is not to the swift, nor the battle to the strong, neither yet riches to men of understanding, nor yet favor to men of skill; but time and chance happeneth to them all.

To be, or not to be; that is the question:
Whether 'tis nobler in the mind to suffer
The slings and arrows of outrageous
    fortune,
Or to take arms against a sea of troubles,
And by opposing end them? To die:
    to sleep;
No more; and by a sleep to say we end
The heart-ache and the thousand natural
    shocks
That flesh is heir to, 'tis a consummation
Devoutly to be wish'd.

To be or the contrary? Whether the former or the latter be preferable would seem to admit of some difference of opinion; the answer in the present case being of an affirmative or of a negative character according as to whether one elects on the one hand to mentally suffer the disfavour of fortune, albeit in an extreme degree, or on the other to boldly envisage adverse conditions in the prospect of eventually bringing them to a conclusion. The condition of sleep is similar to, if not indistinguishable from that of death; and with the addition of finality the former might be considered identical with the latter: so that in this connection it might be argued with regard to sleep that, could the addition be effected, a termination would be put to the endurance of a multiplicity of inconveniences, not to mention a number of down-right evils incidental to our fallen humanity, and thus a consummation achieved of a most gratifying nature.

12

▶ B. Attempt to understand what the authors of the following two pieces of jargon are saying. Then rewrite their ideas (if you can uncover them) in clear, honest language.

• The typical, dominant speech-mode of the middle class is one where speech becomes an object of perceptual activity, and a "theoretical attitude" is developed towards the structural possibilities of sentence organization. This speech-mode facilitates the verbal elaboration of subjective intent, sensitivity to the implications of separateness and difference, and point to the possibilities inherent in a complex conceptual hierarchy for the organization of experience. [The lower working class] are limited to a form of language use which, though allowing for a vast range of possibilities, provides a speech form which discourages the speaker from verbally elaborating subjective intent, and progressively orients the user to descriptive rather than abstract concepts.

• The home then is the specific zone of functional potency that grows about a live parenthood; a zone at the periphery of which is an active interfacial membrane or surface furthering exchange—from within outwards and from without inwards—a mutualising membrane between the family and the society in which it lives.

Examples from H. W. FOWLER

▶ C. Following are examples of inflated prose along with simplifications of their meaning. To what extent do you think the simplifications clarify or distort meaning?

He shows a real ability in plastic conception.

He can make a snake out of clay.

He does seem to have developed late in large-muscle control.

He falls on his head frequently.

A period of unfavorable weather set in.

It rained every day for a week.

WRITING EXERCISES

▶ A. About the person in the first picture (facing page) we know nothing. The other picture is of Marilyn Monroe, who, during these last few years, has become a symbol for one kind of enslavement of the individual by society.

Look at the two pictures closely. Then dig into yourself and discover what one aspect of one or both of these pictures leaves the deepest impression on you. Write a couple of paragraphs about your impression. Give the details that caused the impression.

Following is a student theme that grew out of this exercise. Do you think it is honest and clear?

Physically the old lady and Marilyn Monroe are opposites. The old lady with her unstyled, unkempt hair and
wrinkled skin presses her lips together looking at her
photographer as if she hopes that he will soon be done
with this picture taking. She looks like she always
looks and probably wonders why anyone would want to take
a picture of her. Her eyes are clear, defiant, determined, strong. Marilyn Monroe poses for her photographer
knowing what is expected of her. Her hair is styled in
typical '50's fashion, her make-up including beauty
mark are used to make her the desirable beauty queen she
was. Her eyes seem a little anonymous as if they don't
belong to anyone.

What difference did their looks make in their lives?
Everyone knows that Marilyn Monroe's life was not
happy, that she committed suicide. She avoided becoming
old and wrinkled. The old woman avoided the pain of
being America's famous sex symbol. Her life may not
have been happy but she probably did her duty and lived
to an old age. She was most likely somebody's wife
and mother and grandmother. She looks like she could
make a good pie. Marilyn Monroe, we are told, longed
for the kind of life the old lady may have had—husband,
children, work. It's doubtful that the old lady
would have, if she could have, traded places with
Marilyn.

But one thing is similar about these women's lives—
both the old lady and Marilyn Monroe fell into their
lives and let society, not themselves, decide what their
roles would be. The old lady looks as if she spent
her life doing all those things women traditionally do
whether she liked them or not. She seems to have forgotten herself, beauty, adventure, fun. Marilyn Monroe
spent her life being all those things men are supposed
to want. She let society trap her into becoming those
things instead of the person she wanted to be.

Neither of these women look as if they lived
balanced lives.

Susan Wolfe

▶ B. If you have notes on an opposition that interests you, organize them and use them to write the first draft of a paper.

Or select one of the oppositions suggested below, think of an experience in your life connected with it, and write a short paper about it. You may take one side or the other or both. You need not set out formal similarities and differences between the two. But try to say what you have to say as "clearly and purely and simply" as you can.

then/now—the economic situation in America ten years ago, the economic situation in America today

here/there—where you were an hour, a day, a year ago and where you are now

like/dislike—two activities, two people, or two kinds of work

for/against—two ideas, two political issues

advantages/disadvantages—staying in college, dropping out

And so on.

Here is one student theme that grew out of this exercise:

TRAPPED AND TRAPPED

One hot afternoon during last semester I was having a
hard time concentrating on what my history professor was
saying. My eyes drooped uncontrollably. It seemed to
me that I had been sitting in classrooms all my life. I
looked around at the other students in the class. They
looked bored. The professor even looked bored.
     All but one of the windows in the room was closed.
I got up and pushed open another window at the rear of
the room. I leaned out and let the cool air revive me.
     A sudden realization startled me out of my grog-
giness. I did not want to be here. I did not want to
hear any more lectures. I did not want to become an
engineer. I wanted out. There was nothing, no desire
or need, nothing which held me back from dropping
the whole lot and walking off. I turned around and
walked out of the room leaving my expensive books and
notes and the lecturer who was talking about the Battle
Born State.
     Water seeks its own level, it is said, and I
promptly found mine. For a few days I passed time with
people who "hang around." It was exhilarating. We
were always going somewhere, but beyond that somewhere

lay I didn't know what. Usually it was a park concert, somebody's pad, a bar, or an aimless car ride. I never spent more than one or two days with the same person, nor more than a week in the same town.

My vagabond meanderings took me as far as Nogales, Mexico. I had hitched a ride with a couple of Mississippians who wanted to spend everything they had in Mexican bars. They were buying the rounds and since my money had run out that morning, our relationship had changed. They didn't include me in the conversation any more. I listened. A map of Northern Mexico lay before us on the table, and they were trying to figure out where they were going. Neither of them were very clear about their directions. They weren't even sure whether Nogales was on the border or not.

I didn't want to listen to what they were saying any more. They were getting ready to bid me adios. Meanwhile I could think of nothing but the Nogales sun frying everything outside in the street. The thought of all that sun on top of the tequila made me feel like I was caught in a trap.

I got up and walked to the door. The barkeeper bid me farewell in Spanish, and someone else made a remark which made everyone in the bar laugh.

The sun hit my eyes so I sat down, leaning against a wall. I sat there for a long time. Eventually it cooled down. I remembered leaning out the window in the history class. That moment had begun a whole series of experiences which had somehow ended here on this very spot at this moment.

I felt that I had escaped one trap only to get caught in another. "From the classroom to the street," I thought. If drifting was my way to be free then I must continue drifting, but I did not want to go on. Old and familiar desires came rushing back—food, clothing, money. In the midst of my floundering a string of words went through my mind: "I wonder if my notebooks were turned in?"

The University seemed to possess a kind of magnetism to it. I went along the streets to the border gate, and almost effortlessly hitched back home.

From the classroom window the world outside had looked like less of a trap than I found it to be.

Frank Johnson

UNIT 3

SELECTIONS

You can't write about people out of textbooks, and you can't use a jargon. You have to speak clearly and simply and purely in a language that a six-year-old child can understand; and yet have the meanings and the overtones of language, and the implications, that appeal to the highest intelligence—that is, the highest intelligence that one is able to reach.

KATHERINE ANNE PORTER

(A short story of Katherine Anne Porter's is included in Unit 12.)

One wants to get something off one's chest. One doesn't know quite what it is that one wants to get off the chest until one's got it off.

T. S. ELIOT

(There are poems by T. S. Eliot in Units 9 and 12.)

If the emotion is strong enough, the words are unambiguous. Someone asked Robert Frost (is this right?) if he was selective. He said, "Call it passionate preference." Must a man be good to write good poems? . . . rectitude has a ring that is implicative I would say. And with no integrity, a man is not likely to write the kind of book I read.

MARIANNE MOORE

(A poem by Marianne Moore follows in this unit.)

But finally for me the difficulty is to remain in touch with the private life. The private life, his own and that of others, is the writer's subject—his key and ours to his achievement. . . . The writer trapped among a speechless people is in danger of becoming speechless himself. For then he has no mirror, no corroborations of his essential reality; and this means that he has no grasp of the reality of the people around him. What the times demand, and in an unprecedented fashion, is that one be—not seem—outrageous, independent, anarchical. That one be thoroughly disciplined—as a means of being spontaneous. That one resist at whatever cost the fearful pressures placed on one to lie about one's own experience.

JAMES BALDWIN

(James Baldwin's essay "Stranger in the Village" is in Unit 21.)

I could remember anything,
whether it happened or not.

MARK TWAIN

(A portion of Mark Twain's novel *Roughing It* appears in this unit.)

At night I practiced writing and studied Joyce,
Dostoevski, Stein, and Hemingway. Especially
Hemingway; I read him to learn his sentence
structure and how to organize a story. I guess
many young writers were doing this, but I also
used his description of hunting when I went
into the fields the next day. I had been hunting
since I was eleven, but no one had broken down
the process of wing-shooting for me, and it was
from reading Hemingway that I learned to lead
a bird. When he describes something in print,
believe him; believe him even when he describes the process of art in terms of baseball or
boxing; he's been there.

RALPH ELLISON

(A portion of Ralph Ellison's *Invisible Man* is in Unit 9.)

from An Ethic of Clarity

DONALD HALL

In the expression "good writing" or "good style," the word "good" has usually meant "beautiful" or "proficient"—like a good Rembrandt or a good kind of soap. In our time it has come to mean honest as opposed to fake. Bad writing happens when the writer lies to himself, to others, or to both. Probably, it is usually necessary to lie to oneself in order to lie to others; advertising men use the products they praise. Bad writing may be proficient; it may persuade us to buy a poor car or vote for an imbecile, but it is bad because it is tricky, false in its enthusiasm, and falsely motivated. It appeals to a part of us that wants to deceive itself. I am encouraged to tell myself that I am enjoying my favorite beverage when, really, I am only getting sloshed.

"If a man writes clearly enough any one can see if he fakes," says Hemingway. Orwell reverses the terms: "The great enemy of clear language is insincerity. . . . When there is a gap between one's real and one's declared aims, one turns as it were instinctively to long words and exhausted idioms, like a cuttlefish squirting out ink." Pound talks about the "gap between one's real and one's declared aims" as the distance between expression and meaning. In "The New Vocabularianism," Thurber speaks of the political use of clichés to hide a "menacing Alice in Wonderland meaninglessness."

As Robert Graves says, "The writing of good English is thus a moral matter." And the morality is a morality of truth-telling. Herbert Read declares that "the only thing that is indispensible for the possession of a good style is personal sincerity." We can agree, but we must add that personal sincerity is not always an easy matter, nor is it always available to the will. Real aims, we must understand, are not necessarily conscious ones. The worst liars in the world may consider themselves sincere. Analysis of one's own style, in fact, can be a test of one's own feelings. And certainly, many habits of bad style are bad habits of thinking as well as of feeling.

There are examples of the modern attitude toward style in older writers. Jonathan Swift, maybe the best prose writer of the language, sounds like George Orwell when he writes:

> . . . Our English tongue is too little cultivated in this kingdom, yet the faults are nine in ten owing to affectation, not to want of understanding. When a man's thoughts are clear, the properest words will generally offer themselves first, and his own judgment will direct him in what order to place them, so as they may be best understood.

Here Swift appears tautological; clear thoughts only *exist* when they are embodied in clear words. But he goes on: "When men err against this method, it is usually on purpose," purposes, we may add, that we often disguise from ourselves.

Aristotle in his *Rhetoric* makes a case for plainness and truth-telling. "The right thing in speaking really is that we should be satisfied not to annoy our hearers, without trying to delight them: we ought in fairness to fight our case with no help beyond the bare facts." And he anticipates the modern stylist's avoidance of unusual words: "Clearness is secured by using the words . . . that are current and ordinary." Cicero attacks the Sophists because they are "on the lookout for ideas that are neatly put rather than reasonable. . . ."

Yet, when we quote Cicero, the master rhetorician, on behalf of honest clarity, we must remember that the ancients did not really think of style as we do. Style until recent times has been a division of rhetoric. To learn style, one learned the types of figures of speech and the appropriateness of each to different levels of discourse—high, middle, and low. The study of style was complex, but it was technical rather than moral. For some writers, Latin was high and the vernacular low, but in the Renaissance the vernacular took in all levels. It is only in modern times that style divorces itself from rhetoric—rhetoric belongs to the enemy, to the advertisers and the propagandists—and becomes a matter of ethics and introspection.

Ezra Pound, like some French writers before him, makes the writer's function social. "Good writers are those who keep the language efficient. That is to say, keep it accurate, keep it clear." We must ask why this idea of the function of good style is so predominantly a modern phenomenon. Pound elsewhere speaks of the "assault," by which he means the attack upon our ears and eyes of words used dishonestly to persuade us, to convince us to buy or to believe. Never before have men been exposed to so many words—written words, from newspapers and billboards and paperbacks and flashing signs and the sides of buses, and spoken words, from radio and television and loudspeakers. Everyone who wishes to keep his mind clear and his feelings his own must make an effort to brush away these words like cobwebs from the face. The assault of the phoney is a result of technology combined with a morality that excuses any technique which is useful for persuasion. The persuasion is for purposes of making money, as in advertising, or winning power, as in war propaganda and the slogans of politicians. Politicians have always had slogans, but they never before had the means to spread their words so widely. The cold war of rhetoric between communism and capitalism has killed no soldiers, but the air is full of the small corpses of words that were once alive: "democracy," "freedom," "liberation."

It is because of this assault, primarily, that writers have become increasingly concerned with the honesty of their style to the exclusion of other qualities. Concentration on honesty is the only way to exclude the sounds of the bad style that assault us all. These writers are concerned finally *to be honest about what they see, feel, and know.* For some of them, like William Carlos Williams, we can only trust the evidence of our eyes and ears, our real knowledge of our immediate environment.

Our reading of good writers and our attempt to write like them can help to guard us against the dulling onslaught. But we can only do this if we are able to look into ourselves with some honesty. An ethic of clarity demands intelligence and self-knowledge. Really, the ethic is not only a defense against the assault (nothing good is ever merely defensive), but is a development of the same inwardness that is reflected in psychoanalysis. One cannot, after all, examine one's motives and feelings carefully if one takes a naïve view that the appearance of a feeling is the reality of that feeling. . . .

The style is the man. Again and again, the modern stylists repeat this idea. By a man's metaphors you shall know him. When a commencement orator advises students to enrich themselves culturally, chances are that he is more interested in money than in poetry. When a university president says that his institution turned out 1,432 B.A.s last year, he tells us that he thinks he is running General Motors. The style is the man. Remy de Gourmont used the analogy that the bird's song is conditioned by the shape of the beak. And Paul Valery said, ". . . what makes the style is not merely the mind applied to a particular action; it is the whole of a living system extended, imprinted and recognizable in expression." These statements are fine, but they sound too deterministic, as if one expresses an unalterable self and can no more change the style of that self than a bird can change the shape of its beak. Man is a kind of bird that can change his beak.

A writer of bad prose, to become a writer of good prose, must alter his character. He does not have to become good in terms of conventional morality, but he must become honest in the expression of himself, which means that he must know himself. There must be no gap between expression and meaning, between real and declared aims. For some people, some of the time, this simply means *not* telling deliberate lies. For most people, it means learning when they are lying and when they are not. It means learning the real names of their feelings. It means not saying or thinking, "I didn't *mean* to hurt your feelings," when there really existed a desire to hurt. It means not saying "luncheon" or "home" for the purpose of appearing upper-class or well-educated. It means not using the passive mood to attribute to no one in particular opinions that one is unwilling to call one's own. It means not disguising banal thinking by polysyllabic writing or the lack of feeling by clichés that purport to display feeling.

The style is the man, and the man can change himself by changing his style. Prose style is the way you think and the way you understand what you feel. Frequently, we feel for one another a mixture of strong love and strong hate; if we call it love and disguise the hate to ourselves by sentimentalizing over love, we are thinking and feeling badly. Style is ethics and psychology; clarity is a psychological sort of ethic, since it involves not general moral laws, but truth to the individual self. The scrutiny of style is a moral and psychological study. . . . Editing our own writing, or going over in memory our own spoken words, or even inwardly examining our thought, we can ask *why* we resorted to the passive in this case or to clichés in that. When the smoke of bad prose fills the air, something is always on fire somewhere. If the style is really the man, the style becomes an instrument for discovering and changing the man. Language is expression of self, but language is also the instrument by which to know that self.

According to this essay, what is "good writing?"

How does Hall define "style"? "clarity"?

Hall suggests that we edit our writing and examine our thoughts. What do you see as the relationship between thoughts and words?

Poetry

MARIANNE MOORE

I, too, dislike it; there are things that are important beyond all this fiddle.
   Reading it, however, with a perfect contempt for it, one discovers in
   it after all, a place for the genuine.
      Hands that can grasp, eyes
      that can dilate, hair that can rise
         if it must, these things are important not because a

high-sounding interpretation can be put upon them but because they are
    useful. When they become so derivative as to become unintelligible,
    the same thing may be said for all of us, that we
      do not admire what
      we cannot understand: the bat
         holding on upside down or in quest of something to

eat, elephants pushing, a wild horse taking a roll, a tireless wolf under
    a tree, the immovable critic twitching his skin like a horse that feels a
       flea, the base-
   ball fan, the statistician—
     nor is it valid
       to discriminate against 'business documents and

school-books'; all these phenomena are important. One must make a dis-
     tinction however: when dragged into prominence by half poets, the
     result is not poetry,
nor til the poets among us can be
     'literalists of
     the imagination'—above
       insolence and triviality and can present

for inspection, 'imaginary gardens with real toads in them', shall we have
  it. In the meantime, if you demand on the one hand,
    the raw material of poetry in
      all its rawness and
      that which is on the other hand
        genuine, you are interested in poetry.

What are some of the images you see in your mind's eye as you read this poem? How clear are they?

Why must poetry "present for inspection imaginary gardens with real toads in them"? What does the poet mean by this?

What argument does the speaker make in support of poetry?

from **Roughing It**

MARK TWAIN

Somebody has said that in order to know a community, one must observe the style of its funerals and know what manner of men they bury with most ceremony. I cannot say which class we buried with most eclat in our "flush times," the distinguished public benefactor or the distinguished rough—possibly the two chief grades or grand divisions of society honored their illustrious dead about equally; and hence, no doubt the philosopher I have quoted from would have needed to see two representative funerals in Virginia before forming his estimate of the people.

    There was a grand time over Buck Fanshaw when he died. He was a representative citizen. He had "killed his man"—not in his own quarrel, it is true, but in defence of a stranger unfairly beset by numbers. He had kept a sumptuous saloon. He had been the proprietor of a dashing help-meet whom he could have discarded without the formality of a divorce. He had held a high position in the fire department and been a very Warwick in politics. When he died there was great lamentation throughout the town, but especially in the vast bottom-stratum of society.

    On the inquest it was shown that Buck Fanshaw, in the delirium of a wasting typhoid fever, had taken arsenic, shot himself through the body, cut his throat, and jumped out of a four-story window and broken his neck—and after due deliberation, the jury, sad and tearful, but with intelligence unblinded by its sorrow, brought in a verdict of death "by the visitation of God." What could the world do without juries?

Prodigious preparations were made for the funeral. All the vehicles in town were hired, all the saloons put in mourning, all the municipal and fire-company flags hung at half-mast, and all the firemen ordered to muster in uniform and bring their machines duly draped in black. Now—let us remark in parenthesis—as all the peoples of the earth had representative adventurers in the Silverland, and as each adventurer had brought the slang of his nation or his locality with him, the combination made the slang of Nevada the richest and the most infinitely varied and copious that had ever existed anywhere in the world, perhaps, except in the mines of California in the "early days." Slang was the language of Nevada. It was hard to preach a sermon without it, and be understood. Such phrases as "You bet!" "Oh, no, I reckon not!" "No Irish need apply," and a hundred others, became so common as to fall from the lips of a speaker unconsciously—and very often when they did not touch the subject under discussion and consequently failed to mean anything.

After Buck Fanshaw's inquest, a meeting of the short-haired brotherhood was held, for nothing can be done on the Pacific coast without a public meeting and an expression of sentiment. Regretful resolutions were passed and various committees appointed; among others, a committee of one was deputed to call on the minister, a fragile, gentle, spirituel new fledgling from an Eastern theological seminary, and as yet unacquainted with the ways of the mines. The committeeman, "Scotty" Briggs, made his visit; and in after days it was worth something to hear the minister tell about it. Scotty was a stalwart rough, whose customary suit, when on weighty official business, like committee work, was a fire helmet, flaming red flannel shirt, patent leather belt with spanner and revolver attached, coat hung over arm, and pants stuffed into boot tops. He formed something of a contrast to the pale theological student. It is fair to say of Scotty, however, in passing, that he had a warm heart, and a strong love for his friends, and never entered into a quarrel when he could reasonably keep out of it. Indeed, it was commonly said that whenever one of Scotty's fights was investigated, it always turned out that it had originally been no affair of his, but that out of native goodheartedness he had dropped in of his own accord to help the man who was getting the worst of it. He and Buck Fanshaw were bosom friends, for years, and had often taken adventurous "pot-luck" together. On one occasion, they had thrown off their coats and taken the weaker side in a fight among strangers, and after gaining a hard-earned victory, turned and found that the men they were helping had deserted early, and not only that, but had stolen their coats and made off with them! But to return to Scotty's visit to the minister. He was on a sorrowful mission, now, and his face was the picture of woe. Being admitted to the presence he sat down before the clergyman, placed his fire-hat on an unfinished manuscript sermon under the minister's nose, took from it a red silk handkerchief, wiped his brow and heaved a sigh of dismal impressiveness, explanatory of his business. He choked, and even shed tears; but with an effort he mastered his voice and said in lugubrious tones:

"Are you the duck that runs the gospel-mill next door?"

"Am I the—pardon me, I believe I do not understand?"

With another sigh and a half-sob, Scotty rejoined:

"Why you see we are in a bit of trouble, and the boys thought maybe you would give us a lift, if we'd tackle you—that is, if I've got the rights of it and you are the head clerk of the doxology-works next door."

"I am the shepherd in charge of the flock whose fold is next door."

"The which?"

"The spiritual adviser of the little company of believers whose sanctuary adjoins these premises."

Scotty scratched his head, reflected a moment, and then said:

"You ruther hold over me, pard. I reckon I can't call that hand. Ante and pass the buck."

"How? I beg pardon. What did I understand you to say?"

"Well, you've ruther got the bulge on me. Or maybe we've both got the bulge, somehow. You don't smoke me and I don't smoke you. You see, one of the boys has passed in his checks and we want to give him a good send-off, and so the thing I'm on now is to roust out somebody to jerk a little chin-music for us and waltz him through handsome."

"My friend, I seem to grow more and more bewildered. Your observations are wholly incomprehensible to me. Cannot you simplify them in some way? At first I thought perhaps I understood you, but I grope now. Would it not expedite matters if you restricted yourself to categorical statements of fact unencumbered with obstructing accumulations of metaphor and allegory?"

Another pause, and more reflection. Then, said Scotty:

"I'll have to pass, I judge."

"How?"

"You've raised me out, pard."

"I still fail to catch your meaning."

"Why, that last lead of yourn is too many for me—that's the idea. I can't neither trump nor follow suit."

The clergyman sank back in his chair perplexed. Scotty leaned his head on his hand and gave himself up to thought. Presently his face came up, sorrowful but confident.

"I've got it now, so's you can savvy," he said. "What we want is a gospel-sharp. See?"

"A what?"

"Gospel-sharp. Parson."

"Oh! Why did you not say so before? I am a clergyman—a parson."

"Now you talk! You see my blind and straddle it like a man. Put it there!"—extending a brawny paw, which closed over the minister's small hand and gave it a shake indicative of fraternal sympathy and fervent gratification.

"Now we're all right, pard. Let's start fresh. Don't you mind my snuffling a little—becuz we're in a power of trouble. You see, one of the boys has gone up the flume—"

"Gone where?"

"Up the flume—throwed up the sponge, you understand."

"Thrown up the sponge?"

"Yes—kicked the bucket—"

"Ah—has departed to that mysterious country from whose bourne no traveler returns."

"Return! I reckon not. Why pard, he's *dead!*"

"Yes, I understand."

"Oh, you do? Well I thought maybe you might be getting tangled some more. Yes, you see he's dead again—"

"*Again*? Why, has he ever been dead before?"

"Dead before? No! Do you reckon a man has got as many lives as a cat? But you bet you he's awful dead now, poor old boy, and I wish I'd never seen this day. I don't want no better friend than Buck Fanshaw. I knowed him by the back; and when I know a man and like him, I freeze to him—you hear *me*. Take him all round, pard, there never was a bullier man in the mines. No man ever knowed Buck Fanshaw to go back on a friend. But it's all up, you know, it's all up. It ain't no use. They've scooped him."

"Scooped him?"

"Yes—death has. Well, well, well, we've got to give him up. Yes indeed. It's a kind of a hard world, after all, *ain't* it! But pard, he was a rustler! You ought to seen him get started once. He was a bully boy with a glass eye! Just spit in his face and give him room according to his strength, and it was just beautiful to see him peel and go in. He was the worst son of a thief that ever drawed breath. Pard, he was *on* it! He was on it bigger than an Injun!"

"On it? On what?"

"On the shoot. On the shoulder. On the fight, you understand. *He* didn't give a continental for *any*body. *Beg* your pardon, friend, for coming so near saying a cuss-word—but you see I'm on an awful strain, in this pala-ver, on account of having to cramp down and draw everything so mild. But we've got to give him up. There ain't any getting around that, I don't reckon. Now if we can get you to help plant him—"

"Preach the funeral discourse? Assist at the obsequies?"

"Obs'quies is good. Yes. That's it—that's our little game. We are going to get the thing up regardless, you know. He was always nifty himself, and so you bet you his funeral ain't going to be no slouch—solid silver door-plate on his coffin, six plumes on the hearse, and a nigger on the box in a biled shirt and a plug hat—how's that for high? And we'll take care of *you*, pard. We'll fix you all right. There'll be a kerridge for you; and whatever you want, you just 'scape out and we'll 'tend to it. We've got a shebang fixed up for you to stand behind, in No. 1's house, and don't you be afraid. Just go in and toot your horn, if you don't sell a clam. Put Buck through as bully as you can, pard, for anybody that knowed him will tell you that he was one of the whitest men that was ever in the mines. You can't draw it too strong. He never could stand it to see things going wrong. He's done more to make this town quiet and peaceable than any man in it. I've seen him lick four Greasers in eleven minutes, myself. If a thing wanted regu-lating, *he* warn't a man to go browsing around after somebody to do it, but he would prance in and regulate it himself. He warn't a Catholic. Scasely. He was down on 'em. His word was, 'No Irish need apply!' But it didn't make no difference about that when it came down to what a man's rights was—and so, when some roughs jumped the Catholic bone-yard and started in to stake out town-lots in it he *went* for 'em! And he *cleaned* 'em, too! I was there, pard, and I seen it myself."

"That was very well indeed—at least the impulse was—whether the act was strictly defensible or not. Had deceased any religious convictions?

That is to say, did he feel a dependence upon, or acknowledge allegiance to a higher power?"

More reflection.

"I reckon you've stumped me again, pard. Could you say it over once more, and say it slow?"

"Well, to simplify it somewhat, was he, or rather had he ever been connected with any organization sequestered from secular concerns and devoted to self-sacrifice in the interests of morality?"

"All down but nine—set 'em up on the other alley, pard."

"What did I understand you to say?"

"Why, you're most too many for me, you know. When you get in with your left I hunt grass every time. Every time you draw, you fill; but I don't seem to have any luck. Lets have a new deal."

"How? Begin again?"

"That's it."

"Very well. Was he a good man, and—"

"There—I see that; don't put up another chip till I look at my hand. A good man, says you? Pard, it ain't no name for it. He was the best man that ever—pard, you would have doted on that man. He could lam any galoot of his inches in America. It was him that put down the riot last election before it got a start; and everybody said he was the only man that could have done it. He waltzed in with a spanner in one hand and a trumpet in the other, and sent fourteen men home on a shutter in less than three minutes. He had that riot all broke up and prevented nice before anybody ever got a chance to strike a blow. He was always for peace, and he would *have* peace—he could not stand disturbances. Pard, he was a great loss to this town. It would please the boys if you could chip in something like that and do him justice. Here once when the Micks got to throwing stones through the Methodis' Sunday school windows, Buck Fanshaw, all of his own notion, shut up his saloon and took a couple of six-shooters and mounted guard over the Sunday school. Says he, 'No Irish need apply!' And they didn't. He was the bulliest man in the mountains, pard! He could run faster, jump higher, hit harder, and hold more tangle-foot whisky without spilling it than any man in seventeen counties. Put that in, pard—it'll please the boys more than anything you could say. And you can say, pard, that he never shook his mother."

"Never shook his mother?"

"That's it—any of the boys will tell you so."

"Well, but why *should* he shake her?"

"That's what *I* say—but some people does."

"Not people of any repute?"

"Well, some that averages pretty so-so."

"In my opinion the man that would offer personal violence to his own mother, ought to—"

"Cheese it, pard; you've banked your ball clean outside the string. What I was a drivin' at, was, that he never *throwed off* on his mother—don't you see? No indeedy. He give her a house to live in, and town lots, and plenty of money; and he looked after her and took care of her all the time; and when she was down with the small-pox I'm d—d if he didn't set up nights and nuss her himself! *Beg* your pardon for saying it, but it hopped out too quick for yours truly. You've treated me like a gentleman, pard, and I ain't the man to hurt your feelings intentional. I think you're white. I think you're a square man, pard. I like you, and I'll lick any man that don't. I'll lick him till he can't tell himself from a last year's corpse! Put it *there!*" [Another fraternal handshake—and exit.]

The obsequies were all that "the boys" could desire. Such a marvel of funeral pomp had never been seen in Virginia. The plumed hearse, the dirge-breathing brass bands, the closed marts of business, the flags drooping at half mast, the long, plodding procession of uniformed secret societies, military battalions and fire companies, draped engines, carriages of officials, and citizens in vehicles and on foot, attracted multitudes of spectators to the sidewalks, roofs and windows; and for years afterward, the degree of grandeur attained by any civic display in Virginia was determined by comparison with Buck Fanshaw's funeral.

Scotty Briggs, as a pall-bearer and a mourner, occupied a prominent place at the funeral, and when the sermon was finished and the last sentence of the prayer for the dead man's soul ascended, he responded, in a low voice, but with feeling:

"AMEN. No Irish need apply."

As the bulk of the response was without apparent relevancy, it was probably nothing more than a humble tribute to the memory of the friend that was gone; for, as Scotty had once said, it was "his word."

Scotty Briggs, in after days, achieved the distinction of becoming the only convert to religion that was ever gathered from the Virginia roughs; and it transpired that the man who had it in him to espouse the quarrel of the weak out of inborn nobility of spirit was no mean timber whereof to construct a Christian. The making him one did not warp his generosity or diminish his courage; on the contrary it gave intelligent direction to the one and a broader field to the other. If his Sunday school class progressed faster than the other classes, was it matter for wonder? I think not. He talked to his pioneer small-fry in a language they understood! It was my large privilege, a month before he died, to hear him tell the beautiful story of Joseph and his brethren to his class "without looking at the book." I leave it to the reader to fancy what it was like, as it fell, riddled with slang, from the lips of that grave, earnest teacher, and was listened to by his little learners with a consuming interest that showed that they were as unconscious as he was that any violence was being done to the sacred proprieties!

How does their speech reveal the essential differences between Scotty and the minister? Discuss their word choice, tone, honesty, originality. Does each speak in his own voice?

Donald Hall says (in his essay in this unit) that "by a man's metaphors you shall know him." Analyze Scotty Briggs' metaphors and tell what you know about him.

Why do we prefer Scotty's voice to the minister's? Is it actually more honest? Is his speech any freer of jargon than the minister's?

UNIT 4

PREWRITING

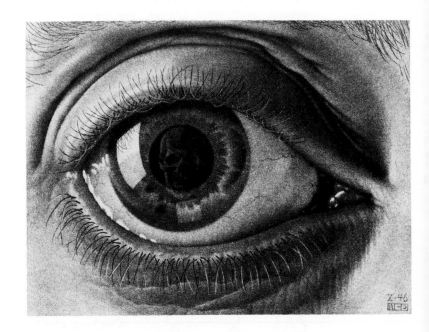

M. C. Escher, *Eye.*
Escher Foundation—
Haags Gemeente-
museum—The Hague

"The fact that we have to die is unalterable for man. Man is aware of this fact, and this very awareness profoundly influences his life. But death remains the very opposite of life ... there is nothing for us to do but to accept the fact of death; ... "the wise man," ... "thinks not of death but of life."

ERICH FROMM

33

The Latin phrase *memento mori,* "remember that you must die," has long reminded people of the final fact of life. Some have heightened their consciousness of this fact by keeping death heads on their desks, and skulls in place of flowers as centerpieces for their dining-room tables. For the same reasons both John Donne, the seventeenth-century poet, and Sarah Bernhardt, the twentieth-century actress, slept in coffins. These devices remind people that life is soon gone and that it must be lived more fully and correctly now, while there is time.

We ask you to become (in a similar but less bizarre way) more aware of the different stages of your life by looking more carefully at your daily experiences of youth and age. Observe your reactions to this opposition in your personal life and begin gathering material to write about. As you walk along the street or sit in a classroom you may realize that, at the very moment, you are making the journey shown in the American Indian pictographs that follow.

DISCUSSION

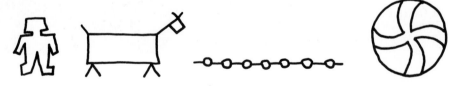

American Indian signs for man, journey, days and nights, and the four ages of man.

Keeping in mind the order of the pictographs, what do you read the message to be? Would the message have a different emotional effect if it were in our language?

❝Prudence is not a deity to cultivate in youth. Youth is the time to go flashing from one end of the world to the other both in mind and body; to try the manners of different nations; to hear the chimes at midnight; to see sunrise in town and country; to be converted at a revival; to circumnavigate the metaphysics, write halting verse, run a mile to see a fire. ❞

ROBERT LOUIS STEVENSON

Do you agree: youth is a time to flash . . . to try . . . to hear . . . to see . . . to be converted . . . to circumnavigate . . . to write . . . to run? Why?

❝At ten [man] is led by cakes, at twenty by a mistress, at thirty by amusements, at forty by ambition, and at fifty by avarice. When does he make wisdom his sole pursuit? ❞

JEAN JACQUES ROUSSEAU

Find examples within your experience that support or deny this statement.

❝A man that is young in years may be old in hours, if he have lost no time. But that happeneth rarely. Generally youth is like the first cogitations, not so wise as the second. For there is a youth in thoughts as well as in ages. And yet the invention of young men is more lively than that of old; and imaginations stream into their minds better, and, as it were, more divinely.

Natures that have much heat, and great and violent desires and perturbations, are not ripe for action till they have passed the meridian of their years. ❞

FRANCIS BACON

What do you see as the chief difference between the thoughts of old people and those of young people? Give examples to support your statements.

❝No young man ever thinks he shall die. He may believe that others will, or assent to the doctrine that "all men are mortal" as an abstract proposition, but he is far enough from bringing it home to himself individually. Youth, buoyant activity, and animal spirits hold absolute antipathy with old age as well as with death. . . . We eye the farthest verge of the horizon and think what a way we shall have to look back

Picasso, *La Vie*.

upon ere we arrive at our journey's end; and without our in the least suspecting it, the mists are at our feet, and the shadows of age encompass us. The two divisions of our lives have melted into each other: the extreme points close and meet with none of that romantic interval stretching out between them, that we had reckoned upon; and for the rich, melancholy, solemn hues of age, "the sear, the yellow leaf" the deepening shadows of an autumnal evening, we only feel a dank, cold mist encircling all objects, after the spirit of youth is fled. 99

WILLIAM HAZLITT

Have you felt the shadows of age? What was your reaction?

66 Youth is a blunder; manhood a struggle; old age a regret. 99

BENJAMIN DISRAELI

How do you see youth, manhood, and old age?

66 "La Vie" is one of the most moving and one of the most enigmatic of Picasso's early works. Basically it belongs to the "Cycle of Life" type of painting. . . . The main theme is evidently the contrast between the naked lovers on the left and the older emaciated figure of the mother carrying a child on the right. The mood of melancholy which this juxtaposition suggests is intensified by the two canvases which appear in the background between the two groups. These seem to provide a further contrast with the lovers in the foreground, since they, too, are naked and apparently young, but in the deepest dejection. 99

ANTHONY BLUNT and PHOEBE POOL

What does this painting say to you about the cycle of life? Why this dejection? Why this melancholy?

CONNECTING EXERCISES

▶A. Observe two people at different stages of life, in childhood, youth, middle age, and old age. Take notes. See them as they are physically, mentally, and emotionally. Here are some things you might look at in detail:
—eyes, skin, hair
—the speed and smoothness of their movements; their walk, their gestures; their facial expressions
—things they say and how they say them; words they use, sentence structure, tone of voice, and amount of talk
—their interests and desires; likes and dislikes

▶B. Describe a scene or line in a recent movie, book, or song that deals with the theme of youth and age. What statement about youth/age does the movie, book, or song make? What details are used to support this statement?

UNIT 5

FREE WRITING

The first words of a paper are often as difficult as the proverbial first step of a thousand-mile journey. Getting started is a problem, even for veteran writers. The petty clerk Monsieur Grand in Albert Camus' novel *The Plague* has been struggling with this problem for years. Grand is writing a novel and cannot get the first sentence right. And he cannot go on until he has it right:

> What I really want . . . is this. One day when the manuscript reaches the publisher, I want him to stand up—after he's read it through, of course—and say to his staff: "Gentlemen, hats off!" . . . So you see, . . . it's got to be flawless. . . . Evenings, whole weeks, spent on one word, just think! Sometimes on a mere conjunction! . . . I'd like you to understand. . . . I grant you it's easy enough to choose between a "but" and an "and." It's a bit more difficult to decide between "and" and "then." But definitely the hardest thing may be to know whether one should put an "and" or leave it out.

Grand says that the first sentence of his novel is giving him "no end of trouble." It reads:

> One fine morning in May an elegant young horse-woman might have been seen riding a handsome sorrel mare along the flowery avenues of the Bois de Boulogne.

66 That's only a rough draft. Once I've succeeded in rendering perfectly the picture in my mind's eye, once my words have the exact tempo of this ride, the horse trotting one-two-three, one-two-three, see what I mean?—the rest will come more easily and, what's even more important, the illusion will be such that from the very first words it will be possible to say: "Hats off!" 99

Grand has given himself a mental charley horse because he wants the first sentence to be flawless. In his effort to make it flawless he has made it artificial. Compare Grand's sentence with the first sentence of Herman Melville's *Moby Dick:* "Call me Ishmael." The narrator starts simply and his words follow naturally from this beginning.

Free writing is a technique for getting started and going on before paralysis or artificiality take hold. You begin simply by writing freely, discovering yourself, your material, your idea in the act of writing. In this way you bypass inertia and give yourself a chance to say what you have to say before borrowed words, emotions, and ideas creep in.

Interviewer: What about working habits? How do you start? . . .

Frank O'Connor: "Get black on white" used to be Maupassant's advice—that's what I always do. I don't give a hoot about what the writing's like, I write any sort of rubbish. . . . When I write . . . I never think of writing nice sentences about, "It was a nice August evening when Elizabeth Jane Moriarty was coming down the road." I just write roughly what happened.

WRITING EXERCISES

▶ A. Review any notes you have on youth and age and begin writing. Write out of your personal experience of the subject. Write freely for about twenty minutes, not giving a "hoot about what the writing's like," just getting "black on white" as fast as you can.

Here's a sample of one student's revised free writing:

WHEN I AM OLD

I know it but I don't believe it. If I don't die
before, I too will be stiff, stooped, watery and dim-
eyed and shuffle along with a palsied hand all wrinkles
and warts. Why don't old people just move along like
the rest of us?

When I'm old I'll do sit-ups, stretching exercises,
and stand on my head. I'll be young when I'm old.
But that's not possible? Old Paterson's knuckles,
knarled, arthritic, the clippers going clack, clack in
his hands. That morning when he was down clipping the
lawn and pushed himself up—those knuckles knotted
on the ground for support. And when he came up, nearly
went over backwards before he got his balance. Didn't
know whether to take his arm to help steady him or act
as if nothing had happened. Tip of his tongue moving
lightly from corner to corner of his mouth. His hand as
palsied as a tuning fork affecting me like the tremors
of an earthquake beneath my feet. I feeling his age
more than he. If I go that far, live that long, is it
possible I'll be like that?

Or that old man on the street last winter, his back
to the building, watery eyes, grey whiskers stiff in
the cold.

I'll be successful and avoid that.

Yet old Robinson—clean, with a plaid wool muffler
and polished cane—crabbed, crotchety, righteous, and
bitter. I'll be free and open, generous and kind. How
to live now to be that way then? Fly into it—dance,
sing, run and burst with energy and love—or conserve,
saving something in preparation. Save what can't be
saved? The thought of age . . . This hand here before
me, pushing the pen, could it be knarled and ache
one day? The same hand turtle-skinned? Move fast now
while I can? More life by remembering this hand? Whenever I'm feeling lifeless I'll look at this hand,
imagine what is to come, see the knuckles swollen and
twisted with age (then I'll know it and believe it) and
like an alarm clock the sight of what is to come will
set me off running.

Bob Owen

▶B. When you write freely, you may succeed in overcoming inertia and in avoiding stilted language. But free writing, like all writing, requires rewriting and careful revision:

(1) After a day or two read through your free writing to discover what ideas and details in it are most interesting to you. Or read it aloud to the class to get their opinions.

(2) Rewrite using one idea or detail as a focal point. Let everything you say support or emphasize this focal point.

(3) Do a careful revision, paying attention to word choice and sentence structure.

WRITING HINT:
TRUST YOUR EYES AND EARS.

You may discover in your free writing that many of your words are the names of things or people as in Bob Owen's paper above: Paterson . . . clack . . . knuckles . . . watery eyes . . . grey whiskers . . . polished cane. If they are, you probably trusted your eyes and ears.

> **"** If those who have studied the art of writing are in accord on any one point, it is on this: The surest way to arouse and hold the attention of the reader is by being specific, definite and concrete. The greatest writers . . . are effective because they deal in particulars and report the details that matter. Their words call up pictures. **"**
>
> WILLIAM STRUNK, JR.

You should have a good foundation for your writing if you have collected specific details. Without them, your writing may be only a series of vague abstractions, lacking vitality. Here is an opening sentence from a student paper: "Age is a condition of time that results in an uncomfortable situation that one does not look forward to but one which must be faced (and I will face it) with courage."

The student has missed the specific, the definite, the concrete—things you can hear, taste, touch, or smell. His writing calls up no pictures because he has not written about what he has seen or heard. He has begun with a vague emotional response to his subject, and the expression of a vague emotion usually fails unless it is nailed down with facts. Without facts, writing lacks freshness. This writer has gotten off on the wrong foot—a very easy thing to do. He needs now to scratch out and rewrite.

Here is another opening sentence from a student paper: "Every night assistant coach Troxel (old let-me-show-you-young-fellows-how-to-do-it) bustles into the shower, sweat sparkling on the curve of his bald head, in his gray mustache and in the curly gray hairs on his chest, turns on the cold shower, says, 'Ahg! Ahg! Ahg!' steps into the stream of icy water, and lets out his usual middle-aged yodel."

The student has trusted his eyes and ears. Reading the words, you see and hear. You can anticipate the meaning the writer has discovered in his experience from the details of his opening sentence. Compare the concrete terms used in this sentence with the abstract words used in the first opening sentence quoted:

First opening sentence	Second opening sentence
age	sweat sparkling
condition	curve of bald head
time	gray beard
uncomfortable	curly gray hairs
situation	ahg, ahg, ahg!
courage	

Read your paper aloud to yourself or to the class. See if your words "call up pictures," if you have been "specific, definite, and concrete." In Unit 2 the suggestion was to free yourself from jargon. In Unit 8 we will show, without denying what we have said here, the value of abstract ideas.

Remember that the surest way to free yourself from vagueness is to write what happened—what you saw and heard. Later you may need to give your account a governing idea; but first collect concrete facts.

UNIT 6

SELECTIONS

Francoise Gilot, one of many women in Picasso's life, was 21 when she met the 61-year-old artist. Before their relationship soured, Francoise lived with Picasso over 10 years and bore two of his children, Claude and Paloma. In the following passage from her book *Life with Picasso*, Francoise recalls the time when she realized that the difference in their ages was one of the many problems that would eventually cause their separation:

> **"**. . . I saw him, for the first time, from outside. I realized that passing his seventieth birthday had made him feel a whole decade older and that the strength he ordinarily kept concentrated within him for his creative work, he was suddenly eager to spend in "living." And so all the standards he had set up and so carefully observed until now were completely thrown aside. His constant dread of death had moved into a critical phase and, as one of its effects, had apparently provoked a taste for "life" in a form which he had abandoned years earlier. He was anxious to appear youthful, whatever the cost, and he kept asking me if I wasn't afraid of death. He often said, "I'd give anything to be twenty years younger.**"**

After Francoise left Picasso, Claude and Paloma often spent their holidays with their father. Francoise writes:

43

66 Pablo has never let Claude return without taking at least one, sometimes more than one, article of clothing from his luggage. The first thing his father took was a new Tyrolean hat.... Another time it was a light-blue poplin raincoat ... his pajamas and very often one or more neckties.

I finally became convinced that Pablo hoped by this method that some of Claude's youth would enter into his own body. It was a metaphorical way of appropriating someone else's substance, and in that way, I believe, he hoped to prolong his own life. 99

Compare and contrast the young and the older Picasso. Indicate how the concrete physical characteristics (eyes, mouth, facial lines, expression) suggest abstract qualities of character (sensitivity, self-possession, power, kindness, vulnerability).

What do you think underlies the desire "to appear youthful, whatever the cost"? (p. 43)

from **The Pump House Gang**

TOM WOLFE

All these kids, seventeen of them, members of the Pump House crowd, are lollygagging around the stairs down to Windansea Beach, La Jolla, California, about 11 a.m., and they all look at the black feet, which are a woman's pair of black street shoes, out of which stick a pair of old veiny white ankles, which lead up like a senile cone to a fudge of tallowy, edematous flesh, her thighs, squeezing out of her bathing suit, with old faded yellow bruises on them, which she probably got from running eight feet to catch a bus or something. She is standing with her old work-a-hubby, who has on *san*dals: you know, a pair of navy-blue anklet socks and these sandals with big, wide, new-smelling tan straps going this way and that, *for keeps.* Man, they look like orthopedic sandals, if one can imagine that. Obviously, these people come from Tucson or Albuquerque or one of those hincty adobe towns. All these hincty, crumbling black feet come to La Jolla-by-the-sea from the adobe towns for the weekend. They even drive in cars all full of thermos bottles and mayonnaisey sandwiches and some kind of latticework wooden-back support for the old crock who drives and Venetian blinds on the back window....

God, they must be practically 50 years old. Naturally, they're carrying every piece of garbage imaginable: the folding aluminum chairs, the newspapers, the lending-library book with the clear plastic wrapper on it, the sunglasses, the sun ointment, about a vat of goo—

It is a Mexican standoff. In a Mexican standoff, both parties narrow their eyes and glare but nobody throws a punch. Of course, nobody in the Pump House crowd would ever even jostle these people or say anything right to them; they are too cool for that.

Everybody in the Pump House crowd looks over, even Tom Coman, who is a cool person. Tom Coman, 16 years old, got thrown out of his garage last night. He is sitting up on top of the railing, near the stairs, up over the beach, with his legs apart. Some nice long willowy girl in yellow slacks is standing on the sidewalk but leaning into him with her arms around his body, just resting. Neale Jones, 16, a boy with great lank perfect surfer's hair, is standing nearby with a Band-Aid on his upper lip, where the sun has burnt it raw. Little Vicki Ballard is up on the sidewalk. Her older sister, Liz, is down the stairs by the Pump House itself, a concrete block, 15 feet high, full of machinery for the La Jolla water system. Liz is wearing her great "Liz" styles, a hulking rabbit-fur vest and black-leather boots over her Levis, even though it is about 85 out here and the sun is plugged in up there like God's own dentist lamp and the Pacific is heaving in with some fair-to-middling surf. Kit Tilden is lollygagging around, and Tom Jones, Connie Carter, Roger Johnson, Sharon Sandquist, Mary Beth White, Rupert Fellows, Glenn Jackson, Dan Watson from San Diego, they are all out here, and everybody takes a look at the panthers.

The old guy, one means, you know, he must be practically 50 years old, he says to his wife, "Come on, let's go farther up," and he takes her by her fat upper arm as if to wheel her around and aim her away from here.

But she says, "No! We have just as much right to be here as they do."

"That's *not the point—*"

"Are you going to—"

"Mrs. Roberts," the work-a-hubby says, calling his own wife by her official married name, as if to say she took a vow once and his word is law, even if he is not testing it with the blond kids here—"farther up, *Mrs. Roberts."*

They start to walk up the sidewalk, but one kid won't move his feet, and, oh, god, her work-a-hubby breaks into a terrible shaking Jello smile as she steps over them, as if to say, Excuse me, sir, I don't mean to make trouble, please, and don't you and your colleagues rise up and jump me, screaming *Gotcha—*

But exactly! This beach *is* verboten for people practically 50 years old. This is a segregated beach. They can look down on Windansea Beach and see nothing but lean tan kids. It is posted "no swimming" (for safety reasons), meaning surfing only. In effect, it is segregated by age. From Los Angeles on down the California coast, this is an era of age segregation. People have always tended to segregate themselves by age, teenagers hanging around with teenagers, old people with old people, like the old men who sit on the benches up near the Bronx Zoo and smoke black cigars. But before, age segregation has gone on within a larger community. Sooner or later during the day everybody has melted back into the old community network that embraces practically everyone, all ages.

But in California today surfers, not to mention rock n' roll kids and the hot-rodders or Hair Boys, named for their fanciful pompadours—all sorts of sets of kids—they don't merely hang around together. They establish whole little societies for themselves. In some cases they live with one another for months at a time. The "Sunset Strip" on Sunset Boulevard used to be a kind of Times Square for Hollywood hot dogs of all ages, anyone who wanted to promenade in his version of the high life. Today "The Strip" is almost completely the preserve of kids from about 16 to 25. It is lined with go-go clubs. One of them, a place called It's Boss, is set up for people 16 to 25 and won't let in anybody over 25, and there are some terrible I'm-dying-a-thousand-deaths scenes when a girl comes up with her boyfriend and the guy at the door at It's Boss doesn't think she looks under 25 and tells her she will have to produce some identification proving she is young enough to come in here and live The Strip kind of life and—she's *had* it, because she can't get up the I.D. and nothing in the world is going to make a woman look stupider than to stand around trying to argue *I'm younger than I look, I'm younger than I look.* So she practically shrivels up like a Peruvian shrunken head in front of her boyfriend and he trundles her off, looking for some place you can get an old doll like this into. One of the few remaining clubs for "older people," curiously, is the Playboy Club. There are apartment houses for people 20 to 30 only, such as the Sheri Plaza in Hollywood and the E'Questre Inn in Burbank. There are whole suburban housing developments, mostly private developments, where only people over 45 or 50 can buy a house. Whole towns, meantime, have become identified as "young": Venice, Newport Beach, Balboa—or "old": Pasadena, Riverside, Coronado Island. . . .

There is a built-in trouble with age segregation. Eventually one *does* reach the horror age of 25, the horror dividing line. Surfing and the surfing life have been going big since 1958, and already there are kids who—well, who aren't kids anymore, they are pushing 30, and they are stagnating on the beach. Pretty soon the California littoral will be littered with these guys, stroked out on the beach like beached white whales, and girls, too, who can't give up the mystique, the mysterioso mystique, Oh Mighty Hulking Sea, who can't *conceive* of living any other life. It is pathetic when they are edged out of groups like the Pump House gang. Already there are some guys who hang around with the older crowd around the Shack who are stagnating on the beach. Some of the older guys, like Gary Wickham, who is 24, are still in *The Life,* they still have it, but even Gary Wickham will be 25 one day and then 26 and then. . . . and then even pan-thuh age. Is one really going to be pan-thuh age one day? Watch those black feet go. And Tom Coman still snuggles with Yellow Slacks, and Liz still roosts moodily in her rabbit fur at the bottom of the Pump House and Pam still sits on the steps contemplating the mysterioso mysteries of Pump House ascension and John and Artie still bob, tiny pink porcelain shells, way out there waiting for godsown bitchen *set,* and godsown sun is still turned on like a dentist's lamp and so far— . . . They are at just about the point Leonard Anderson and Donna Blanchard got that day, December 6, 1964, when Leonard said, Pipe it, and fired two shots, one at her and one at himself. Leonard was 18 and Donna was 21—21!—god, for a girl in the Pump House gang that is almost the horror line right there. But it was all so mysterioso. Leonard was just lying down on the beach at the foot of the Pump House, near the stairs, just talking to John K. Weldon down there, and then Donna appeared at the top of the stairs and Leonard got up and went up the stairs to meet her, and they didn't say anything, they weren't *angry* over anything, they never had been, although the police said they had, they just turned and went a few feet down the sidewalk, away from the Pump House and—blam blam!—these two shots. Leonard fell dead on the sidewalk and Donna died that afternoon in Scripps Memorial Hospital. Nobody knew what to think. But one thing it seemed like—well, it seemed like Donna and Leonard thought they had lived *The Life* as far as it would go and now it was running out. All that was left to do was—but that is an *insane* idea. It can't be like that, *The Life* can't run out, people can't change all that much just because godsown chronometer runs on and the body packing starts deteriorating and the fudgy tallow shows up at the thighs where they squeeze out of the bathing suit—

Tom, boy! John, boy! Gary, boy! Neale, boy! Artie, boy! Pam, Liz, Vicki, Jackie Haddad! After all this—just a pair of . . . bunions inching down the sidewalk away from the old Pump House stairs?

Contrast the life-styles of the older couple and the members of the Pump House Gang.

What age do you consider "the horror line"? Why?

Think of an example of "age segregation." What caused it? What advantages and disadvantages did it offer?

from **As You Like It**

WILLIAM SHAKESPEARE

Jacques: All the world's a stage,
And all the men and women merely players.
They have their exits and their entrances,
And one man in his time plays many parts,
His acts being seven ages. At first the infant,
Mewling, and puking in the nurse's arms.
Then the whining schoolboy with his satchel
And shining morning face, creeping like snail
Unwillingly to school. And then the lover,
Sighing like furnace, with a woeful ballad
Made to his mistress' eyebrow. Then, a soldier.
Full of strange oaths, and bearded like the pard,
Jealous in honour, sudden and quick in quarrel,
Seeking the bubble reputation
Even in the cannon's mouth. And then, the justice,
In fair round belly, with good capon lined,
With eyes severe, and beard of formal cut,
Full of wise saws and modern instances.
And so he plays his part. The sixth age shifts
Into the lean and slippered pantaloon,
With spectacles on nose, and pouch on side;
His youthful hose well saved, a world too wide
For his shrunk shank, and his big manly voice,
Turning again toward childish treble pipes
And whistles in his sound. Last scene of all,
That ends this strange eventful history,
Is second childishness and mere oblivion,
Sans teeth, sans eyes, sans taste, sans everything.

The Force that Through the Green Fuse Drives the Flower

DYLAN THOMAS

The force that through the green fuse drives the flower
Drives my green age; that blasts the roots of trees
Is my destroyer.
And I am dumb to tell the crooked rose
My youth is bent by the same wintry fever.

The force that drives the water through the rocks
Drives my red blood; that dries the mouthing streams
Turns mine to wax.
And I am dumb to mouth unto my veins
How at the mountain spring the same mouth sucks.

The hand that whirls the water in the pool
Stirs the quicksand; that ropes the blowing wind
Hauls my shroud sail.
And I am dumb to tell the hanging man
How of my clay is made the hangman's lime.

The lips of time leech to the fountain head;
Love drips and gathers, but the fallen blood
Shall calm her sores.
And I am dumb to tell a weather's wind
How time has ticked a heaven round the stars.

And I am dumb to tell the lover's tomb
How at my sheet goes the same crooked worm.

Note the concrete words in the two preceding poems. Divide them according to those that make you see something; then those that let your hear, smell, taste, and feel something.

What do you see as the attitude toward life of the speaker in each of these poems?

Do you think that man ends as he begins—"sans everything"?

What is the force that through the green fuse drives the flower? What is ironic about this force?

What parts have you played so far in your life? What were the characteristics of those parts? What parts do you expect to play? How do you expect to play them?

For Jacques, one period of life turns into another and there are seven distinct turnings. For the poet Dylan Thomas one force runs through all life and that force gives both youth and life/age and death. What is your view of the youth/age process?

O Youth and Beauty!

JOHN CHEEVER

At the tag end of nearly every long, large Saturday-night party in the suburb of Shady Hill, when almost everybody who was going to play golf or tennis in the morning had gone home hours ago and the ten or twelve people remaining seemed powerless to bring the evening to an end although the gin and whiskey were running low, and here and there a woman who was sitting out her husband would have begun to drink milk; when everybody had lost track of time, and the baby sitters who were waiting at home for these diehards would have long since stretched out on the sofa and fallen into a deep sleep, to dream about cooking-contest prizes, ocean voyages, and romance; when the bellicose drunk, the crapshooter, the pianist, and the woman faced with the expiration of her hopes had all expressed themselves; when every proposal—to go to the Farquarsons' for breakfast, to go swimming, to go and wake up the Townsends, to go here and go there—died as soon as it was made, then Trace Bearden would begin to chide Cash Bentley about his age and thinning hair. The chiding was preliminary to moving the living-room furniture. Trace and Cash moved the tables and the chairs, the sofas and the fire screen, the woodbox and the footstool; and when they had finished, you wouldn't know the place. Then if the host had a revolver, he would be asked to produce it. Cash would take off his shoes and assume a starting crouch behind a sofa. Trace would fire the weapon out of an open window, and if you were new to the community and had not understood what the preparations were about, you would then realize that you were watching a hurdle race. Over the sofa went Cash, over the tables, over the fire screen and the woodbox. It was not exactly a race, since Cash ran it alone, but it was extraordinary to see this man of forty surmount so many obstacles so gracefully. There was not a piece of furniture in Shady Hill that Cash could not take in his stride. The race ended with cheers, and presently the party would break up.

Cash was, of course, an old track star, but he was never aggressive or tiresome about his brilliant past. The college where he had spent his youth had offered him a paying job on the alumni council, but he had refused it, realizing that that part of his life was ended. Cash and his wife, Louise, had two children, and they lived in a medium-cost ranchhouse on Ale-wives Lane. They belonged to the country club, although they could not afford it, but in the case of the Bentleys nobody ever pointed this out, and Cash was one of the best liked men in Shady Hill. He was still slender—he was careful about his weight—and he walked to the train in the morning with a light and vigorous step that marked him as an athlete. His hair was thin, and there were mornings when his eyes looked bloodshot, but this did not detract much from a charming quality of stubborn youthfulness.

In business Cash had suffered reverses and disappointments, and the Bentleys had many money worries. They were always late with their tax payments and their mortgage payments, and the drawer of the hall table was stuffed with unpaid bills; it was always touch and go with the Bentleys and the bank. Louise looked pretty enough on Saturday night, but her life was exacting and monotonous. In the pockets of her suits, coats, and dresses there were little wads and scraps of paper on which was written: "Oleomargarine, frozen spinach, Kleenex, dog biscuit, hamburger, pepper, lard . . ." When she was still half awake in the morning, she was putting on the water for coffee and diluting the frozen orange juice. Then she would be wanted by the children. She would crawl under the bureau on her hands and knees to find a sock for Toby. She would lie flat on her belly and wiggle under the bed (getting dust up her nose) to find a shoe for Rachel. Then there were the housework, the laundry, and the cooking, as well as the demands of the children. There always seemed to be shoes to put on and shoes to take off, snowsuits to be zipped and unzipped, bottoms to be wiped, tears to be dried, and when the sun went down (she saw it set from the kitchen window) there was the supper to be cooked, the baths, the bed-time story, and the Lord's Prayer. With the sonorous words of the Our Fa-ther in a darkened room the children's day was over, but the day was far from over for Louise Bentley. There were the darning, the mending, and some ironing to do, and after sixteen years of housework she did not seem able to escape her chores even while she slept. Snowsuits, shoes, baths, and groceries seemed to have permeated her subconscious. Now and then she would speak in her sleep—so loudly that she woke her husband. "I can't *af-ford* veal cutlets," she said one night. Then she sighed uneasily and was quiet again.

By the standards of Shady Hill, the Bentleys were a happily married couple, but they had their ups and downs. Cash could be very touchy at times. When he came home after a bad day at the office and found that Louise, for some good reason, had not started supper, he would be ugly. "Oh, for Christ sake!" he would say, and go into the kitchen and heat up some frozen food. He drank some whiskey to relax himself during this or-deal, but it never seemed to relax him, and he usually burned the bottom out of a pan, and when they sat down for supper the dining space would be full of smoke. It was only a question of time before they were plunged into a bitter quarrel. Louise would run upstairs, throw herself onto the bed, and sob. Cash would grab the whiskey bottle and dose himself. These rows, in spite of the vigor with which Cash and Louise entered into them, were the source of a great deal of pain for both of them. Cash would sleep downstairs on the sofa, but sleep never repaired the damage, once the trouble had begun, and if they met in the morning, they would be at one another's throats in a second. Then Cash would leave for the train, and, as soon as the children had been taken to nursery school, Louise would put on her coat and cross the grass to the Beardens' house. She would cry into a cup of warmed-up coffee and tell Lucy Bearden her troubles. What was the meaning of marriage? What was the meaning of love? Lucy always suggested that Louise get a job. It would give her emotional and financial independence, and that, Lucy said, was what she needed.

The next night, things would get worse. Cash would not come home for dinner at all, but would stumble in at about eleven, and the whole sordid wrangle would be repeated, with Louise going to bed in tears upstairs and Cash again stretching out on the living-room sofa. After a few days and nights of this, Louise would decide that she was at the end of her rope. She would decide to go and stay with her married sister in Mamaroneck. She usually chose a Saturday, when Cash would be at home, for her departure. She would pack a suitcase and get her War Bonds from the desk. Then she would take a bath and put on her best slip. Cash, passing the bedroom door, would see her. Her slip was transparent, and suddenly he was all repentance, tenderness, charm, wisdom, and love. "Oh, my darling!" he would groan, and when they went downstairs to get a bite to eat an hour later, they would be sighing and making cow eyes at one another; they would be the happiest married couple in the whole Eastern United States. It was usually at about this time that Lucy Bearden turned up with the good news that she had found a job for Louise. Lucy would ring the doorbell, and Cash, wearing a bathrobe, would let her in. She would be brief with Cash, naturally, and hurry into the dining room to tell poor Louise the good news. "Well that's very nice of you to have looked," Louise would say wanly, "but I don't think that I want a job any more. I don't think that Cash wants me to work, do you, sweetheart?" Then she would turn her big dark eyes on Cash, and you could practically smell smoke. Lucy would excuse herself hurriedly from this scene of depravity, but she never left with any hard feelings, because she had been married for nineteen years herself and she knew that every union has its ups and downs. She didn't seem to leave any wiser, either; the next time the Bentleys quarreled, she would be just as intent as ever on getting Louise a job. But these quarrels and reunions, like the hurdle race, didn't seem to lose their interest through repetition.

On a Saturday night in the spring, the Farquarsons gave the Bentleys an anniversary party. It was their seventeenth anniversary. Saturday afternoon, Louise Bentley put herself through preparations nearly as arduous as the Monday wash. She rested for an hour, by the clock, with her feet high in the air, her chin in a sling, and her eyes bathed in some astringent solution. The clay packs, the too tight girdle, and the plucking and curling and painting that went on were all aimed at rejuvenation. Feeling in the end that she had not been entirely successful, she tied a piece of veiling over her eyes—but she was a lovely woman, and all the cosmetics that she had struggled with seemed, like her veil, to be drawn transparently over a face where mature beauty and a capacity for wit and passion were undisguisable. The Farquarsons' party was nifty, and the Bentleys had a wonderful time. The only person who drank too much was Trace Bearden. Late in the party, he began to chide Cash about his thinning hair and Cash good-naturedly began to move the furniture around. Harry Farquarson had a pistol, and Trace went out onto the terrace to fire it up at the sky. Over the sofa went Cash, over the end table, over the arms of the wing chair and the fire screen. It was a piece of carving on a chest that brought him down, and down he came like a ton of bricks.

Louise screamed and ran to where he lay. He had cut a gash in his forehead, and someone made a bandage to stop the flow of blood. When he tried to get up, he stumbled and fell again, and his face turned a terrible green. Harry telephoned Dr. Parminter, Dr. Hopewell, Dr. Altman, and Dr. Barnstable, but it was two in the morning and none of them answered. Finally, a Dr. Yerkes—a total stranger—agreed to come. Yerkes was a young man—he did not seem old enough to be a doctor—and he looked around at the disordered room and the anxious company as if there was something weird about the scene. He got off on the wrong foot with Cash. "What seems to be the matter, old-timer?" he asked.

Cash's leg was broken. The doctor put a splint on it, and Harry and Trace carried the injured man out to the doctor's car. Louise followed them in her own car to the hospital, where Cash was bedded down in a ward. The doctor gave Cash a sedative, and Louise kissed him and drove home in the dawn.

Cash was in the hospital for two weeks, and when he came home he walked with a crutch and his broken leg was in a heavy cast. It was another ten days before he could limp to the morning train. "I won't be able to run the hurdle race any more, sweetheart," he told Louise sadly. She said that it didn't matter, but while it didn't matter to her, it seemed to matter to Cash. He had lost weight in the hospital. His spirits were low. He seemed discontented. He did not himself understand what had happened. He, or everything around him, seemed subtly to have changed for the worse. Even his senses seemed to conspire to damage the ingenuous world that he had enjoyed for so many years. He went into the kitchen late one night to make himself a sandwich, and when he opened the icebox door he noticed a rank smell. He dumped the spoiled meat into the garbage, but the smell clung to his nostrils. A few days later he was in the attic, looking for his old varsity sweater. There were no windows in the attic and his flashlight was dim. Kneeling on the floor to unlock a trunk, he broke a spider web with his lips. The frail web covered his mouth as if a hand had been put over it. He wiped it impatiently, but also with the feeling of having been gagged. A few nights later, he was walking down a New York side street in the rain and saw an old whore standing in a doorway. She was so sluttish and ugly that she looked like a cartoon of Death, but before he could appraise her—the instant his eyes took an impression of her crooked figure—his lips swelled, his breathing quickened, and he experienced all the other symptoms of erotic excitement. A few nights later, while he was reading *Time* in the living room he noticed that the faded roses Louise had brought in from the garden smelled more of earth than of anything else. It was a putrid, compelling smell. He dropped the roses into a wastebasket, but not before they had reminded him of the spoiled meat, the whore, and the spider web.

He had started going to parties again, but without the hurdle race to run, the parties of his friends and neighbors seemed to him interminable and stale. He listened to their dirty jokes with an irritability that was hard for him to conceal. Even their countenances discouraged him, and, slumped in a chair, he would regard their skin and their teeth narrowly, as if he were himself a much younger man.

The brunt of his irritability fell on Louise, and it seemed to her that Cash, in losing the hurdle race, had lost the thing that had preserved his equilibrium. He was rude to his friends when they stopped in for a drink. He was rude and gloomy when he and Louise went out. When Louise asked him what was the matter, he only murmured, "Nothing, nothing, nothing," and poured himself some bourbon. May and June passed, and then the first part of July, without his showing any improvement.

Then it is a summer night, a wonderful summer night. The passengers on the eight-fifteen see Shady Hill—if they notice it at all—in a bath of placid golden light. The noise of the train is muffled in the heavy foliage, and the long car windows look like a string of lighted aquarium tanks before they flicker out of sight. Up on the hill, the ladies say to one another, "Smell the grass! Smell the trees!" The Farquarsons are giving another party, and Harry has hung a sign, WHISKY GULCH, from the rose arbor, and is wearing a chef's white hat and an apron. His guests are still drinking, and the smoke from his meat fire rises, on this windless evening, straight up into the trees.

In the clubhouse on the hill, the first of the formal dances for the young people begins around nine. On Alewives Lane sprinklers continue to play after dark. You can smell the water. The air seems as fragrant as it is dark—it is a delicious element to walk through—and most of the windows on Alewives Lane are open to it. You can see Mr. and Mrs. Bearden, as you pass, looking at their television. Joe Lockwood, the young lawyer who lives on the corner, is practicing a speech to the jury before his wife. "I intend to show you," he says, "that a man of probity, a man whose reputation for honesty and reliability . . ." He waves his bare arms as he speaks. His wife goes on knitting. Mrs. Carver—Harry Farquarson's mother-in-law—glances up at the sky and asks, "*Where* did all the stars come from?" She is old and foolish, and yet she is right: Last night's stars seem to have drawn to themselves a new range of galaxies, and the night sky is not dark at all, except where there is a tear in the membrane of light. In the unsold house lots near the track a hermit thrush is singing.

The Bentleys are at home. Poor Cash has been so rude and gloomy that the Farquarsons have not asked him to their party. He sits on the sofa beside Louise, who is sewing elastic into the children's underpants. Through the open window he can hear the pleasant sounds of the summer night. There is another party, in the Rogerses' garden, behind the Bentleys'. The music from the dance drifts down the hill. The band is sketchy—saxophone, drums, and piano—and all the selections are twenty years old. The band plays "Valencia," and Cash looks tenderly toward Louise, but Louise, tonight, is a discouraging figure. The lamp picks out the gray in her hair. Her apron is stained. Her face seems colorless and drawn. Suddenly, Cash begins frenziedly to beat his feet in time to the music. He sings some gibberish—Jabajabajabajaba—to the distant saxophone. He sighs and goes into the kitchen.

Here a faint, stale smell of cooking clings to the dark. From the kitchen window Cash can see the lights and figures of the Rogerses' party. It is a young people's party. The Rogers girl has asked some friends in for dinner before the dance, and now they seem to be leaving. Cars are driving away. "I'm covered with grass stains," a girl says. "I hope the old man remembered to buy gasoline," a boy says, and a girl laughs. There is nothing on their minds but the passing summer night. Taxes and the elastic in underpants—all the unbeautiful facts of life that threaten to crush the breath out of Cash—have not touched a single figure in this garden. Then jealousy seizes him—such savage and bitter jealousy that he feels ill.

He does not understand what separates him from these children in the garden next door. He has been a young man. He has been a hero. He has been adored and happy and full of animal spirits, and now he stands in a dark kitchen, deprived of his athletic prowess, his impetuousness, his good looks—of everything that means anything to him. He feels as if the figures in the next yard are the specters from some party in that past where all his tastes and desires lie, and from which he has been cruelly removed. He feels like a ghost of the summer evening. He is sick with longing. Then he hears voices in the front of the house. Louise turns on the kitchen light. "Oh, here you are," she said. "The Beardens stopped in. I think they'd like a drink."

Cash went to the front of the house to greet the Beardens. They wanted to go up to the club, for one dance. They saw, at a glance, that Cash was at loose ends, and they urged the Bentleys to come. Louise got someone to stay with the children and then went upstairs to change.

When they got to the club, they found a few friends of their age hanging around the bar, but Cash did not stay in the bar. He seemed restless and perhaps drunk. He banged into a table on his way through the lounge to the ballroom. He cut in on a young girl. He seized her too vehemently and jigged her off in an ancient two-step. She signaled openly for help to a boy in the stag line, and Cash was cut out. He walked angrily off the dance floor onto the terrace. Some young couples there withdrew from one another's arms as he pushed open the screen door. He walked to the end of the terrace, where he hoped to be alone, but here he surprised another young couple, who got up from the lawn, where they seemed to have been lying, and walked off in the dark toward the pool.

Louise remained in the bar with the Beardens. "Poor Cash is tight," she said. And then, "He told me this afternoon that he was going to paint the storm windows," she said. "Well, he mixed the paint and washed the brushes and put on some old fatigues and went into the cellar. There was a telephone call for him at around five, and when I went down to tell him, do you know what he was doing? He was just sitting there in the dark with a cocktail shaker. He hadn't touched the storm windows. He was just sitting there in the dark, drinking Martinis."

"Poor Cash," Trace said.

"You ought to get a job," Lucy said. "That would give you emotional and financial independence." As she spoke, they all heard the noise of furniture being moved around in the lounge.

"Oh, my God!" Louise said. "He's going to run the race. Stop him, Trace, stop him! He'll hurt himself. He'll kill himself!"

They all went to the door of the lounge. Louise again asked Trace to interfere, but she could see by Cash's face that he was way beyond remonstrating with. A few couples left the dance floor and stood watching the preparations. Trace didn't try to stop Cash—he helped him. There was no pistol, so he slammed a couple of books together for the start.

Over the sofa went Cash, over the coffee table, the lamp table, the fire screen, and the hassock. All his grace and strength seemed to have returned to him. He cleared the big sofa at the end of the room and instead of stopping there, he turned and started back over the course. His face was strained. His mouth hung open. The tendons of his neck protruded hideously. He made the hassock, the fire screen, the lamp table, and the coffee table. People held their breath when he approached the final sofa, but he cleared it and landed on his feet. There was some applause. Then he groaned and fell. Louise ran to his side. His clothes were soaked with sweat and he gasped for breath. She knelt down beside him and took his head in her lap and stroked his thin hair.

Cash had a terrible hangover on Sunday, and Louise let him sleep until it was nearly time for church. The family went off to Christ Church together at eleven, as they always did. Cash sang, prayed, and got to his knees, but the most he ever felt in church was that he stood outside the realm of God's infinite mercy, and, to tell the truth, he no more believed in the Father, the Son, and the Holy Ghost than does my bull terrier. They returned home at one to eat the overcooked meat and stony potatoes that were their customary Sunday lunch. At around five, the Parminters called up and asked them over for a drink. Louise didn't want to go, so Cash went alone. (Oh, those suburban Sunday nights, those Sunday-night blues! Those departing weekend guests, those stale cocktails, those half-dead flowers, those trips to Harmon to catch the Century, those post-mortems and pickup suppers!) It was sultry and overcast. The dog days were beginning. He drank gin with the Parminters for an hour or two and then went over to the Townsends' for a drink. The Farquarsons called up the Townsends and asked them over and bring Cash with them, and at the Farquarsons' they had some more drinks and ate the leftover party food. The Farquarsons were glad to see that Cash seemed like himself again. It was half past ten or eleven when he got home. Louise was upstairs, cutting out of the current copy of *Life* those scenes of mayhem, disaster, and violent death that she felt might corrupt her children. She always did this. Cash came upstairs and spoke to her and then went down again. In a little while, she heard him moving the living-room furniture around. Then he called to her, and when she went down, he was standing at the foot of the stairs in his stocking feet, holding the pistol out to her. She had never fired it before, and the directions he gave her were not much help.

"Hurry up," he said. "I can't wait all night."

He had forgotten to tell her about the safety, and when she pulled the trigger nothing happened.

"It's that little lever," he said. "Press that little lever." Then, in his impatience, he hurdled the sofa anyhow.

The pistol went off and Louise got him in midair. She shot him dead.

What does the sofa-jumping mean to Cash? Is it only his youth, his glory as a track star that he is seeking?

What significance do the spoiled meat, the whore, and the spider have within the context of the story? Why do you think life has become stale for Cash?

Why does Cash feel "like a ghost of the summer evening" when he glances at the young people having a party?

How do you feel about the shooting? Is it accidental? Ironic? Deserved?

ANXIETY

AND

3

TRANQUILLITY

UNIT 7

PREWRITING

Paul Klee, *Outburst of Fear III.*

disturbance
[L. disturbare, **to drive asunder; tear in pieces]**

harmony
[Gr. harmozein, **to fit together]**

In this chapter we suggest a few ways you may discover anxiety and tranquillity (and the related feelings of worry, frustration, and peacefulness) in your life. Anxiety and tranquillity cannot exist in one person at the same time. When you are anxious you are "torn to pieces"; when you are tranquil the elements of your inner world "fit together."

Anxiety and tranquillity, like Hell and Paradise, are in opposition. Hell in Dante Aligheri's poem *The Divine Comedy* is a place of torment and anguish, paradise a realm of peace and acceptance. In hell one victim is blown by fierce winds and hurled about in incessant grief and pain. Another trembles in eternal chill, frozen in ice up to his neck. One of a pair gnaws the other's skull as the two suffer in their hate through eternity. But in another world, in paradise, there are souls completely fulfilled in their peace.

Dante's hell and paradise are emotional states realized to a lesser degree here on earth. Like the characters in Dante's poem we all live within the circle of our feelings. It has been said that emotions are the most important aspect of any person's life. If now we hate, we are hate itself. If now we love, then this emotion colors the whole of our existence. Emotions are fundamental.

But writing about emotions isn't always easy. They are elusive and complex because we are always passing rapidly from one to another. Furthermore, as our thinking influences our emotions, so do our emotions permeate and influence our thinking.

How is it possible to write about emotions then? Perhaps it isn't—at least not directly. But it is possible to write about the things you see. If you can't actually see an emotion you can see a mouth with the corners turned up or a mouth with the corners turned down and you can write about that. In the next few pages we ask you to find an emotion and to look at it closely until you have details and a purpose for writing about it.

DISCUSSION

"Both anxiety and fear . . . are in fact emotional reactions to danger and may be accompanied by physical sensations, such as trembling, perspiration, violent heartbeat. . . . Yet there is a difference between the two . . . fear is a reaction that is proportionate to the danger one has to face, whereas anxiety is a disproportionate reaction to danger, or even a reaction to imaginary danger. . . . Not only . . . may we have anxiety without knowing it, but anxiety may be the determining factor in our lives without our being conscious of it. "

KAREN HORNEY

When was the last time you trembled or perspired from fear or an uneasy situation? When in your life have you shown a "disproportionate reaction to danger"?

> " The price of hating other human beings is loving oneself less. "
>
> ELDRIDGE CLEAVER

Can you find an example of this in your own life?

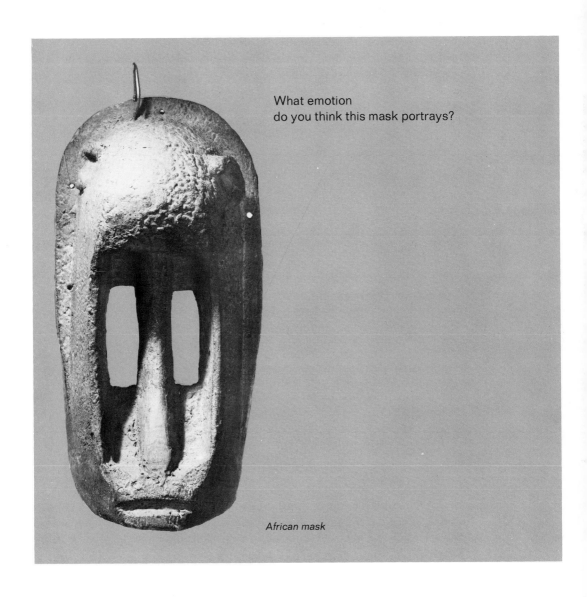

What emotion
do you think this mask portrays?

African mask

66One evening there fell upon me without warning a horrible fear of my own existence. There arose in my mind the image of an epileptic patient whom I had seen in the asylum, a black-haired youth with greenish skin, looking absolutely non-human. *That shape am I,* I felt, potentially. Nothing that I possess can defend me against that fate if the hour for it should strike for me as it struck for him. I became a mass of quivering fear. I remember wondering how other people could live, how I myself had ever lived, so unconscious of that pit of insecurity beneath the surface of life. **99**

WILLIAM JAMES

Recall an instance in your life of anxiety coming from an awareness of "that pit of insecurity beneath the surface of life."

66 No need at all of hills and streams
For quiet meditation;
When the mind has been extinguished,
Even fire is refreshing. **99**

THE ZENRIN KUSHU

Remember a time when you felt completely quiet. Describe it.

66Every age but ours has its model, its ideal. All of these have been given up by our culture: the saint, the hero, the gentleman, the knight, the mystic. About all we have left is the well-adjusted man without problems, a very pale and doubtful substitute. Perhaps we shall soon be able to use as our guide and model the fully growing and self-fulfilling human being, the one in whom all his potentialities are coming to full development, the one whose inner nature expresses itself freely, rather than being warped, suppressed, or denied. **99**

ABRAHAM H. MASLOW

Do you know a well-adjusted man? Can you describe him? What would you need to do in your life to develop your potentialities? What do you see as the differences between the emotions of a self-fulfilling man and a well-adjusted person?

66 Zen makes a religion of tranquillity. Zen is not a religion which arouses emotions, causing tears to roll from our eyes or stirring us to shout aloud the name of God. When the soul and the mind meet in a perpendicular line, so to speak, in that moment complete unity between the universe and the self will be realized. 99

SOKEI-AN

Distinguish between tranquillity arising from the comfort of unity and comfort arising from self-satisfaction.

CONNECTING EXERCISES

▶ A. Make notes on the most anxious or most tranquil experience you had this last year. Or keep notes for the next few days on what is usually the most anxious or tranquil period of your average day. Recall the details: Where were you? What objects were nearby? Who was there? What happened? What did you do? Say? Think? In one sentence say what significance this particular situation has for you.

▶ B. Find an example of anxiety or tranquillity in a TV show, advertisement, movie, book, or current political event.

UNIT 8

WRITING PERSONAL EXPERIENCES

At times we have all had an impulse to record and relate something we have seen or done. Following are statements by two writers who explain why they wrote about their experiences.

> **❝**I began these pages for myself, in order to think out my own particular pattern of living, my own individual balance of life, work and human relationships. And since I think best with a pencil in my hand, I started naturally to write. I had the feeling, when the thoughts first clarified on paper, that my experience was very different from other people's. . . . But as I went on writing . . . I found that my point of view was not unique. In varying settings and under different forms, I discovered that many women, and men, too, were grappling with essentially the same questions as I, and were hungry to discuss and argue and hammer out possible answers. **❞**
>
> ANNE MORROW LINDBERGH

> **❝**I desire to set before my fellows the likeness of a man in all the truth of nature, and that man myself.
>
> Myself alone! I know the feelings of my heart, and I know men. I am not made like any of those I have seen; I venture to believe that I am not made like any of those who are in existence. If I am not better, at least I am different. Whether Nature has acted rightly or wrongly in destroying the mould in which she cast me, can only be decided after I have been read.

I . . . say boldly: "This is what I have done, what I have thought, what I was. . . ." I have shown myself as I was: mean and contemptible, good, high-minded and sublime, according as I was one or the other.   **"**

JEAN-JACQUES ROUSSEAU

You are the subject of the personal experience paper you write. The essential quality of your writing is that the material for it comes from something *you* have lived, something only you could have thought and felt about something that happened in your day-by-day life.

Along the street you walk every day is a subject for your paper. But finding a subject in some one daily activity, discovering your emotional response to that activity, your understanding of it, and putting all this into language is not always a simple task. You have to see, think, and communicate so your reader can understand, as nearly as possible, your experience. Following is a record of one person's experience:

It was my custom to go out every morning on horseback . . . to ride away from the valley; and no sooner would I climb the terrace and plunge into the gray, universal thicket, than I would find myself as completely alone as if five hundred instead of only five miles separated me from the valley and river. So wild and solitary and remote seemed that gray waste, stretching away into infinitude, a waste untrodden by man, and where the wild animals are so few that they have made no discoverable path in the wilderness of thorns. . . . Not once nor twice nor thrice but day after day I returned to this solitude, going to it in the morning as if to attend a festival, and leaving it only when hunger and thirst and the westering sun compelled me. And yet I had no object in going, no motive which could be put into words; . . . Sometimes I would pass a whole day without seeing one mammal, and perhaps not more than a dozen birds of any size. The weather at that time was cheerless, generally with a gray film of cloud spread over the sky, and a bleak wind, often cold enough to make my bridle-hand quite numb. . . . At a slow pace, which would have seemed intolerable under other circumstance, I would ride about for hours together at a stretch. On arriving at a hill, I would slowly ride to its summit, and stand there to survey the prospect. On every side it stretched away in great undulations, wild and irregular. How gray it all was! Hardly less so near at hand than on the haze-wrapped horizon where the hills were dim and the outline obscured by distance. Descending from my outlook, I would take up my aimless wanderings again and visit other elevations to gaze on the same landscape from another point; and so on for hours. And at noon I would dismount and sit or lie on folded poncho for an hour or longer. One day in these rambles I discovered a small grove composed of twenty or thirty trees, growing at a convenient distance apart, that had evidently been resorted to by a herd of deer or other wild animals. The grove was on a hill differing in shape from other hills in its neighborhood, and after a time I made a point of finding and using it as a resting-place every day at noon. I did not ask myself why I made choice of that one spot, sometimes going out of my way to sit there instead of sitting down under any one of the millions of trees and bushes on any other hillside. I thought nothing about it, but acted unconsciously. Only afterward it seemed to me that, after having rested there once, each time I wished to rest again the wish came associated with the image of that particular clump of trees with polished stems and clean bed of sand beneath; and in a short time I formed a habit of returning, animal like, to repose at that same spot.

It was, perhaps, a mistake to say that I would sit down and rest, since I was never tired; and yet, without being tired, that noonday pause, during which I sat for an hour without moving, was strangely grateful. All day there would be no sound, not even the rustling of a leaf. One day, while *listening* to the silence, it occurred to my mind to wonder what the effect would be if I were to shout aloud. This seemed at the time a horrible suggestion, which almost made me shudder. But during those solitary days it was a rare thing for any thought to cross my mind. In the state of mind I was in, thought had become impossible. My state was one of *suspense* and *watchfulness*, yet I had no expectation of meeting an adventure and felt . . . free from apprehension. . . . The state seemed familiar rather than strange, and accompanied by a strong feeling of elation; and I did not know that something had come between me and my intellect until I returned to my former self—to thinking, and the old insipid existence.

I had undoubtedly *gone back;* and that state of intense watchfulness or alertness, rather, with suspension of the higher intellectual faculties, represented the mental state of the pure savage. He thinks little, reasons little, having a surer guide in his [mere sensory perceptions]. He is in perfect harmony with nature.

W. H. HUDSON

WRITING HINT: TRUST YOUR INTERPRETATION OF YOUR EXPERIENCE.

In Unit 5 we talked of trusting your eyes and ears, of using words that are "specific . . . definite . . . concrete." But you also need to trust your feelings and thoughts. If you don't trust your interpretation of your experience, your language will lack meaning. Your reader wants to know what the details you use mean to you.

In the account of the personal experience given above on pages 67–68, note the combination of concrete detail and abstract idea. The author takes the reader along with him, giving him a sense of the experience:

> I climb . . . and plunge into the gray . . . thicket . . .

> a bleak wind, often cold enough to make my bridle-hand quite numb . . .

> I would dismount and sit or lie on folded poncho . . .

> that particular clump of trees with polished stems and the clean bed of sand beneath . . .

> no sound, not even the rustling of a leaf . . .

In these passages nouns are concrete: thicket, bridle-hand, poncho, sand, rustling, leaf; adjectives are specific: grey, bleak, numb, folded, polished; verbs are exact: climb, plunge, dismount.

But Hudson also uses abstract terms to communicate his understanding of his experience:

> I had no object in going, no motive which could be put into words . . .

> I thought nothing about it, but acted unconsciously . . .

> My state was one of *suspense* and *watchfulness* . . . free from apprehension . . . something had come between me and my intellect . . .

> I had undoubtedly *gone back* . . .

Hudson has discovered the meaning his experience has for him. He communicates this meaning to his reader. The words that interpret the experience are more abstract than the ones that record it. In your writing you will also find that when you show what happened, your words will be more concrete. And when you tell your reader the meaning the experience had for you, your words will be more abstract.

In Hudson's account concrete details of the experience join abstract interpretation of it. Like Hudson's account, most successful writing reflects the union of abstract and concrete. In their earliest stages picture languages mirrored this union. In hieroglyphic, picture language of ancient Egypt, legs, a hand gripping a stick, the sun, an animal, are concrete things denoting abstract concepts:

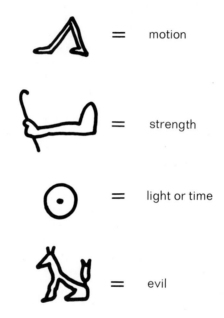

The very hieroglyph for "abstract" was itself a concrete image indicating "that which cannot be pictured":

As you write, shuttle back and forth between concrete detail and abstract idea, between specific and general, between fact and judgment, experience and meaning.

Ask yourself: What are the facts of my experience? What do they mean to me?

WRITING EXERCISES

▶A. Write a personal-experience paper on the main source of anxiety and of tranquillity for you. What one aspect of modern society (pace, noise, general stress, competition, bureaucracy, laws, comforts, entertainment) disorders or brings harmony to your emotional world?

▶B. Write a paper on how you deal with your anxiety. Do you give free expression to your inner desires? Work? Analyze the anxiety? Run? Go to a movie?

▶C. Write a personal-experience paper on the effect anxiety or tranquillity has on other emotions. For example, you might write about what seems to you to be a common sequence of emotions: frustration—anxiety—hate—self-hate.

CLASS EXERCISE

▶As you read the following student theme: (1) Check those words "attached to things" (as opposed to those words that are more abstract). (2) Underline the statements that most clearly indicate the meaning the experience has for its author.

"I'LL EAT THE APRICOTS"

An argument I had with my husband a few months ago proved to me that most emotional states I experience give the impression of permanence; actually, even the strongest emotions are short-lived.

He and I decided to exchange Christmas gifts this year; last year we didn't. A few days before Christmas I saw some rather healthy looking plants for sale in a store and I decided to give him one of them. The idea behind the gift was to give something living. When I bought the plant, I recall having an uneasy feeling that I made a mistake. This condition lingered until I talked myself into feeling confident and happy that I made the right decision.

Christmas Eve arrived. We were at his parents' house for dinner and the unwrapping. He opened my present and was really pleased with it; I was relieved. I opened his and was disappointed. My eyes fell on a

package of dried prunes, apricots and dates. Through
the cellophane, it was obvious that the fruit was hard
and withered. I covered my dismay and made it through
the evening with his family.

By the time we reached home I was depressed. Everything about our marriage seemed hopeless. We had a
tense talk about the dried fruit and I got increasingly
angry over the gift. I decided it represented our
decaying relationship. Within an hour both of us were
convinced a divorce must be the next step for us. We
didn't speak to each other for a long while. During
this time I recall that I felt a tightness in my chest
attended by thoughts of despair and general worry. I
saw the apricots and the plant on the table. I realized
my anxiety over giving the plant had changed into
my depression over receiving the dried fruit. And both
anxiety and depression had been dissipated by my
anger. Suddenly, everything changed. I said to my
husband, "All right, I'll eat the apricots!" We broke
out laughing at the absurdity of the situation.

My emotions are changeable and impermanent and yet I
still believe in each emotion's permanence when I
experience it.

Sally Massa

UNIT 9

SELECTIONS

> **"**I walked with two friends. Then the sun sank. Suddenly the sky turned red as blood, and I felt a touch of sadness. I stood still and leant against the railings. Above the blueish-black fjord and above the city the sky was like blood and flames. My friends walked on, and I was left alone, trembling with fear. I felt as if all nature were filled with one mighty, and unending shriek.**"**
>
> EDVARD MUNCH
> (quoted by Werner Timm)

"Every day Edvard Munch was at the theatre; he lived right amongst us, worked through the day, drank at night, and painted. . . . Sometimes he sat for quite a while in my office, completely still and without moving, very serious, scarcely saying a word to anybody. He seemed not to see or hear what went on around him, entirely taken up with himself, with not a muscle moving in his face! What went on behind this calm facade? What was working behind these strong features, this strange strong forehead? Then, some small thing was enough to startle him. He became bright and laughed: the simple merry laugh of a child. He was always equable and friendly, yet still somehow reserved, a stiff Northerner, difficult to penetrate. For us he remained a stranger, a puzzle. He had something of the child and the savage, an almost animal primitiveness . . . he was immensely

73

complicated, with his knowledge of deepest secrets. One only had to see his pictures: where was there another to be so completely man, to experience woman, and suffer through her? Sometimes he was ridiculously obstinate, did not look up or listen, neither to left or right, remained untouched, not deflected by praise or censure. But behind this obstinacy was a gigantic iron will, sure of itself in a somnolent kind of way. There was a will for freedom which appeared to burst all social conventions, and could arise and grow only in an essentially deep loneliness.

WERNER TIMM

Edvard Munch, *The Scream.*

Leonardo da Vinci, *Mona Lisa.*

“In his *Treatise on Painting* Leonardo had recommended painters not to work on portraits in the hard light of a bright day, but when the clouds hang low and a pale light filters through; when rain pours down in silver streams; or when the bluish dusk effaces every hard gleam, enticing the shadows and giving men and women the unreal charm of faces seen between dreaming and waking. In such hours of subdued light he painted Mona Lisa. The room would be filled with the unusual tones of musical instruments of his own making. (At this time he made many new instruments, of strange richness and peculiar timbre, like a voice floating in from another world.) Meanwhile one of the readers would recite the verses of great poets of the past. Mona Lisa sat resting with folded hands in her chair, with the poise of any Florentine woman of good family.

Leonardo had probably been at work for some time on this portrait of Mona Lisa, the young wife of the rich Francesco del Giocondo . . . the story of its subject is as fragmentary as the history of the picture. It was in any case a commonplace story. Francesco del Giocondo, rich and growing old, had been twice a widower when he married this dowerless girl, twenty years younger than he, the daughter of a Florentine named Antonio Maria di Noldo Gherardini; she, like Leonardo's successive stepmothers, had looked on her marriage as a sort of refuge for the needy. This is all that was known in Florence of Messer Giocondo's wife, Madonna Lisa (Mona Lisa for short, or alternatively, after her husband, La Gioconda)—this, and that a little daughter was born to the couple but died young; they seem to have had no other children. When Leonardo began her portrait, Mona Lisa was something over twenty-four years of age; when she last sat to him she was nearly thirty and, in the eyes of the people of that time, a woman past her prime. . . . Her face was . . . a commonplace one, the product of a commonplace existence—a face that revealed perfect health and imperturbable calm, the face of a woman whose senses had been dulled by the lazy flow of her existence and who whiled away her days with little to expect or desire.

And yet this thoroughly bourgeois woman, ripened and not very happy and not particularly unhappy, had been able to fascinate Leonardo more than any other woman he met in all his life. . . .

Did Leonardo unconsciously assimilate Mona Lisa's features to his soul's ideal? Is it his own gaze, burdened with some unfathomable problem, that peers from her eyes; is it his own smile, a smile of consciously superior knowledge, that flits around her firm little mouth, expressing a haughty inaccessibility that has nothing in common with her good-natured face?

99

ANTONIA VALLENTIN

Compare the details of the two works, *The Scream* and *Mona Lisa*, noting eyes, mouth, cheeks eyebrows, forehead lines, hands, posture, expression, pattern of lines, light and shade.

Compare the total emotional effects of the Munch and Da Vinci works: soft/loud, angular/rounded, empty/full, light/heavy.

Munch tells of an experience one evening before he drew *The Scream*: ". . . above the city the sky was like blood and flames. . . . I was left alone, trembling with fear." And we are told that while Leonardo painted *Mona Lisa* he arranged his surroundings to harmonize with the emotional effect he wished to produce in the painting. In the two works what is the relation between the figure in the foreground and the landscape in the background? In what way does emotion distort surroundings and surroundings affect emotions?

The Anatomy of Angst

TIME

The automatic elevator stops with a jolt. The doors slide open, but instead of the accustomed exit, the passenger faces only a blank wall. His fingers stab at buttons: nothing happens. Finally, he presses the alarm signal, and a starter's gruff voice inquires from below: "What's the matter?" The passenger explains that he wants to get off on the 25th floor. "There is no 25th floor in this building," comes the voice over the loudspeaker. The passenger explains that, nonsense, he has worked here for years. He gives his name. "Never heard of you," says the loudspeaker. "Easy," the passenger tells himself. "They are just trying to frighten me."

But time passes and nothing changes. In that endless moment, the variously pleading and angry exchanges over the loudspeaker are the passenger's only communication with the outside world. Finally, even that ceases; the man below says that he cannot waste any more time. "Wait! Please!" cries the passenger in panic—"Keep on talking to me!" But the loudspeaker clicks into silence. Hours, days or ages go by. The passenger cowers in a corner of his steel box, staring at the shining metal grille through which the voice once spoke. The grille must be worshiped; perhaps the voice will be heard again.

This is not a story by Franz Kafka or by one of his contemporary imitators. It is a recent dream remembered in precise detail by a successful New Yorker (one wife, three children, fair income, no analyst) who works with every outward appearance of contentment in one of Manhattan's new, midtown office buildings. Whatever Freudian or other analysis might make of it, the dream could serve as a perfect allegory for an era that is almost universally regarded as the Age of Anxiety. It speaks of big city towers in which life is lived in compartments and cubicles. It speaks of the century's increasingly complex machines that no one man can control. It speaks of the swift ascents and descents not only in a competitive business existence but in an ever-fluid society. It speaks of man's dreaded loss of identity, of a desperate need to make contact with his fellow man, with the world and with whatever may be beyond the world. Above all, it speaks of God grown silent.

Stage Whines. Anxiety seems to be the dominant fact—and is threatening to become the dominant cliché—of modern life. It shouts in the headlines, laughs nervously at cocktail parties, nags from advertisements, speaks suavely in the board room, whines from the stage, clatters from the Wall Street ticker, jokes with fake youthfulness on the golf course and whispers in privacy each day before the shaving mirror and the dressing table. Not merely the black statistics of murder, suicide, alcoholism and divorce betray anxiety (or that special form of anxiety which is guilt), but almost any innocent, everyday act: the limp or overhearty handshake, the second pack of cigarettes or the third martini, the forgotten appointment, the stammer in mid-sentence, the wasted hour before the TV set, the spanked child, the new car unpaid for.

Although he died in 1855, the great Danish existentialist Sören Kierkegaard described the effects of anxiety in terms that are strikingly apt today. He spoke of his "cowardly age," in which "one does everything possible by way of diversions and the Janizary music of loud-voiced enterprises to keep lonely thoughts away." Yet all the noise is in vain: "No Grand Inquisitor has in readiness such terrible tortures as has anxiety, and no spy knows how to attack more artfully the man he suspects, choosing the instant when he is weakest, nor knows how to lay traps where he will be caught and ensnared, and no sharp-witted judge knows how to interrogate, to examine the accused, as anxiety does, which never lets him escape, neither by diversion nor by noise, neither at work not at play, neither by day nor by night."

War or Peace. When a fact is as universal as love, death or anxiety, it becomes difficult to measure and classify. Man would not be human were he not anxious. Is his anxiety today really greater than ever before—different from Job's? Or is modern man simply a victim of distorted historical vision that always sees the present as bigger and worse than the past?

There is general agreement among psychiatrists, theologians, sociologists and even poets that in this era, anxiety is indeed different both in quantity and quality.

Other eras were turbulent, insecure and complex—the great migrations after the fall of the Roman Empire; the age of discovery; Copernicus and Galileo's tinkering with the universe, removing the earth and man from its center; the industrial revolution. But in a sense, the 20th century U.S. is the culmination of all these upheavals—itself the product of a gigantic migration, itself both champion and victim of the industrial revolution, itself faced with the necessity not only of accepting a new universe but of exploring it.

The American today is told without pause that the world is up to him—war or peace, prosperity or famine, the welfare or literacy of the last, remotest Congolese, Tibetan or Laotian. And he is facing his demanding destiny in a state of psychological and religious confusion.

For centuries of Christian civilization (and not Christian alone), man assumed that anxiety and guilt were part of his nature and that as a finite and fallen being, he had plenty to be guilty about. The only remedies were grace and faith. When the age of reason repealed the Fall, man was thrust back onto himself and, for a time, reason seemed to be an adequate substitute for the certainties of faith. Spinoza could write confidently: "Fear arises from a weakness of mind and therefore does not appertain to the use of reason." But it was soon clear that reason alone could not answer all man's questions, could not provide what he desperately needs: order and purpose in the universe. And so man invented substitute deities—History, the State, Environment. But in the end all these only led back to the nearly unbearable message that man is alone in a meaningless cosmos, subject only to the blind forces of evolution and responsible only to himself. As Kirilov puts it in Dostoevsky's *The Possessed:* "If there is no God, then I am god."

The discovery of the unconscious depths of man's mind by Schopenhauer, Freud and others seemed to offer an escape; here was a dark, mysterious realm, irrational as man knew himself to be irrational, to which he might shift responsibility for his acts. But this worked only partly; ultimately even the cult of the unconscious (psychoanalysis) directed man back to himself and his own resources. Many rejoice that man has been freed from the fear of demons, not realizing that it may be worse to have to fear himself. Many similarly rejoice that, to some extent, he has been freed from the fear of hell-fire, not realizing that he has instead been condemned to the fear of nothingness—what Paul Tillich calls the fear of "nonbeing."

Widespread awareness of all this has itself contributed to the change. Psychologists report that 30 years ago the U.S. was in an "age of covert anxiety." It is now in an age of "overt anxiety." People tend to believe that it is wrong and "sick" to feel anxious or guilty; they are beset by guilt about guilt, by anxiety about anxiety.

Bound and Free. Psychiatrists and theologians know, of course, that a certain amount of guilt and anxiety is inevitable and necessary in man. They are like pain: "bad" because they are discomforting, but in normal quantities necessary for survival because they warn of danger and because they make a human being responsible to others. The rare individual who feels neither guilt nor anxiety is a monster—a psychopath with no conscience. What psychologists call *Urangst,* or original anxiety, the anxiety that is inevitably part of any human being, is well described by Theologian Reinhold Niebuhr, who believes that it springs from man's dual character: on the one hand, man is involved in the contingencies of nature, like the animals; on the other, he has freedom and understanding of his position. "In short, man, being both bound and free, both limited and limitless, is anxious."

This basic, or existential, anxiety (which Niebuhr sees as the precondition of sin) is no more disturbing, in normal quantities, than is rational fear of danger. In contrast, neurotic anxiety is irrational fear, a response to a danger that is unknown, internal, intangible or unreal. Anxiety is fear in search of a cause. Authorities differ on the relationship of guilt to anxiety, but Dr. John Donnelly of Hartford's Institute of Living offers what is for laymen the most sense-making distinction: guilt is apprehension over some transgression in the past, whether actually committed or merely contemplated, whereas anxiety involves only the possible and the future. Because the German equivalent, *die Angst*, carries a stronger connotation of dread, many psychiatrists prefer this term to the English word. Of itself, anxiety is not a neurosis, but it is an essential ingredient in almost all neuroses, most major mental and psychosomatic illnesses. Its victims fall into three broad categories:

1. The whole men and women, who have such minor emotional disturbances as fear about the war or a compulsion to twist and untwist paper clips (symbolically twisting the boss's neck). Their aggressiveness, perfectionism or shyness are not exaggerated.

2. The walking wounded, who can usually control their anxiety and its symptoms well enough to function as breadwinners or housewives, but periodically break down and wind up, in a severe anxiety state, in a psychiatrist's office or, briefly, in a mental hospital.

3. The ambulance cases, who spend months or years or drag out their lives in mental hospitals, or (in some cases still not recognized often enough) land in the emergency rooms of general hospitals with psychosomatic illnesses often mistaken for heart attacks, asthma or pregnancy complications.

All the neurotic symptoms, major or minor, originate in the same way: they are defenses against anxiety. The most common are the phobias in which—to cover up anxiety and guilt too' painful to be acknowledged—people develop an irrational aversion to some act or object seemingly unconnected with their anxiety. Phobias seem to occur in dazzling profusion: Blakiston's *New Gould Medical Dictionary* lists 217 of them. More prevalent but less generally recognized as cover-ups for anxiety are compulsive forms of behavior and addictions to alcohol and narcotics.

Little Hans. How does a man become anxious to the point of phobia or compulsion? After decades of debate psychologists and psychiatrists are at last substantially agreed that anxiety arises from feelings of helplessness.* According to the best modern thinking, Freud never fully understood the essential nature of anxiety. His first theory, propounded in 1894, was that repressed libido (sexual energy) becomes anxiety, which later reappears as free-floating anxiety or a symptom (phobia of compulsion) that is equivalent to it. This, as critics pointed out, was a theory of mechanism and not an explanation of causes. So he tried again, and decided in 1923 that a totally different process was involved: anxiety was the cause of repression.

Freud's classic example was of little Hans, aged five, who was panic-stricken at the idea of having to go out in the street. Why? Freud explained that little Hans had strong Oedipal feelings toward his mother; therefore he had hostility toward his father and therefore anxiety. He repressed the anxiety and converted it into hippophobia—he was afraid to go out because he was afraid of being castrated by the bite of a horse. To Freud the horse represented little Hans's father. This elaborate hypothesis neatly fitted Freud's preoccupation with castration fears, which Psycho-

---

*Anxiety is not the same as depression. While anxiety is helplessness, depression is hopelessness. But helplessness unendurably prolonged leads inevitably to hopelessness. So anxiety and depression are seen together as often as not, in many classes of mental patients.

analyst Rollo May now interprets as the fear of losing mother's love and, hence, self-esteem.

Otto Rank (1884-1939), disciple of Freud, who later split with him, made a cult of birth trauma. To him life was a process of individuation, which meant a series of separations–birth, weaning, going to school, heading a household. To Rank, anxiety was the apprehension involved in these separations. Alfred Adler, apostle of inferiority feelings, never formulated a full-blown theory of anxiety, but showed more insight than his Vienna rivals in seeing the uses that the neurotic makes of anxiety. If it blocks his activity, it permits him to retreat to a previous state of security, to evade decisions and responsibility–and, therefore, dangers. Also, as happens in many families, it can be forged into a weapon for dominating others, who would rather yield to unreasonable demands than be made to feel guilty.

Power Drive. Anxiety won belated recognition as a social phenomenon in the U.S. from Karen Horney, Erich Fromm and Harry Stack Sullivan. To Fromm, the Freudian frustration of sex energy becomes anxiety only when it involves some value or way of life that the individual holds vital to his security–for instance, the prestige of having a pretty wife. Horney believed that Freud put the cart before the horse; anxiety, she held, came before the instinctual drives–the instincts developed into drives only under the whiplash of anxiety. To Sullivan, devotee of the "power motive," which drives man to pursue security, anxiety arose from the infant's apprehension of disapproval. And Sullivan had one significant insight: experiences that create anxiety not only limit the victim's activities, but also actually set limits to his awareness and hence to his learning ability.

University of Illinois Psychologist O. Hobart Mowrer agrees with Freud on the mechanism of anxiety's creation. But Mowrer differs on basic cause. To him the conflicts that cause anxiety are not so much animal and sexual as human and ethical. They involve the repression of moral strivings. Mowrer notes that anxiety arises when the person feared is also loved. Similarly, Psychoanalyst May sees anxiety in his patients not only when sexual or aggressive urges are revealed but also when the need or desire for constructive new powers is exposed. Thus, it is from the repression of *agape,* love of one's fellow men, as well as from the repression of *eros,* or sexual love, that anxiety springs.

As the earth-moving machines have bulldozed the landscape, so have the technologists bulldozed the manscape. Human nature, says Dr. May, has been made the object of control measures, just like any other part of nature. "Keeping busy" for its own sake has become a neurotic anxiety. While it may allay superficial anxiety, Dr. May holds that it exacerbates the deeper and more pervasive existential anxiety, about being and nonbeing. A do-it-yourselfer in a basement workshop may be too busy watching the guard on his bench saw to worry about traditional causes of anxiety, but at heart he eventually begins to wonder what is the meaning of life for him. That existential question, says May, is now the prevailing cause of the anxiety states that send patients to psychoanalysts. They are dealing less with *"Sexschmerz"* than with *Weltschmerz.*

Orthodoxy of Change. In the U.S. today, causes for such *Weltschmerz* are easy to find. Psychologists know that all change is threat and that all threat produces anxiety. The U.S., more than any other society in history, believes in change. Conservative in many ways, the U.S. has never been conservative in the sense of trying to preserve things the way they were yesterday. Its very orthodoxy is based on the idea of change: the most orthodox tenet in the American creed is that the individual can accomplish anything if he tries hard enough. It may be one of the glories of a free society, but it also carries great potential danger and may well be the greatest single cause of anxiety on the American scene. From the noble notion that man is free to do anything that he can do, the U.S. somehow subtly proceeds to the notion that he *must* do anything he can and, finally, that there is nothing he cannot do.

This leads to a kind of compulsory freedom that encourages people not only to ignore their limitations but to defy them: the dominant myth is that the old can grow young, the indecisive can become leaders of men, the housewives can become glamour girls, the glamour girls can become actresses, the slow-witted can become intellectuals.

Almost every boy in the U.S. has dinned into him the idea that he must excel his father—a guaranteed producer of anxiety, by Freudian theory, if the boy has grown up idolizing his father as a paragon of power and virtues. The process is severest in the sons of outstandingly successful men: their anxiety neuroses are as notorious as the traditional case of the preacher's son becoming a drunkard. A career girl is shredded by the need to excel father or mother or both, and for her the problem may be complicated by Oedipal feelings toward mother.

Many people feel guilty simply about not being talented enough or intelligent enough or well-informed enough. If anybody can be anything he wishes, no wonder the businessman is made to feel guilty—he has neither ear nor taste for modern music (but somehow, the artist never seems to feel guilty about not understanding business). No wonder, too, that the adman thinks he ought to be able to write a novel or to know all about the atom. In an absurd misapplication of the ideal of equality, one man's opinions become as valid as another's. Thus, every man competes not only in his own job or his own social setting; he also somehow feels he must compete with the TV newscaster and the editorial writer (not very difficult), with the physics professor and the philosopher (very difficult indeed).

Why Grow Old? Every girl is tight-corseted with the propaganda that she must have a slim, svelte figure, no matter what her natural body build or bone structure. She may react to this either by trimming down mercilessly and suffering near starvation; or she may surrender to the neurotic pleasures of overeating—all the time rationalizing that the trouble is in her glands (which it almost never is). Another deliberate anxiety builder is the slogan, "Why grow old?" It introduces a prescription containing a teaspoonful of wisdom, such as the values of exercise and a balanced diet, diluted in an ocean of nonsense about wrinkle erasers and pep medicines. Actually, the less anxiety is associated with the inevitable aging process, the better are people's chances of growing old gracefully and with a sense of fulfillment.

The phenomenon of change in the U.S. contributes to anxiety in another way: no one "knows his place," and even if he does and likes it, there are no easy ways of announcing the fact to others. The worker can indeed still become boss, the immigrant a settled American. But how do they show their newly acquired place in life? No aristocratic titles, no rigid distinctions of dress are available; man's achievements can be signaled only by the fascinating game of displaying "status symbols." Hence the endless American preoccupation with what is "in" and what is "out"–clothes, addresses, speech, schools, cars. The phenomenon (well understood by U.S. novelists, most notably John O'Hara) tends to force Americans into infinite patterns of snobbery and reverse snobbery. The first step after success is to display wealth; the second step is to learn that flashy display is wrong; the third step is to learn that, if one is really "secure," one can afford even to be flashy. This interminable dialectic of snobbery can produce genuine anxiety, as is shown by the innumerable cases of people who frantically seek to hide their families, change their names, tailor their accents–and wind up losing their identities.

This particular form of social anxiety is the most potent of the "hidden persuaders" used by admen. Vance *(The Status Seekers)* Packard, while superficial in much of his work, is correct in pointing out that a key element in selling is to present a product so that it promises to satisfy some need for security or power.

Abstract and Atonal.   Two of the forces that might be counted on to reduce anxiety in U.S. life–the artists and the social scientists–are contributing to it. In abstract painting and atonal music, the modern artist has largely destroyed recognizable reality, creating a world in which he is master because it is incomprehensible to others: he is alone, but at least he is boss. In literature and drama, he has just moved through a long period of writing psychiatric case histories, and is now experimenting with improvised works that seek to destroy the barrier between audience and artist. His traditional role is to assume the burdens of guilt and anxiety freely, transforming them in his own soul into works of art that can offer the audience catharsis or clarity. This is the function for which the artist is applauded, adored–and paid. More and more today, he rejects that function and insists on dragging his audiences into his own neurosis, shifting the burden of guilt and anxiety on to them.

The social scientists have helped make the U.S. the most self-analytic civilization ever known. Rome was not conscious of the "fall of the Roman Empire"; the Crusaders scarcely analyzed the infectious new ideas they brought back from the East; the romantics wrote new kinds of poetry, but did not turn out essays on the alarming death wishes in those poems. Americans cannot make a move without having it declared a trend, viewed critically in innumerable books deploring *The Lonely Crowd, The Status Seekers, The Organization Man.* The exhortations offered to the U.S. public are always contradictory. No sooner had Americans learned that they must not be rugged individualists but must practice "adjustment," than they were told that they were all turning into conformists. No sooner had they learned that children must be raised progressively and permissively than they were told that children desperately want discipline. No sooner had they accepted the fact that women deserved and needed equal rights than they were informed that women had become too much like men.

Anxious Intellectuals.   This kind of ever-contradictory ferment gives the U.S. an exciting intellectual life, but it also makes anxious intellectuals. The intellectuals, in turn, carry their anxiety to the rest of the country through the immensely fast popularization of new ideas. U.S. intellectuals are forever complaining that no one pays attention to their opinions. This is patently untrue: very likely, they complain merely to cover their own guilt at not being as certain about things as they secretly feel they should be—in short, at not being leaders.

This points to what may be the ultimate cause of anxiety in the U.S.: pragmatism. It not only—legitimately—questions every truth, but it also questions whether the concept of truth itself has any meaning. When mixed with logical positivism, it leads to the notion that philosophy, the search for truth beyond mere language or mathematical symbols, is impossible. Few things could produce more anxiety in people who either believe in, or want to believe in, a moral order.

High Places and Dirt. Fantastic and confused though symptoms of anxiety can be, there is often a kind of logic, even a dramatic beauty or poetic justice, about them. They seek to compensate for what is lacking. Thus, according to the Jungian school, the unconscious tries to correct or heal disorganization of the ego—or of society—by doggedly creating images of value, order and meaning. This process can produce fanatics, prophets and saints; it did produce, according to the analytic view of history, Torquemada, Calvin, Knox and Jonathan Edwards. No one can say what prophets or fanatics the U.S. may produce to combat its Age of Anxiety, but its people are certain to react—possibly in futile and less spectacular ways—to the disorder and the threats of their environment.

Logically enough, considering the environment, the phobias most often found in U.S. metropolitan areas have to do with high places, airplanes and dirt. Fear of heights is not a serious matter if it involves only skyscrapers: an occasional high-steel worker or window-washer has to change his job because of this. But many people, as they grow older, become neurotically cautious, get to the stage where they cannot even go near a window above the ground floor. In such severe cases, the anxiety usually extends far beyond this symptom and pervades the whole personality. Airplanes evoke a comparable phobia. In practical terms, such case histories seem relatively simple:

A traveling salesman may be economically crippled and have to change jobs if his company orders him to leave the rails and take to the air. Viewed more philosophically, such cases may suggest a protest against man's high-flying pride.

Dread of dirt (mysophobia) goes hand in overwashed hand with the cleanliness compulsion. The victim must carry out his cleansing routine even though he knows it is unreasonable. Otherwise, he finds himself the prisoner of intolerable anxiety. The cleanliness compulsion commonly arises from conflict involving a strict and perfectionist parent. The victim begins by being simply overneat and fussy about cleanliness. Then he gets into conflict with all the people around him who do not comply with his compulsive standards. His compulsion may drive him to excessive washing of his body, of clothes, and even doorknobs. (One legendary American tycoon would not shake hands or touch a doorknob unless he had on white cotton gloves.) He gets to the point where he actually washes the skin off hands and has to go into a hospital.

Most in the Middle. Research in recent years has shown some fairly clear patterns about where anxiety develops. It is greatest where change is swiftest. Children are not very susceptible to it; their problems of adjustment are normal for their age (adolescents show confusing symptoms). Anxiety is most apparent in the 20-to-40 age group. These youngish adults may not suffer from it more than their elders, but they talk more about it. In any case, they are the most active and mobile members of society, constantly making decisions, changing jobs or moving to new locations. From 40 to 70, anxiety is usually better controlled or concealed. Above 70, it breaks out again, now that modern medicine has so greatly prolonged the lives of so many people who are financially and socially insecure, who feel unwanted, useless and rejected.

By social stratification, reports Cornell University's Dr. Lawrence Hinkle, there is least anxiety at the top and bottom, and most in between. An upsurge of anxiety has begun, and more is predicted, among Negroes, for whom possibilities of social and economic advancement, to a degree undreamed of at war's end, are now developing. Puerto Rican and Mexican immigrants will have their innings with anxiety later; opportunities for mobility and morbidity go together.

Wherever there is opportunity, there is anxiety: it is just as severe in the ivied halls of research institutions as it is in the garment district—or in some Government offices. And it is far more severe than it used to be on farms. Big business, on the other hand, is not, as often described, a single pail of anxiously writhing worms. Some giant corporations have become "settled societies" of their own, in which the rungs of the promotion ladder are neatly numbered and everybody knows when he may have his chance to step up. But in advertising, communications and entertainment, anxiety is extensive and vociferously proclaimed; half the name actors on Broadway and in Hollywood have been analyzed, and the others should never be allowed off the couch.

Priests and Prisoners. It is among writers and other editorial workers that Raymond B. Cattell and Ivan H. Sheier of the University of Illinois have found the highest anxiety ratings, based on complex personality tests. That they come just ahead of the Navy's underwater demolition teams (frogmen) is probably due more to their higher verbal abilities than to on-the-job hazards. Air pilots in training have, naturally, more anxiety than business executives; priests have less—but this may be a reflection of their having found a certainty of faith and of a rigid routine that conceals if it does not catharize anxiety. Convicts have far less than average. This reflects both routine and the high prison population of conscienceless psychopaths. Least anxious of all, on the Cattell-Sheier scale, are university administrators.

Cattell and Sheier give the U.S. a lower anxiety rating than Britain. Explaining this apparent surprise, they suggest that what passes for anxiety in the U.S. is really the stress of effort in a land of ambition, competition and challenge. More convincingly, they note that anxiety is higher in situations where the individual feels unable to save himself. The anxiety of waiting for D-day is worse than the fear of walking through a field of land mines. This principle may help explain the attitude of many U.S.

scientists and liberal intellectuals toward The Bomb. The possibility of civilization's total destruction is usually cited as one of the great factors contributing to anxiety in the U.S. But there is a strong suggestion that The Bomb is merely a handy device, welcomed almost with relief, for the release of anxiety and guilt that have little to do with the subject as such. For many Bomb worriers, it seems to be a true phobia, a kind of secular substitute for the Last Judgment, and a truly effective nuclear ban would undoubtedly deprive them of a highly comforting sense of doom.

Drugs for the Mind. What can psychiatry do to combat anxiety and the various mental illnesses it feeds? The Joint Commission on Mental Illness and Health, set up by Congress in 1955, last week issued an ambitious prescription in a report asking for $3 billion to be spent annually by 1971 (three times the present amount) and for other sweeping reforms to make better psychiatric service more generally available. It also called for a study to find out what is "the public's image of the psychiatrist," suggesting that there is guilt and anxiety within the profession itself.

As for treatment of patients, sedatives ranging in potency from aspirin to barbiturates and narcotics have no effect on the underlying emotional state; all they can do is relieve the symptoms temporarily. Only since 1954 have there been tranquilizing drugs specifically designed and directed toward relieving signs of anxiety. For depression, psychiatrists are now prescribing the psychic energizers, of which half a dozen, such as Marplan and Niamid, have won fairly general acceptance. But talking it out in psychotherapy is generally recognized as the only measure that offers the possibility of a true cure. There is still controversy as to the value of different types of treatment, especially between the advocates of the analytic schools and the psychiatrists who favor shorter, more "directive" therapy. There is some question as to whether guilt feelings should be relieved in all cases. Dr. May reports that diluting a patient's guilt feelings allays superficial anxiety but sometimes obscures the "genuine if confused insights of the patient into himself."

Order Out of Chaos. Beyond curing the obviously sick, psychologists and psychiatrists evidently must make an effort to teach people not so much to eliminate guilt and anxiety as to understand them and live with them constructively. That is the point made by Hans Hofmann, associate professor of theology at Harvard Divinity School, in a new book called *Religion and Mental Health* (Harper). Writes Hofmann:

"Our time is one of ferment and potential rebirth. This is so precisely because it is a time full of chaos. . . . It was only natural that Sigmund Freud should at the beginning of his career have thought of the irrational aspects of the human personality as chaotic and potentially dangerous powers. . . . It did not occur to him that chaos in itself may represent a very positive and fertile current of life. For the people of the Old Testament, especially in the creation story, the question was not: 'Why is there chaos?' but rather: 'Why is there order?' For them, order was the outgrowth of daily living. . . . The unique function of man, in their view, is to live in close, creative touch with chaos, and thereby experience the birth of order. . . . Surprisingly enough, modern psychotherapists share this ancient knowledge."

Fear of:

achluophobia	darkness
aichmophobia	pointed objects
ailurophobia	cats
anthophobia	flowers
astrophobia	stars
ballistophobia	missiles
barophobia	gravity
cherophobia	gaiety
chionophobia	snow
chronophobia	time
climacophobia	staircases
dextrophobia	objects on the right side of the body
erythrophobia	red
gephyrophobia	crossing bridges
graphophobia	writing
hypengyophobia	responsibility
kathisophobia	sitting down
levophobia	objects on the left side of the body
linonophobia	string
ophidiophobia	snakes
pantophobia	everything
phobophobia	being afraid
phonophobia	one's own voice
photophobia	light
phronemophobia	thinking
scopophobia	being seen
siderodromo-	
phobia	railroad traveling
sitophobia	eating
stasibasiphobia	walking or standing
thalassophobia	the ocean
vermiphobia	infestation with worms

Do you see indications that the United States is in an age of "overt anxiety"?

One category of the victims of anxiety is "whole men and women . . . who have such minor emotional disturbances as . . . a compulsion to twist and untwist paper clips" (p. 80). Describe a similar disturbance that you have observed and what you believe to be the emotion and the reason for it. Indicate the meaning it had for you.

Is the notion that "the individual can accomplish anything if he tries hard enough" (p. 82) a source of or a relief from anxiety?

The Love Song of J. Alfred Prufrock

T. S. ELIOT

> *S'io credesse che mia risposta fosse*
> *A persona che mai tornasse al mondo,*
> *Questa fiamma staria senza piu scosse.*
> *Ma perciocche giammai di questo fondo*
> *Non torno vivo alcun, s'i'odo il vero,*
> *Senza tema d'infamia ti rispondo.*

Let us go then, you and I,
When the evening is spread out against the sky
Like a patient etherized upon a table;
Let us go, through certain half-deserted streets,
The muttering retreats
Of restless nights in one-night cheap hotels
And sawdust restaurants with oyster-shells:
Streets that follow like a tedious argument
Of insidious intent
To lead you to an overwhelming question . . .
Oh, do not ask, "What is it?"
Let us go and make our visit.

In the room the women come and go
Talking of Michelangelo.

The yellow fog that rubs its back upon the window-panes,
The yellow smoke that rubs its muzzle on the window-panes
Licked its tongue into the corners of the evening,
Lingered upon the pools that stand in drains,
Let fall upon its back the soot that falls from chimneys,
Slipped by the terrace, made a sudden leap,
And seeing that it was a soft October night,
Curled once about the house, and fell asleep.

And indeed there will be time
For the yellow smoke that slides along the street,
Rubbing its back upon the window-panes;
There will be time, there will be time
To prepare a face to meet the faces that you meet;
There will be time to murder and create,
And time for all the works and days of hands
That lift and drop a question on your plate;
Time for you and time for me,
And time yet for a hundred indecisions,

And for a hundred visions and revisions,
Before the taking of a toast and tea.   *In England having tea + bisqutes.*

    In the room the women come and go
Talking of Michelangelo.

    And indeed there will be time
To wonder, "Do I dare?" and, "Do I dare?"
Time to turn back and descend the stair,
With a bald spot in the middle of my hair—
[They will say: "How his hair is growing thin!"]
My morning coat, my collar mounting firmly to the chin,
My necktie rich and modest, but asserted by a simple pin—
[They will say: "But how his arms and legs are thin!"]
Do I dare
Disturb the universe?   *poet must make people think (his goal)*
In a minute there is time
For decisions and revisions which a minute will reverse.

    For I have known them all already, known them all:—
Have known the evenings, mornings, afternoons,
I have measured out my life with coffee spoons;
I known the voices dying with a dying fall
Beneath the music from a farther room.
    So how should I presume?

    And I have known the eyes already, known them all—
The eyes that fix you in a formulated phrase,
And when I am formulated, sprawling on a pin,
When I am pinned and wriggling on the wall,
Then how should I begin
To spit out all the butt-ends of my days and ways?
    And how should I presume?

    And I have known the arms already, known them all—
Arms that are braceleted and white and bare
[But in the lamplight, downed with light brown hair!]
Is it perfume from a dress
That makes me so digress?
Arms that lie along a table, or wrap about a shawl.
    And should I then presume?
    And how should I begin?

        · · ·

Shall I say, I have gone at dusk through narrow streets
And watched the smoke that rises from the pipes
Of lonely men in shirt-sleeves, leaning out of windows? . . .

    I should have been a pair of ragged claws
Scuttling across the floors of silent seas.

        · · ·

And the afternoon, the evening, sleeps so peacefully!
Smoothed by long fingers,
Asleep . . . tired . . . or it malingers,
Stretched on the floor, here beside you and me.
Should I, after tea and cakes and ices,
Have the strength to force the moment to its crisis?
But though I have wept and fasted, wept and prayed,
Though I have seen my head [grown slightly bald] brought in
→ upon a platter,
I am no prophet—and here's no great matter;
I have seen the moment of my greatness flicker,
And I have seen the eternal Footman hold my coat, and snicker,
And in short, I was afraid.

   And would it have been worth it, after all,
After the cups, the marmalade, the tea,
Among the porcelain, among some talk of you and me,
Would it have been worth while,
To have bitten off the matter with a smile,
To have squeezed the universe into a ball
To roll it toward some overwhelming question,
To say: "I am Lazarus, come from the dead,
Come back to tell you all, I shall tell you all"—
If one, settling a pillow by her head,
   Should say: "That is not what I meant at all.
   That is not it, at all."

   And would it have been worth it, after all,
Would it have been worth while,
After the sunsets and the dooryards and the sprinkled streets,
After the novels, after the teacups, after the skirts that trail
   along the floor—
And this, and so much more?—
It is impossible to say just what I mean!
But as if a magic lantern threw the nerves in patterns on a screen:
Would it have been worth while
If one, settling a pillow or throwing off a shawl,
And turning toward the window, should say:
   "That is not it at all,
   That is not what I meant, at all."

           . . .

No! I am not Prince Hamlet, nor was meant to be;
Am an attendant lord, one that will do
To swell a progress, start a scene or two,
Advise the prince; no doubt, an easy tool,
Deferential, glad to be of use,
Politic, cautious, and meticulous;
Full of high sentence, but a bit obtuse;
At times, indeed, almost ridiculous—
Almost, at times, the Fool.

I grow old . . . I grow old . . .
I shall wear the bottoms of my trousers rolled.

Shall I part my hair behind? Do I dare to eat a peach?
I shall wear white flannel trousers, and walk upon the beach.
I have heard the mermaids singing, each to each.
I do not think that they will sing to me. *A love song.*

*I have seen
life but no
more.*

I have seen them riding seaward on the waves
Combing the white hair of the waves blown back
When the wind blows the water white and black.

We have lingered in the chambers of the sea *(by the water)*
By sea-girls wreathed with seaweed red and brown *He can not be
awakened by love*
Till human voices wake us, and we drown.
*so he
drowns*

What are the various manifestations of Prufrock's anxiety?

Consider Prufrock from the point of view of psychologist Abraham Maslow's statement: "Every age but ours has its model, its ideal. All of these have been given up by our culture: the saint, the hero, the gentleman, the knight, the mystic. About all we have left is the well-adjusted man without problems, a very pale and doubtful substitute."

In your opinion is Prufrock one of the "whole men," the "walking wounded," or the "ambulance cases"? (p. 80)

The Lake Isle of Innisfree

WILLIAM BUTLER YEATS

I will arise and go now, and go to Innisfree,
And a small cabin build there, of clay and wattles made;
Nine bean rows will I have there, a hive for the honey bee,
    And live alone in the bee-loud glade.

And I shall have some peace there, for peace comes dropping
    slow,
Dropping from the veils of the morning to where the cricket
    sings;
There midnight's all a glimmer, and noon a purple glow,
    And evening full of the linnet's wings.

I will arise and go now, for always night and day
I hear lake water lapping with low sounds by the shore;
While I stand on the roadway, or on the pavements gray,
    I hear it in the deep heart's core.

Which lines in this poem express a desire for tranquillity arising out of a deep feeling of anxiety? About the origin of this poem Yeats wrote that one day while walking along a London street "[I felt] very home-sick . . . heard a little tinkle of water and saw a fountain in a shop window . . . and began to remember [that I had planned] to live some day in a cottage on a little island called Innisfree."

How do you understand the last line of the poem?

The poet is in one place and wishes to be in another. Recall a similar experience in your life and your emotional response to it.

Preface to a Twenty Volume Suicide Note

LEROI JONES

(For Kellie Jones, Born 16 May, 1959)
Lately, I've become accustomed to the way
The ground opens up and envelops me
Each time I go out to walk the dog.
Or the broad-edged silly music the wind
Makes when I run for a bus . . .

Things have come to that.

And now, each night I count the stars,
And each night I get the same number.
And when they will not come to be counted,
I count the holes they leave.

Nobody sings anymore.

And then last night, I tiptoed up
To my daughter's room and heard her

Talking to someone, and when I opened
The door, there was no one there...
Only she on her knees, peeking into

Her own clasped hands.

What images in this poem suggest anxiety?

How does the poet interpret his experience? (See p. 69.)

Compare the emotional effect of the last line of this poem with the last line of
Lake Isle of Innisfree. (p. 92)

from **The Invisible Man**

RALPH ELLISON

I had been away long enough for the streets to seem strange. The uptown
rhythms were slower and yet were somehow faster; a different tension
was in the hot night air. I made my way through the summer crowds, not
to the district but to Barrelhouse's Jolly Dollar, a dark hole of a bar and
grill on upper Eighth Avenue, where one of my best contacts, Brother
Maceo, could usually be found about this time, having his evening's beer.

Looking through the window, I could see men in working clothes and
a few rummy women leaning at the bar, and down the aisle between the
bar and counter were a couple of men in black and blue checked sport
shirts eating barbecue. A cluster of men and women hovered near the juke
box at the rear. But when I went in Brother Maceo wasn't among them
and I pushed to the bar, deciding to wait over a beer.

"Good evening, Brothers," I said, finding myself beside two men whom
I had seen around before; only to have them look at me oddly, the eyebrows of the tall one raising at a drunken angle as he looked at the other.

"Shit," the tall man said.

"You said it, man; he a relative of yourn?"

"Shit, he goddam sho ain't no kin of mine!"

I turned and looked at them, the room suddenly cloudy.

"He must be drunk," the second man said. "Maybe he thinks he's kin to
you."

"Then his whiskey's telling him a damn lie. I wouldn't be his kin even
if I was—Hey, Barrelhouse!"

I moved away, down the bar, looking at them out of a feeling of suspense. They didn't sound drunk and I had said nothing to offend, and I was certain that they knew who I was. What was it? The Brotherhood greeting was as familiar as "Give me some skin" or "Peace, it's wonderful."

I saw Barrelhouse rolling down from the other end of the bar, his white apron indented by the tension of its cord so that he looked like that kind of metal beer barrel which has a groove around its middle; and seeing me now, he began to smile.

"Well, I'll be damned if it ain't the good brother," he said, stretching out his hand. "Brother, where you been keeping yourself?"

"I've been working downtown," I said, feeling a surge of gratitude.

"Fine, fine!" Barrelhouse said.

"Business good?"

"I'd rather not discuss it, Brother. Business is bad. Very bad."

"I'm sorry to hear it. You'd better give me a beer," I said, "after you've served these gentlemen." I watched them in the mirror.

"Sure thing," Barrelhouse said, reaching for a glass and drawing a beer. "What you putting down, ole man?" he said to the tall man.

"Look here, Barrel, we wanted to ask you one question," the tall one said. "We just wanted to know if you could tell us just whose brother this here cat's supposed to be? He come in here just now calling everybody brother."

"He's *my* brother," Barrel said, holding the foaming glass between his long fingers. "Anything wrong with that?"

"Look, fellow," I said down the bar, "that's our way of speaking. I meant no harm in calling you brother. I'm sorry you misunderstood me."

"Brother, here's your beer," Barrelhouse said.

"So he's *your* brother, eh, Barrel?"

Barrel's eyes narrowed as he pressed his huge chest across the bar, looking suddenly sad. "You enjoying yourself, MacAdams?" he said gloomily. "You like your beer?"

"Sho," MacAdams said.

"It cold enough?"

"Sho, but Barrel—"

"You like the groovy music on the juke?" Barrelhouse said.

"Hell, yes, but—"

"And you like our good, clean, sociable atmosphere?"

"Sho, but that ain't what I'm talking about," the man said.

"Yeah, but that's what *I'm* talking about," Barrelhouse said mournfully. "And if you like it, *like* it, and don't start trying to bug my other customers. This here man's done more for the community than you'll ever do."

"*What* community?" MacAdams said, cutting his eyes around toward me. "I hear he got the white fever and left . . . ."

"You liable to *hear* anything," Barrelhouse said. "There's some paper back there in the gents' room. You ought to wipe out your ears."

"Never mind my ears."

"Aw come on, Mac," his friend said. "Forget it. Ain't the man done apologized?"

"I said never mind my ears," MacAdams said. "You just tell your brother he ought to be careful 'bout who he claims as kinfolks. Some of us don't think so much of his kind of politics."

I looked from one to the other. I considered myself beyond the stage of street-fighting, and one of the worst things I could do upon returning to the community was to engage in a brawl. I looked at MacAdams and was glad when the other man pushed him down the bar.

"That MacAdams thinks he's right," Barrelhouse said. "He's the kind caint nobody please. Be frank though, there's lots feel like that now."

I shook my head in bafflement. I'd never met that kind of antagonism before. "What's happened to Brother Maceo?" I said.

"I don't know, Brother. He don't come in so regular these days. Things are kinda changing up here. Ain't much money floating around."

"Times are hard everywhere. But what's been going on up here, Barrel?" I said.

"Oh, you know how it is, Brother; things are tight and lots of folks who got jobs through you people have lost them. You know how it goes."

"You mean people in our organization?"

"Quite a few of them are. Fellows like Brother Maceo."

"But why? They were doing all right."

"Sure they was—as long as you people was fighting for 'em. But the minute y'all stopped, they started throwing folks out on the street."

I looked at him, big and sincere before me. It was unbelievable that the Brotherhood had stopped its work, and yet he wasn't lying. "Give me another beer," I said. Then someone called him from the back, and he drew the beer and left.

I drank it slowly, hoping Brother Maceo would appear before I had finished. When he didn't I waved to Barrelhouse and left for the district. Perhaps Brother Tarp could explain; or at least tell me something about Clifton.

I walked through the dark block over to Seventh and started down; things were beginning to look serious. Along the way I saw not a single sign of Brotherhood activity. In a hot side street I came upon a couple striking matches along the curb, kneeling as though looking for a lost coin, the matches flaring dimly in their faces. Then I found myself in a strangely familiar block and broke out in a sweat: I had walked almost to Mary's door, and turned now and hurried away.

Barrelhouse had prepared me for the darkened windows of the district, but not, when I let myself in, to call in vain through the dark to Brother Tarp. I went to the room where he slept, but he was not there; then I went through the dark hall to my old office and threw myself into my desk chair, exhausted. Everything seemed to be slipping away from me and I could find no quick absorbing action that would get it under control. I tried to think of whom among the district committee I might call for information concerning Clifton, but here again I was balked. For if I selected one who believed that I had requested to be transferred because I hated my own people it would only complicate matters. No doubt there would be some who'd resent my return, so it was best to confront them all at once without giving any one of them the opportunity to organize any sentiment against me. It was best that I talk with Brother Tarp, whom I trusted. When he came in he could give me an idea of the state of affairs, and perhaps tell me what had actually happened to Clifton.

But Brother Tarp didn't arrive. I went out and got a container of coffee and returned to spend the night poring over the district's records. When he hadn't returned by three A.M. I went to his room and took a look around. It was empty, even the bed was gone. I'm all alone, I thought. A lot has occurred about which I wasn't told; something that had not only stifled the members' interest but which, according to the records, had sent them away in droves. Barrelhouse had said that the organization had quit fighting, and that was the only explanation I could find for Brother Tarp's leaving. Unless, of course, he'd had disagreements with Clifton or some of the other leaders. And now returning to my desk I noticed his gift of Douglass' portrait was gone. I felt in my pocket for the leg chain, at least I hadn't forgotten to take that along. I pushed the records aside; they told me nothing of why things were as they were. Picking up the telephone I called Clifton's number, hearing it ring on and on. Finally I gave it up and went to sleep in my chair. Everything had to wait until the strategy meeting. Returning to the district was like returning to a city of the dead.

Somewhat to my surprise there were a good number of members in the hall when I awoke, and having no directives from the committee on how to proceed I organized them into teams to search for Brother Clifton. Not one could give me any definite information. Brother Clifton had appeared at the district as usual up to the time of his disappearance. There had been no quarrels with committee members, and he was as popular as ever. Nor had there been any clashes with Ras the Exhorter—although in the past week he had been increasingly active. As for the loss of membership and influence, it was a result of a new program which had called for the shelving of our old techniques of agitation. There had been, to my surprise, a switch in emphasis from local issues to those more national and international in scope, and it was felt that for the moment the interests of Harlem were not of first importance. I didn't know what to make of it, since there had been no such change of program downtown. Clifton was forgotten, everything which I was to do now seemed to depend upon getting an explanation from the committee, and I waited with growing agitation to be called to the strategy meeting.

Such meetings were usually held around one o'clock and we were notified well ahead. But by eleven-thirty I had received no word and I became worried. By twelve an uneasy sense of isolation took hold of me. Something was cooking, but what, how, why? Finally I phoned headquarters, but could reach none of the leaders. What is this, I wondered; then I called the leaders of other districts with the same results. And now I was certain that the meeting was being held. But why without me? Had they investigated Wrestrum's charges and decided they were true? It seemed that the membership *had* fallen off after I had gone downtown. Or was it the woman? Whatever it was, now was not the time to leave me out of a meeting; things were too urgent in the district. I hurried down to headquarters.

When I arrived the meeting was in session, just as I expected, and word had been left that it was not to be disturbed by anyone. It was obvious that they hadn't forgotten to notify me. I left the building in a rage. Very well, I thought, when they do decide to call me they'll have to find me. I should never have been shifted in the first place, and now that I was sent back to clean up the mess they should aid me as quickly as possible. I would do no more running downtown, nor would I accept any program that they sent up without consulting the Harlem committee. Then I decided, of all things, to shop for a pair of new shoes, and walked over to Fifth Avenue.

It was hot, the walks still filled with noontime crowds moving with reluctance back to their jobs. I moved along close to the curb to avoid the bumping and agitated changes of pace, the chattering women in summer dresses, finally entering the leather-smelling, air-cooled interior of the shoe store with a sense of relief.

My feet felt light in the new summer shoes as I went back into the blazing heat, and I recalled the old boyhood pleasure of discarding winter shoes for sneakers and the neighborhood foot races that always followed, that lightfooted, speedy, floating sensation. Well, I thought, you've run your last foot race and you'd better get back to the district in case you're called. I hurried now, my feet feeling trim and light as I moved through the oncoming rush of sunbeaten faces. To avoid the crowd on Forty-second Street I turned off at Forty-third and it was here that things began to boil.

A small fruit wagon with an array of bright peaches and pears stood near the curb, and the vendor, a florid man with bulbous nose and bright black Italian eyes, looked at me knowingly from beneath his huge white-and-orange umbrella then over toward a crowd that had formed alongside the building across the street. What's wrong with him? I thought. Then I was across the street and passing the group standing with their backs to me. A clipped, insinuating voice spieled words whose meaning I couldn't catch and I was about to pass on when I saw the boy. He was a slender brown fellow whom I recognized immediately as a close friend of Clifton's, and who now was looking intently across the tops of cars to where down the block near the post office on the other side a tall policeman was approaching. Perhaps he'll know something, I thought, as he looked around to see me and stopped in confusion.

"Hello, there," I began, and when he turned toward the crowd and whistled I didn't know whether he was telling me to do the same or signalling to someone else. I swung around, seeing him step to where a large carton sat beside the building and sling its canvas straps to his shoulder as once more he looked toward the policeman, ignoring me. Puzzled, I moved into the crowd and pressed to the front where at my feet I saw a square piece of cardboard upon which something was moving with furious action. It was some kind of toy and I glanced at the crowd's fascinated eyes and down again, seeing it clearly this time. I'd seen nothing like it before. A grinning doll of orange-and-black tissue paper with thin flat cardboard disks forming its head and feet and which some mysterious mechanism was causing to move up and down in a loose-jointed, shoulder-shaking, infuriatingly sensuous motion, a dance that was completely detached from the black, mask-like face. It's no jumping-jack, but *what*, I thought, seeing the doll throwing itself about with the fierce defiance of someone performing a degrading act in public, dancing as though it received a perverse pleasure from its motions. And beneath the chuckles of the crowd I could hear the swishing of its ruffled paper, while the same out-of-the-corner-of-the-mouth voice continued to spiel:

Shake it up! Shake it up!
He's Sambo, the dancing doll, ladies and gentlemen.
Shake him, stretch him by the neck and set him down,
—He'll do the rest. Yes!

He'll make you laugh, he'll make you sigh, si-igh.
He'll make you want to dance, and dance—
Here you are, ladies and gentlemen, Sambo,
The dancing doll.
Buy one for your baby. Take him to your girl friend and
    she'll love you, loove you!
He'll keep you entertained. He'll make you weep sweet—
Tears from laughing.
Shake him, shake him, you cannot break him
For he's Sambo, the dancing, Sambo, the prancing,
Sambo, the entrancing, Sambo Boogie Woogie paper doll.
And all for twenty-five cents, the quarter part of a dollar . . .
Ladies and gentlemen, he'll bring you joy, step up and
    meet him, Sambo the—

I knew I should get back to the district but I was held by the in-
animate, boneless bouncing of the grinning doll and struggled between the
desire to join in the laughter and to leap upon it with both feet, when it
suddenly collapsed and I saw the tip of the spieler's toe press upon the cir-
cular cardboard that formed the feet and a broad black hand come down,
its fingers deftly lifting the doll's head and stretching it upward, twice its
length, then releasing it to dance again. And suddenly the voice didn't go
with the hand. It was as though I had waded out into a shallow pool only
to have the bottom drop out and the water close over my head. I looked up.

"Not you . . ." I began. But his eyes looked past me deliberately unsee-
ing. I was paralyzed, looking at him, knowing I wasn't dreaming, hearing:

What makes him happy, what makes him dance,
This Sambo, this jambo, this high-stepping joy boy?
He's more than a toy, ladies and gentlemen, he's Sambo,
    the dancing doll, the twentieth-century miracle.
Look at that rumba, that suzy-q, he's Sambo-Boogie,
Sambo-Woogie, you don't have to feed him, he sleeps
    collapsed, he'll kill your depression
And your dispossession, he lives upon the sunshine of
    your lordly smile
And only twenty-five cents, the brotherly two bits of a
    dollar because he wants me to eat.
It gives him pleasure to see me eat.
You simply take him and shake him . . . and he does
    the rest.

Thank you, lady . . .

It was Clifton, riding easily back and forth on his knees, flexing his legs without shifting his feet, his right shoulder raised at an angle and his arm pointing stiffly at the bouncing doll as he spieled from the corner of his mouth.

The whistle came again, and I saw him glance quickly toward his lookout, the boy with the carton.

"Who else wants little Sambo before we take it on the lambo? Speak up, ladies and gentlemen, who wants little . . . ?"

And again the whistle. "Who wants Sambo, the dancing, prancing? Hurry, hurry, ladies and gentlemen. There's no license for little Sambo, the joy spreader. You can't tax joy, so speak up, ladies and gentlemen . . . "

For a second our eyes met and he gave me a contemptuous smile, then he spieled again. I felt betrayed. I looked at the doll and felt my throat constrict. The rage welled behind the phlegm as I rocked back on my heels and crouched forward. There was a flash of whiteness and a splatter like heavy rain striking a newspaper and I saw the doll go over backwards, wilting into a dripping rag of frilled tissue, the hateful head upturned on its outstretched neck still grinning toward the sky. The crowd turned on me indignantly. The whistle came again. I saw a short pot-bellied man look down, then up at me with amazement and explode with laughter, pointing from me to the doll, rocking. People backed away from me. I saw Clifton step close to the building where beside the fellow with the carton I now saw a whole chorus-line of dolls flouncing themselves with a perverse increase of energy and the crowd laughing hysterically.

"You, you!" I began, only to see him pick up two of the dolls and step forward. But now the lookout came close. "He's coming," he said, nodding toward the approaching policeman as he swept up the dolls, dropping them into the carton and starting away.

"Follow little Sambo around the corner, ladies and gentlemen," Clifton called. "There's a great show coming up . . ."

It happened so fast that in a second only I and an old lady in a blue polka-dot dress were left. She looked at me then back to the walk, smiling. I saw one of the dolls. I looked. She was still smiling and I raised my foot to crush it, hearing her cry, "Oh, no!" The policeman was just opposite and I reached down instead, picking it up and walking off in the same motion. I examined it, strangely weightless in my hand, half expecting to feel it pulse with life. It was a still frill of paper. I dropped it in the pocket where I carried Brother Tarp's chain link and started after the vanished crowd. But I couldn't face Clifton again. I didn't want to see him. I might forget myself and attack him. I went in the other direction, toward Sixth Avenue, past the policeman. What a way to find him, I thought. What had happened to Clifton? It was all so wrong, so unexpected. How on earth could he drop from Brotherhood to this in so short a time? And why if he had to fall back did he try to carry the whole structure with him? What would non-members who knew him say? It was as though he had chosen—how had he put it the night he fought with Ras?—to fall outside of *history*. I stopped in the middle of the walk with the thought. "To plunge," he had said. But he knew that only in the Brotherhood could we make ourselves known, could we avoid being empty Sambo dolls. Such an obscene flouncing of everything human! My God! And I had been worrying about being left out of a meeting! I'd overlook it a thousand times; no matter why I wasn't called. I'd forget it and hold on desperately to Brotherhood with all my strength. For to break away would be to plunge . . . To plunge! And those dolls, where had they found them? Why had he picked that way to earn a quarter? Why not sell apples or song sheets, or shine shoes?

I wandered past the subway and continued around the corner to Forty-second Street, my mind grappling for meaning. And when I came around the corner onto the crowded walk into the sun, they were already lining the curb and shading their faces with their hands. I saw the traffic moving with the lights, and across the street a few pedestrians were looking back toward the center of the block where the trees of Bryant Park rose above two men. I saw a flight of pigeons whirl out of the trees and it all happened in the swift interval of their circling, very abruptly and in the noise of the traffic—yet seeming to unfold in my mind like a slow-motion movie run off with the sound track dead.

At first I thought it was a cop and a shoeshine boy; then there was a break in the traffic and across the sun-glaring bands of trolley rails I recognized Clifton. His partner had disappeared now and Clifton had the box slung to his left shoulder with the cop moving slowly behind and to one side of him. They were coming my way, passing a newsstand, and I saw the rails in the asphalt and a fire plug at the curb and the flying birds, and thought, You'll have to follow and pay his fine . . . just as the cop pushed him, jolting him forward and Clifton trying to keep the box from swinging against his leg and saying something over his shoulder and going forward as one of the pigeons swung down into the street and up again, leaving a feather floating white in the dazzling backlight of the sun, and I could see the cop push Clifton again, stepping solidly forward in his black shirt, his arm shooting out stiffly, sending him in a head-snapping forward stumble until he caught himself, saying something over his shoulder again, the two moving in a kind of march that I'd seen many times, but never with anyone like Clifton. And I could see the cop bark a command and lunge forward, thrusting out his arm and missing, thrown off balance as suddenly Clifton spun on his toes like a dancer and swung his right arm over and around in a short, jolting arc, his torso carrying forward and to the left in a motion that sent the box strap free as his right foot traveled forward and his left arm followed through in a floating uppercut that sent the cop's cap sailing into the street and his feet flying, to drop him hard, rocking from left to right on the walk as Clifton kicked the box thudding aside and crouched, his left foot forward, his hands high, waiting. And between the flashing of cars I could see the cop propping himself on his elbows like a drunk trying to get his head up, shaking it and thrusting it forward—And somewhere between the dull roar of traffic and the subway vibrating underground I heard rapid explosions and saw each pigeon diving wildly as though blackjacked by the sound, and the cop sitting up straight now, and rising to his knees looking steadily at Clifton, and the pigeons plummeting swiftly into the trees, and Clifton still facing the cop and suddenly crumpling.

He fell forward on his knees, like a man saying his prayers just as a heavy-set man in a hat with a turned-down brim stepped from around the newsstand and yelled a protest. I couldn't move. The sun seemed to scream an inch above my head. Someone shouted. A few men were starting into the street. The cop was standing now and looking down at Clifton as though surprised, the gun in his hand. I took a few steps forward, walking blindly now, unthinking, yet my mind registering it all vividly. Across and starting up on the curb, and seeing Clifton up closer now, lying in the same position, on his side, a huge wetness growing on his shirt, and I couldn't set my foot down. Cars sailed close behind me, but I couldn't take the step that would raise me up to the walk. I stood there, one leg in the street and the other raised above the curb, hearing whistles screeching and looked toward the library to see two cops coming on in a lunging, big-bellied run. I looked back to Clifton, the cop was waving me away with his gun, sounding like a boy with a changing voice.

"Get back on the other side," he said. He was the cop that I'd passed on Forty-third a few minutes before. My mouth was dry.

"He's a friend of mine, I want to help . . ." I said, finally stepping upon the curb.

"He don't need no help, Junior. Get across that street!"

The cop's hair hung on the sides of his face, his uniform was dirty, and I watched him without emotion, hesitated, hearing the sound of footfalls approaching. Everything seemed slowed down. A pool formed slowly on the walk. My eyes blurred. I raised my head. The cop looked at me curiously. Above in the park I could hear the furious flapping of wings; on my neck, the pressure of eyes. I turned. A round-headed, apple-cheeked boy with a thickly freckled nose and Slavic eyes leaned over the fence of the park above, and now as he saw me turn, he shrilled something to someone behind him, his face lighting up with ecstasy . . . What does it mean, I wondered, turning back to that to which I did not wish to turn.

There were three cops now, one watching the crowd and the others looking at Clifton. The first cop had his cap on again.

"Look, Junior," he said very clearly, "I had enough trouble for today— you going to get on across that street?"

I opened my mouth but nothing would come. Kneeling, one of the cops was examining Clifton and making notes on a pad.

"I'm his friend," I said, and the one making notes looked up.

"He's a cooked pigeon, Mac," he said. "You ain't got any friend any more."

I looked at him.

"Hey, Mickey," the boy above us called, "the guy's out cold!"

I looked down. "That's right," the kneeling cop said. "What's your name?"

I told him. I answered his questions about Clifton as best I could until the wagon came. For once it came quickly. I watched numbly as they moved him inside, placing the box of dolls in with him. Across the street the crowd still churned. Then the wagon was gone and I started back toward the subway.

"Say, mister," the boy's voice shrilled down. "Your friend sure knows how to use his dukes. Biff, bang! One, two, and the cop's on his ass!"

I bowed my head to this final tribute, and now walking away in the sun I tried to erase the scene from my mind.

I wandered down the subway stairs seeing nothing, my mind plunging. The subway was cool and I leaned against a pillar, hearing the roar of trains passing across on the other side, feeling the rushing roar of air. Why should a man deliberately plunge outside of history and peddle an obscenity, my mind went on abstractedly. Why should he choose to disarm himself, give up his voice and leave the only organization offering him a change to "define" himself? The platform vibrated and I looked down. Bits of paper whirled up in the passage of air, settling quickly as a train moved past. Why *had* he turned away? Why had he chosen to step off the platform and fall beneath the train? Why did he choose to plunge into nothingness, into the void of faceless faces, of soundless voices, lying outside history? I tried to step away and look at it from a distance of words read in books, half-remembered. For history records the patterns of men's lives, they say: Who slept with whom and with what results; who fought and who won and who lived to lie about it afterwards. All things, it is said, are duly recorded—all things of importance, that is. But not quite, for actually it is only the known, the seen, the heard and only those events that the recorder regards as important that are put down, those lies his keepers keep their power by. But the cop would be Clifton's historian, his judge, his witness, and his executioner, and I was the only brother in the watching crowd. And I, the only witness for the defense, knew neither the extent of his guilt nor the nature of his crime. Where were the historians today? And how would they put it down?

I stood there with the trains plunging in and out, throwing blue sparks. What did they ever think of us transitory ones? Ones such as I had been before I found Brotherhood—birds of passage who were too obscure for learned classification, too silent for the most sensitive recorders of sound; of natures too ambiguous for the most ambiguous words, and too distant from the centers of historical decision to sign or even to applaud the signers of historical documents? We who write no novels, histories or other books. What about us, I thought, seeing Clifton again in my mind and going to sit upon a bench as a cool gust of air rolled up the tunnel.

A body of people came down the platform, some of them Negroes. Yes, I thought, what about those of us who shoot up from the South into the busy city like wild jacks-in-the-box broken loose from our springs—so sudden that our gait becomes like that of deep-sea divers suffering from the bends? What about those fellows waiting still and silent there on the platform, so still and silent that they clash with the crowd in their very immobility; standing noisy in their very silence; harsh as a cry of terror in their quietness? What about those three boys, coming now along the platform, tall and slender, walking stiffly with swinging shoulders in their well-pressed, too-hot-for-summer suits, their collars high and tight about their necks, their identical hats of black cheap felt set upon the crowns of their heads with a severe formality above their hard conked hair? It was as though I'd never seen their like before: Walking slowly, their shoulders swaying, their legs swinging from their hips in trousers that ballooned upward from cuffs fitting snug about their ankles; their coats long and hip-tight with shoulders far too broad to be those of natural western men. These fellows whose bodies seemed—what had one of my teachers said of me?—"You're like one of these African sculptures, distorted in the interest of a design." Well, what design and whose?

I stared as they seemed to move like dancers in some kind of funeral ceremony, swaying, going forward, their black faces secret, moving slowly down the subway platform, the heavy heel-plated shoes making a rhythmical tapping as they moved. Everyone must have seen them, or heard their muted laughter, or smelled the heavy pomade on their hair—or perhaps failed to see them at all. For they were men outside of historical time, they were untouched, they didn't believe in Brotherhood, no doubt had never heard of it; or perhaps like Clifton would mysteriously have rejected its mysteries; men of transition whose faces were immobile.

I got up and went behind them. Women shoppers with bundles and impatient men in straw hats and seersucker suits stood along the platform as they passed. And suddenly I found myself thinking, Do they come to bury the others or to be entombed, to give life or to receive it? Do the others see them, think about them, even those standing close enough to speak? And if they spoke back, would the impatient businessmen in conventional suits and tired housewives with their plunder, understand? What would they say? For the boys speak a jived-up transitional language full of country glamour, think transitional thoughts, though perhaps they dream the same old ancient dreams. They were men out of time—unless they found Brotherhood. Men out of time, who would soon be gone and forgotten . . . But who knew (and now I began to tremble so violently I had to lean against a refuse can)—who knew but that they were the saviors, the true leaders, the bearers of something precious? The stewards of something uncomfortable, burdensome, which they hated because, living outside the realm of history, there was no one to applaud their value and they themselves failed to understand it. What if Brother Jack were wrong? What if history was a gambler, instead of a force in a laboratory experiment, and the boys his ace in the hole? What if history was not a reasonable citizen, but a madman full of paranoid guile and these boys his agents, his big surprise! His own revenge? For they were outside, in the dark with Sambo, the dancing paper doll; taking it on the lambo with my fallen brother, Tod Clifton (Tod, Tod) running and dodging the forces of history instead of making a dominating stand.

A train came. I followed them inside. There were many seats and the three sat together. I stood, holding onto the center pole, looking down the length of the car. On one side I saw a white nun in black telling her beads, and standing before the door across the aisle there was another dressed completely in white, the exact duplicate of the other except that she was black and her black feet bare. Neither of the nuns was looking at the other but at their crucifixes, and suddenly I laughed and a verse I'd heard long ago at the Golden Day paraphrased itself in my mind:

> *Bread and Wine,*
> *Bread and Wine,*
>   *Your cross ain't nearly so*
>   *Heavy as mine . . .*

And the nuns rode on with lowered heads.

I looked at the boys. They sat as formally as they walked. From time to time one of them would look at his reflection in the window and give his hat brim a snap, the others watching him silently, communicating ironically with their eyes, then looking straight ahead. I staggered with the lunging of the train, feeling the overhead fans driving the hot air down upon me. What was I in relation to the boys, I wondered. Perhaps an accident, like Douglass. Perhaps each hundred years or so men like them, like me, appeared in society, drifting through; and yet by all historical logic we, I, should have disappeared around the first part of the nineteenth century, rationalized out of existence. Perhaps, like them, I was a throwback, a small distant meteorite that died several hundred years ago and now lived only by virtue of the light that speeds through space at too great a pace to realize that its source has become a piece of lead . . . This was silly, such thoughts. I looked at the boys; one tapped another on the knee, and I saw him remove three rolled magazines from an inner pocket, passing two around and keeping one for himself. The others took theirs silently and began to read in complete absorption. One held his magazine high before his face and for an instant I saw a vivid scene: The shining rails, the fire hydrant, the fallen policeman, the diving birds and in the mid-ground, Clifton, crumpling. Then I saw the cover of a comic book and thought, Clifton would have known them better than I. He knew them all the time. I studied them closely until they left the train, their shoulders rocking, their heavy heel plates clicking remote, cryptic messages in the brief silence of the train's stop.

I came out of the subway, weak, moving through the heat as though I carried a heavy stone, the weight of a mountain on my shoulders. My new shoes hurt my feet. Now, moving through the crowds along 125th Street, I was painfully aware of other men dressed like the boys, and of girls in dark exotic-colored stockings, their costumes surreal variations of downtown styles. They'd been there all along, but somehow I'd missed them. I'd missed them even when my work had been most successful. They were outside the groove of history, and it was my job to get them in, all of them. I looked into the design of their faces, hardly a one that was unlike someone I'd known down South. Forgotten names sang through my head like forgotten scenes in dreams. I moved with the crowd, the sweat pouring off me, listening to the grinding roar of traffic, the growing sound of a record shop loudspeaker blaring a languid blues. I stopped. Was this all that would be recorded? Was this the only true history of the times, a mood blared by trumpets, trombones, saxophones and drums, a song with turgid, inadequate words? My mind flowed. It was as though in this short block I was forced to walk past everyone I'd ever known and no one would smile or call my name. No one fixed me in his eyes. I walked in feverish isolation. Near the corner now a couple of boys darted out of the Five and Ten with handfuls of candy bars, dropping them along the walks as they ran with a man right behind. They came toward me, pumping past, and I killed an impulse to trip the man and was confused all the more when an old woman standing further along threw out her leg and swung a heavy bag. The man went down, sliding across the walk as she shook her head in triumph. A pressure of guilt came over me. I stood on the edge of the walk watching the crowd threatening to attack the man until a policeman appeared and dispersed them. And although I knew no one man could do much about it, I felt responsible. All our work had been very little, no

great change had been made. And it was all my fault. I'd been so fascinated by the motion that I'd forgotten to measure what it was bringing
forth. I'd been asleep, dreaming.

What is the main cause for the narrator's anxiety? Is he worried about his position in the Brotherhood? What inner conflict is he experiencing?

The narrator observes a crowd of Blacks and describes them as "so still and
silent . . . harsh as a cry of terror in their quietness." How does this description reflect his own position?

The experiences of the narrator in this chapter make him realize that he has
been asleep, dreaming. How has seeing the dancing dolls, Clifton's fight with
the cop, and the crowds helped the narrator to see his true position?

Read the description of the three boys on p. 102. What abstract statement is
the author making about the Black's position in America?

PRIMITIVISM

4 AND

CIVILIZATION

UNIT PREWRITING 10

In this chapter we ask you to look at some aspect of primitivism/civilization in your life—look at it, take notes on it, and write about it.

The primitivism/civilization polarity surrounds us. One of the inescapable conditions of our lives, it constantly pulls us in two directions, compelling us to make decisions.

The primitivism/civilization conflict has been with us for a long time. In A.D. 50, Roman legions crossed the Rhine and Danube Rivers to battle primitive tribes. These tribes (as the Roman historian Tacitus described them) were "rude masses without ornament or attractiveness," yet free of the corruption the civilized Roman had fallen into in his degenerate cities. The barbarians lived in dung huts and, when they were not fighting, lay "buried in sloth." But they lived without "either natural or acquired cunning." And they were a people who did not (as did the civilized Roman) "laugh at vice . . . [or] call it the fashion to corrupt and to be corrupted." Tacitus thought that in this respect the primitive, uncivilized barbarian surpassed the civilized Roman.

Other writers have thought the opposite, believing the virtues of primitive man imaginary. "I beg to say," Charles Dickens wrote, "that I have not the least belief in the Noble Savage. I consider him a prodigious nuisance, and an enormous superstition. . . . If we have anything to learn from the Noble Savage, it is what to avoid. His virtues are a fable; his happiness is a delusion; his nobility nonsense."

109

Give a spontaneous response to the objects in the collage opening this unit and to each of the following pairs:

concrete
↕
bare earth

fluorescent lighting
↕
sunlight and moonlight

electric stove
↕
campfire

jet airliner
↕
horse with trayneau

reed whistle
↕
symphony orchestra

supermarket
↕
buffalo hunt

Pepsi-Cola
↕
water

alarm clock
↕
meadow lark

Chateaubriand and Cabernet Sauvignon
↕
jack rabbit stew and water

flush toilet
↕
outhouse

bank account
↕
compost pile

shod
↕
barefoot

telephones, telegraphs, television
↕
smoke signals

high-rise apartment
↕
tepee

The term "primitive" commonly means "of the earliest ages, crude, simple, rough, uncivilized." If you believe in or practice primitive ways you are a primitivist. The word "civilize" originally meant "to citify" and today means "to bring out of a savage state." If you belong to and take part in a social organization of a "high order" (one highly developed in the arts and sciences), you live in a civilization and are civilized. But these definitions don't take us very far. Here are more thoughtful descriptions of these two terms:

66 As a philosophy of history primitivism is . . . the belief that the earliest condition of man and of human society . . . was the best condition. . . . Man has, through-out a great part of his historic march, walked with face turned backward; and a nostalgia for his original state. . . . Common to primitivism is the conviction that the time . . . is out of joint; that what is wrong with it is due to an abnormal complexity and sophistication in the life of civilized man, to the pathological multiplicity and emulativeness of his desires and the oppressive over-abundance of his belongings, and the factitiousness and want of inner spontaneity of his emotion. **99**

ARTHUR O. LOVEJOY

66 The word "civilization," like many other terms of the philosophy of human nature, is a word of double meaning. It sometimes stands for *human improvement* in general, and sometimes for *certain kinds* of improvement in particular.

We are accustomed to call a country more civilized if we think it more improved; more eminent in the best characteristics of man and society; farther advanced in the road to perfection; happier, nobler, wiser. This is one sense of the word "civilization." But, in another sense, it stands for that kind of improvement only which distinguishes a wealthy and powerful nation from savages or barbarians. It is in this sense that we may speak of the vices or the miseries of civilization; and that the question has been seriously propounded, whether civilization is, on the whole, a good or an evil. **99**

JOHN STUART MILL

Whatever your definitions of primitivism and of civilization, you probably have many opinions about them. You may desire to return to a "simple, rough," primitive life, but not without the comforts and advantages of your present life; return to Nature—but not so far as to spend a short life time sleeping on the bare earth by night and collecting berries by day. Or you may want more civilization, desiring a life free of the need to work constantly for mere existence. Or you may think that living in this social organization of a high order provides enough savagery and barbarism. You may be caught between two undesirables: the tension of modern living may be near overwhelming, but the fear that accompanies primitive life not so pleasant either.

Whether you wish to go back or to go forward in search of a happier way of life, you may not know how far to go. Or how to begin. Or what is possible. Or whether a better life—more civil or more primitive—is but a dream.

DISCUSSION

❝Instead of being more virtuous, as he is less re-
fined, I am inclined to think that man's virtues are
like the fruits of the earth, only excellent when sub-
jected to culture.❞

ELIAS PYM FORDHAM

Do you believe "culture" has made you or the people around you more
virtuous?

❝Does essential savagery lurk beneath the skin of
civilization, or does essential civilization lurk beneath the skin of savagery?❞

JOHN BARTH

How do you see it?

❝There is a dual process going on through history:
... immense progress in man's knowledge and in his
power over nature, and at the same time, a steady increase of rivalries, distrust, [and] hatred.❞

ARTHUR O. LOVEJOY

Do you think there is a relationship between hatred and man's increasing
power over nature?

❝Machines to do what? Telegraphs, telephones, to
transmit what? Schools, universities, academies, to
teach what? Meetings to discuss what? Books and
newspapers, to spread information about what? ...
Hospitals, physicians, pharmacists, to prolong lives
for what?❞

LEO TOLSTOY

What is the object of civilization?

> **"**How has it come about that so many people have adopted this strange attitude of hostility to civilization?**"**
>
> SIGMUND FREUD

Do you know someone who is hostile to civilization? Are you? What is the cause of the hostility?

CONNECTING EXERCISES

Do one of the following.

▶ A. Imagine the ground which the campus now stands on as it was centuries ago. Imagine the people who lived on this ground—the way they lived, their activities, work, fears, pains, joys, desires, loves. Contrast your imagination of their life with present campus life. Compare your ideas with those of others in the class. Keep notes of your thoughts.

▶ B. In your life, which aspect of civilization gives you the most pleasure? the least? In your writing notebook jot down facts and impressions until you feel you have enough material to write the first draft of a paper.

▶ C. Find and take notes on an illustration of some unusual example of primitivism or civilization in a TV show, advertisement, movie, book, or newspaper. (For example, about 1915 the average speed of traffic through New York City was 12 miles per hour. Today the average is 6 miles per hour.)

UNIT 11
WRITING DESCRIPTION

Buffalo Eye (American Indian symbol for alertness)

Before a writer can describe something, he must first see it. The narrator of Ralph Ellison's *Invisible Man* (Unit 9) realizes, "I am invisible . . . simply because people refuse to see me. . . . When [people] approach me they see only my surroundings, themselves, or figments of their imagination—indeed, everything and anything except me." The people and objects you pass every day but do not *see* are invisible to you.

> 66 It is what a bull-dog has in his jaw. We . . . must have that same power to seize with our eyes, ears and all our senses. If [we] . . . listen, let [us] do it intently. If called upon to smell, let [us] smell hard. If [we are] to look at something, let [us] really use [our] eyes. 99
>
> KONSTANTIN STANISLAVSKY

The renowned naturalist Louis Agassiz had a method of teaching observation, for really looking hard at something. Here is a report of one student's experience with that method:

❝While Agassiz questioned me carefully . . . he seemed in . . . no wise concerned to find what I knew about fossils, rocks, animals, and plants; he put aside the offerings of my scanty lore. This offended me a bit, as I recall, for the reason that I thought I knew, and for a self-taught lad really did know, a good deal about such matters, especially as to the habits of insects, particularly spiders. It seemed hard to be denied the chance to make my parade; but I afterward saw what this meant—that he did not intend to let me begin my tasks by posing as a naturalist. . . .

I had assigned to me a small pine table with a rusty tin pan upon it. . . . When I sat me down before my tin pan, Agassiz brought me a small fish, placing it before me with the rather stern requirement that I should study it, but should on no account talk to any one concerning it, nor read anything relating to fishes. . . . To my inquiry, "What shall I do?" he said in effect: "Find out what you can without damaging the specimen. . . ."

In the course of an hour I thought I had compassed that fish; it was rather an unsavory object, giving forth the stench of old alcohol, then loathsome to me, though in time I came to like it. Many of the scales were loosened so that they fell off. It appeared to me to be a case for a summary report, which I was anxious to make and get on to the next stage of the business. But Agassiz, though always within call, concerned himself no further with me that day, nor the next, nor for a week. . . . I saw that it was a game. . . . So I set my wits to work upon the thing, and in the course of a hundred hours or so thought I had done much—a hundred times as much as seemed possible at the start. I got interested in finding out how the scales went in series, their shape, the form and placement of the teeth, etc. Finally, I felt full of the subject. . . . At the end of the hour's telling, Agassiz swung off and away, saying: "That is not right. . . ."

I went at the task anew. . . . and in another week of ten hours a day labor I had results which astonished myself and satisfied him.

NATHANIEL SOUTHGATE SHALER

The problem is that this method consumes more time than you may have. But you will need to use a method something like Agassiz's before you can write description.

In James Joyce's *Portrait of the Artist as a Young Man* the student Stephen Dedalus describes this method of apprehending a subject to his friend Lynch:

“In order to see that basket . . . your mind first of all separates the basket from the rest of the visible universe which is not the basket. The first phase of apprehension is a bounding line drawn about the object to be apprehended. . . . You apprehend it as *one* thing. You see it as one whole. . . .

Then, said Stephen, you pass from point to point, led by its formal lines; you apprehend it as balanced part against part within its limits. . . . In other words, the synthesis of immediate perception is followed by the analysis of apprehension. . . . You apprehend it as complex, multiple, divisible, separable, made up of its parts, the results of its parts and their sum. . . .

When you have apprehended that basket as one thing and have then analysed it according to its form and apprehended it as a thing you make the only synthesis which is logically and esthetically permissible. You see that it is that thing which it is and no other thing.”

Dedalus distinguished three stages in the process of "apprehending" a subject: (1) The observer sets a boundary line around the object. (Agassiz's student is given the fish in a tin pan. He sees the fish within this boundary, separated from the surrounding world.) (2) The observer sees the parts, each in relation to the other parts and to the whole. (The student saw how the scales went in series and noticed the placement of the teeth.) (3) The observer apprehends the individual, unique essence, the "radiance" of the thing. (Agassiz's student does not indicate that he fully experiences this stage of the process other than that he says he "felt full of the subject." This, we may assume, is something akin to sensing its essence.)

WRITING EXERCISES

▶A. After the class has selected an object for observation—either a fish, a basket, a fossil, a cabbage, a rock, the backs of your hands:

- Place the object before you, and, as Agassiz suggests, "Find out what you can without damaging the specimen."
- Take notes and write a paper.

Reading a few papers aloud in class will show you how differently various observers "see" the same object.

▶B. Of the following objects select one associated with the primitive life and/or one associated with our modern technological age: a Navajo rug, a basket, a can opener, power lawn mower, electric toaster or this African ritual mask.

Liberian Mask (Poro Society).
Museum of Primitive Art, New York.

- Set a boundary line around the object.
- Note each part of it in relation to the whole.
- Consider its texture, form, color.
- Note the impressions the object makes on your senses. What is its "feel," its radiance?
- Write your paper.

WRITING HINT: FOCUS—KNOW THE CENTER OF YOUR COMPOSITION.

> "Our eyes are accustomed to fixing upon a specific object."
>
> M. C. ESCHER

M. C. Escher, *Selfportait*. Escher Foundation—Haags Gemeentemuseum—The Hague.

Like your physical eyes, your mind's eye is accustomed to seeking a focal point. Your reader will consciously or unconsciously search for the focal point in your writing: for the object, the statement, the idea, the dominant impression that gives unity to your composition. So you need to know what *one thing* you are saying.

But the mental process of focusing is a great deal more complex than the physical one. If you write on and on, passing from one thing to another without purpose, vaguely searching for something to say, saying a little of everything and nothing much about anything in particular, both you and your reader will be lost.

> 66 There is [a] voice which is a plague of locusts—the voice of a man stumbling drowsily among loose words. Clutching aimlessly at vague ideas. 99
>
> VIRGINIA WOOLF

Give your writing a focus by taking hold of one lucid idea and letting all other ideas and details in your paper contribute to development of this one central idea. Here are suggestions for finding and keeping a focus:

- Ask yourself questions: "What am I trying to do?" "What one thing am I saying?"
- In one sentence write out your answer. Let this sentence accurately say the one main thing you intend to say in your paper. Make it so clear that no one can miss its meaning. You may find that you will not be able to state your central idea until after you have done a rough draft. Often a writer doesn't know exactly what he wants to say until he has tried to say it.
- Once you have formulated your central idea, try writing it at the top of your paper or in some way set it before you so you won't lose sight of it. Ideas have a habit of floating off if they are not tacked down.

In Unit 5 we spoke of the need for specific concrete details; in Unit 8 of the need for an abstract idea. Here we emphasize the interrelationship of abstract and concrete. Writing is a two-part process, a movement from the concrete to the abstract and from the abstract to the concrete that reflects the mental gymnastics we go through when we think.

In most compositions an abstract idea serves as the focal point. In a description paper the abstract idea may take the form of a comprehensive statement controlling the whole composition. The writer achieves focus through one statement that governs, and is supported by, a number of concrete details.

Comprehensive statement
{
detail
detail
detail
detail
}

> 66 The chief rule of Description is to include with the Enumeration of the parts a comprehensive statement, or general Plan, of the whole. 99
>
> ALEXANDER BAIN

When you write a description, you need to include, along with the details that help your reader see the object, your impressions of those details. Personal reflection is often a significant part of description.

In its restricted sense description is concerned with objects in space—with people only if they are viewed as objects. As soon as the writer tells what a person says or does, then, he is no longer writing description. But in a more general sense, description refers to a drawing in words of the appearance of things—of the vital essence of an object or the essential character of a person, whether viewed as still life or not.

WRITING EXERCISES

▶C. Observe two people—one who has lived "close to the land," a life of physical hardship and privation, and one who has lived most of his life in buildings with central heating, free from physical hardship but busy with appointments and paper work. Note:
—details of their daily activity
—their hands, skin, facial lines
—their relationship to family, friends, strangers
—their general response to life
—their conversation and actions

▶D. Without giving an obvious clue, describe a person or group of persons with whom the whole class is probably acquainted. Or describe one of the pictures in this book. Read your paper in class. See if the class can identify your subject.

Ho-Wear

The following paper is a description of the picture of the Indian chief Ho-wear on the preceding page.

THE STORY OF A MAN'S FACE

Through many hardships this man has developed a knowledge of himself, of what he can do and of what he will do. Ho-wear's features tell his story.

His hawkish nose, high broad cheekbones, and bow-shaped mouth show his heritage. These traits have been passed on from generation to generation. The granite-like features project the indestructible strength and pride of the Indian, just as the stoney faces of Mt. Rushmore project the strength and pride of the white man.

Unlike granite, which can endure nature's elements and still remain unmarred, this man's skin has become rough and pitted. Seasons of bitter winds, violent rains, extreme heat and cold have toughened his exterior as well as his sense of survival. This man has learned to live in harmony with Mother Earth, not to fight against her. Though he seems tough and strong on the outside, he knows tenderness and love. He has a love and respect for Mother Earth, and all her living creatures. He worships the sun and seasons of the year through songs, prayers, and dance. These are not things that have died with the old people; even today my own father practices his religion through ancient songs and prayers. There are many Indians young and old that still follow the ceremonies of their ancestors.

Ho-wear's long-thick dusty black hair, worn in the traditional style of his tribe, openly proclaims his pride. One can imagine the wind softly blowing through his hair as he stands high on a hilltop while giving thanks to the Great Spirit. His expressionless mouth works as a shield to hide his thoughts, for it would be a sign of weakness to give a clue to his emotion.

He is a young man, as the tightness of his skin over his sculptured features shows. The smooth fatty flesh that is so obvious in the faces of many people today is not present in the face of this man who went for days without a decent meal, if any at all. Yes, this man is young, chronologically, but not mentally. He has the knowledge of life and nature which can never be obtained from books.

Finally, his most striking feature—his eyes. Deep set under his heavy brow, his dark eyes seem to reflect his whole story by themselves. The endurance and patience dominant in his dark eyes seem indestructible. Only the blood line through the white of his left eye gives a hint to his vulnerability. Protecting his hunting grounds and people may have brought about battles where this wound was inflicted as well as others. His eyes have seen the excitement and horror of battle and his heart has felt the glory and the sorrow. But none of his battles can compare with the overwhelming sorrow that would sweep his soul if his eyes could see his land desecrated by so called civilization, and his once proud people living in despair and shame.

One cannot overlook the glint of uncertainty in his eyes. He could not have begun to imagine all that has come to pass with the civilization of the settlers. To ponder the future of his people must have brought clouds of uncertainty which concluded in a thunderstorm of defeat and rejection.

It is sad to know that such a powerful society, one that has tamed the "wild savage" and has advanced so far in technology, lacks the simple elements of respect, understanding, and love for nature and mankind. These elements burned in this man's life but were drowned out until his people carry only a smouldering fire which must be preserved, rekindled, and spread to others if the Indian people are to survive. Ho-wear knew what he could and what he would do. He had the strength of his pride, but he had no control over the civilization that was settling around him.

Ellen Nez Johnson

CLASS EXERCISE

▶What do you see as the focal point, the comprehensive statement, of this paper? What details, what parts, are enumerated to support the comprehensive statement? Indicate a few of the places where the writer introduces her personal reflections about the subject.

UNIT 12

Who Killed King Kong?

X. J. KENNEDY

The ordeal and spectacular death of King Kong, the giant ape, undoubtedly have been witnessed by more Americans than have ever seen a performance of *Hamlet, Iphigenia at Aulis,* or even *Tobacco Road.* Since RKO Radio Pictures first released *King Kong,* a quarter-century has gone by; yet year after year, from prints that grow more rain-beaten, from sound tracks that grow more tinny, ticket-buyers by thousands still pursue Kong's luckless fight against the forces of technology, tabloid journalism, and the DAR. They see him chloroformed to sleep, see him whisked from his jungle isle to New York and placed on show, see him burst his chains to roam the city (lugging a frightened blonde), at last to plunge from the spire of the Empire State Building, machine-gunned by model airplanes.

Though Kong may die, one begins to think his legend unkillable. No clearer proof of his hold upon the popular imagination may be seen than what emerged one catastrophic week in March 1955, when New York WOR-TV programmed *Kong* for seven evenings in a row (a total of sixteen showings). Many a rival network vice-president must have scowled when surveys showed that *Kong*—the 1933 B-picture—had lured away fat segments of the viewing populace from such powerful competitors as Ed Sullivan, Groucho Marx and Bishop Sheen.

But even television has failed to run *King Kong* into oblivion. Coffee-in-the-lobby cinemas still show the old hunk of hokum, with the apology that in its use of composite shots and animated models the film remains technically interesting. And no other monster in movie history has won so devoted a popular audience. None of the plodding mummies, the stultified draculas, the white-coated Lugosis with their shiny pinball-machine laboratories, none of the invisible stranglers, berserk robots, or menaces from Mars has ever enjoyed so many resurrections.

Why does the American public refuse to let King Kong rest in peace? It is true, I'll admit, that *Kong* outdid every monster movie before or since in sheer carnage. Producers Cooper and Schoedsack crammed into it dinosaurs, headhunters, riots, aerial battles, bullets, bombs, bloodletting. Heroine Fay Wray, whose function is mainly to scream, shuts her mouth for hardly one uninterrupted minute from first reel to last. It is also true that *Kong* is larded with good healthy sadism, for those whose joy it is to see the frantic girl dangled from cliffs and harried by pterodactyls. But it seems to me that the abiding appeal of the giant ape rests on other foundations.

Kong has, first of all, the attraction of being manlike. His simian nature gives him one huge advantage over giant ants and walking vegetables in that an audience may conceivably identify with him. Kong's appeal has the quality that established the Tarzan series as American myth—for what man doesn't secretly image himself a huge hairy howler against whom no other monster has a chance? If Tarzan recalls the ape in us, then Kong may well appeal to that great-granddaddy primordial brute from whose tribe we have all deteriorated.

Intentionally or not, the producers of *King Kong* encourage this identification by etching the character of Kong with keen sympathy. For the ape is a figure in a tradition familiar to moviegoers: the tradition of the pitiable monster. We think of Lon Chaney in the role of Quasimodo, of Karloff in the original *Frankenstein*. As we watch the Frankenstein monster's fumbling and disastrous attempts to befriend a flower-picking child, our sympathies are enlisted with the monster in his impenetrable loneliness. And so with Kong. As he roars in his chains, while barkers sell tickets to boobs who gape at him, we perhaps feel something more deep than pathos. We begin to sense something of the problem that engaged Eugene O'Neill in *The Hairy Ape:* the dilemma of a displaced animal spirit forced to live in a jungle built by machines.

King Kong, it is true, had special relevance in 1933. Landscapes of the depression are glimpsed early in the film when an impresario, seeking some desperate pretty girl to play the lead in a jungle movie, visits souplines and a Woman's Home Mission. In Fay Wray—who's been caught snitching an apple from a fruitstand—his search is ended. When he gives her a big feed and a movie contract, the girl is magic-carpeted out of the world of the National Recovery Act. And when, in the film's climax, Kong smashes that very Third Avenue landscape in which Fay had wandered hungry, audiences of 1933 may well have felt a personal satisfaction.

What is curious is that audiences of 1960 remain hooked. For in the heart of urban man, one suspects, lurks the impulse to fling a bomb. Though machines speed him to the scene of his daily grind, though IBM comptometers ("freeing the human mind from drudgery") enable him to drudge more efficiently once he arrives, there comes a moment when he wishes to turn upon his machines and kick hell out of them. He wants to hurl his combination radio-alarmclock out the bedroom window and listen to its smash. What subway commuter wouldn't love—just for once—to see the downtown express smack head-on into the uptown local? Such a wish is gratified in that memorable scene in *Kong* that opens with a wide-angle shot: interior of a railway car on the Third Avenue El. Straphangers are nodding, the literate refold their newspapers. Unknown to them, Kong has torn away a section of trestle toward which the train now speeds. The motorman spies Kong up ahead, jams on the brakes. Passengers hurtle together like so many peas in a pail. In a window of the car appear Kong's bloodshot eyes. Women shriek. Kong picks up the railway car as if it were a rat, flips it to the street and ties knots in it, or something. To any commuter the scene must appear one of the most satisfactory pieces of celluloid ever exposed.

Yet however violent his acts, Kong remains a gentleman. Remarkable is his sense of chivalry. Whenever a fresh boa constrictor threatens Fay, Kong first sees that the lady is safely parked, then manfully thrashes her attacker. (And she, the ingrate, runs away every time his back is turned.) Atop the Empire State Building, ignoring his pursuers, Kong places Fay on a ledge as tenderly as if she were a dozen eggs. He fondles her, then turns to face the Army Air Force. And Kong is perhaps the most disinterested lover since Cyrano: his attentions to the lady are utterly without hope of reward. After all, between a five-foot blonde and a fifty-foot ape, love can hardly be more than an intellectual flirtation. In his simian way King Kong is the hopelessly yearning lover of Petrarchan convention. His forced exit from his jungle, in chains, results directly from his single-minded pursuit of Fay. He smashes a Broadway theater when the notion enters his dull brain that the flashbulbs of photographers somehow endanger the lady. His perilous shinnying up a skyscraper to pluck Fay from her boudoir is an act of the kindliest of hearts. He's impossible to discourage even though the love of his life can't lay eyes on him without shrieking murder.

The tragedy of King Kong then, is to be the beast who at the end of the fable fails to turn into the handsome prince. This is the conviction that the scriptwriters would leave with us in the film's closing line. As Kong's corpse lies blocking traffic in the street, the entrepreneur who brought Kong to New York turns to the assembled reporters and proclaims: "That's your story, boys—it was Beauty killed the Beast!" But greater forces than those of the screaming Lady have combined to lay Kong low, if you ask me. Kong lives for a time as one of those persecuted near-animal souls bewildered in the middle of an industrial order, whose simple desires are thwarted at every turn. He climbs the Empire State Building because in all New York it's the closest thing he can find to the clifftop of his jungle isle. He dies, a pitiful dolt, and the army brass and publicity-men cackle over him. His death is the only possible outcome to as neat a tragic dilemma as you can ask for. The machine-guns do him in, while the manicured human hero (a nice clean Dartmouth boy) carries away Kong's sweetheart to the altar. O, the misery of it all. There's far more truth about upper-middle-class American life in *King Kong* than in the last seven dozen novels of John P. Marquand.

A Negro friend from Atlanta tells me that in movie houses in colored neighborhoods throughout the South, *Kong* does a constant business. They show the thing in Atlanta at least every year, presumably to the same audiences. Perhaps this popularity may simply be due to the fact that *Kong* is one of the most watchable movies ever constructed, but I wonder whether Negro audiences may not find some archetypical appeal in this serio-comic tale of a huge black powerful free spirit whom all the hard-working white policemen are out to kill.

Every day in the week on a screen somewhere in the world, King Kong relives his agony. Again and again he expires on the Empire State Building, as audiences of the devout assist his sacrifice. We watch him die, and by extension kill the ape within our bones, but these little deaths of ours occur in prosaic surroundings. We do not die on a tower, New York before out feet, nor do we give our lives to smash a few flying machines. It is not for us to bring to a momentary standstill the civilization in which we move. King Kong does this for us. And so we kill him again and again, in much-spliced celluloid, while the ape in us expires from day to day, obscure, in desperation.

Why is King Kong more popular than any other monster in movie history? Does the author of this essay suggest that King Kong is popular because he is a good-natured beast? Is this similar to a common romantic notion about primitive man?

To what extent do you see yourself as "one of those persecuted near-animal souls bewildered in the middle of an industrial order, whose simple desires are thwarted at every turn"? Is the "ape" within you expiring, "obscure, in desperation"?

Is there any aspect of civilization that gives you the impulse to turn on it and take revenge?

City Life

D. H. LAWRENCE

When I am in a great city, I know that I despair.
I know there is no hope for us, death waits, it is useless to care.
For oh the poor people, that are flesh of my flesh,
I, that am flesh of their flesh,
when I see the iron hooked into their faces
their poor, their fearful faces
I scream in my soul, for I know I cannot
take the iron hooks out of their faces, that make them so drawn,

nor cut the invisible wires of steel that pull them
back and forth, to work,
back and forth to work,
like fearful and corpse-like fishes hooked and being played
by some malignant fisherman on an unseen shore
where he does not choose to land them yet, hooked fishes of
    the factory world.

Lawrence uses the image of a puppet and of a hooked fish to describe "industrialized" man. Do you think that being in an industrialized society puts man in this position?

Why does the poet despair? Does he seem to agree that city life obscures "the ape in us"? (See page 127.)

To what extent do you think your external environment "hooks" you? Is it possible to live in a city and not become like the components of it—that is, the neon signs, skyscrapers, bustling crowds? Is your response to city life "to scream in your soul"? Or is this your response to country life?

Bustopher Jones: The Cat About Town

T. S. ELIOT

Bustopher Jones is *not* skin and bones—
In fact, he's remarkably fat.
He doesn't haunt pubs—he has eight or nine clubs,
For he's the St. James's Street Cat!
He's the Cat we all greet as he walks down the street
In his coat of fastidious black:
No commonplace mousers have such well-cut trousers
Or such an impeccable back.
In the whole of St. James's the smartest of names is
The name of this Brummell of Cats;
And we're all of us proud to be nodded or bowed to
By Bustopher Jones in white spats!

His visits are occasional to the *Senior Educational*
And it is against the rules
For any one Cat to belong both to that
And the *Joint Superior Schools.*
For a similar reason, when game is in season
He is found, not at *Fox's* but *Blimp's;*
He is frequently seen at the gay *Stage and Screen*
Which is famous for winkles and shrimps.
In the season of venison he gives his ben'son
To the *Pothunter's* succulent bones;
And just before noon's not a moment too soon
To drop in for a drink at the *Drones.*
When he's seen in a hurry there's probably curry
At the *Siamese*—or at the *Glutton;*
If he looks full of gloom then he's lunched at the *Tomb*
On cabbage, rice pudding and mutton.

So, much in this way, passes Bustopher's day—
At one club or another he's found.
It can be no surprise that under our eyes
He has grown unmistakably round.
He's a twenty-five pounder, or I am a bounder,
And he's putting on weight every day:
But he's so well preserved because he's observed
All his life a routine, so he'll say.
Or, to put it in rhyme: "I shall last out my time"
Is the word of this stoutest of Cats.
It must and it shall be Spring in Pall Mall
While Bustopher Jones wears white spats!

The author lets us know what kind of a cat Bustopher is by describing his appearance and his habitual activities. Which details do you think give the clearest picture of Bustopher's character?

In what ways is Bustopher Jones representative of a civilized man? Is his costume appropriate? What aspects of being a "cat" are possible only in civilization?

Can you imagine Bustopher's reaction to having to get his own food as a primitive man has to? Do you believe that hunting or working for his meals would improve the quality of Bustopher's life?

The Basket Maker

MARY AUSTIN

"A man," says Seyavi of the campoodie, "must have a woman, but a woman who has a child will do very well."

That was perhaps why, when she lost her mate in the dying struggle of his race, she never took another, but set her wit to fend for herself and her young son. No doubt she was often put to it in the beginning to find food for them both. The Paiutes had made their last stand at the border of the Bitter Lake; battle-driven they died in its waters, and the land filled with cattle-men and adventurers for gold: this while Seyavi and the boy lay up in the caverns of the Black Rock and ate tule roots and fresh-water clams that they dug out of the slough bottoms with their toes. In the interim, while the tribes swallowed their defeat, and before the rumor of war died out, they must have come very near to the bare core of things. That was the time Seyavi learned the sufficiency of mother wit, and how much more easily one can do without a man than might at first be supposed.

To understand the fashion of any life, one must know the land it is lived in and the procession of the year. This valley is a narrow one, a mere trough between hills, a draught for storms, hardly a crow's flight from the sharp Sierras of the Snows to the curled, red and ochre, uncomforted, bare ribs of Waban. Midway of the groove runs a burrowing, dull river, nearly a hundred miles from where it cuts the lava flats of the north to its widening in a thick, tideless pool of a lake. Hereabouts the ranges have no foothills, but rise up steeply from the bench lands above the river. Down from the Sierras, for the east ranges have almost no rain, pour glancing white floods toward the lowest land, and all beside them lie the campoodies, brown wattled brush heaps, looking east.

In the river are mussels, and reeds that have edible white roots, and in the soddy meadows tubers of joint grass; all these at their best in the spring. On the slope the summer growth affords seeds; up the steep the one-leafed pines, an oily nut. That was really all they could depend upon, and that only at the mercy of the little gods of frost and rain. For the rest it was cunning against cunning, caution against skill, against quacking hordes of wild-fowl in the tulares, against pronghorn and bighorn and deer. You can guess, however, that all this warring of rifles and bowstrings, this influx of overlording whites, had made game wilder and hunters fearful of being hunted. You can surmise also, for it was a crude time and the land was raw, that the women became in turn the game of the conquerors.

There used to be in the Little Antelope a she dog, stray or outcast, that had a litter in some forsaken lair, and ranged and foraged for them, slinking savage and afraid, remembering and mistrusting humankind, wistful, lean, and sufficient for her young. I have thought Seyavi might have had days like that, and have had perfect leave to think, since she will not talk of it. Paiutes have the art of reducing life to its lowest ebb and yet saving it alive on grasshoppers, lizards, and strange herbs; and that time must have left no shift untried. It lasted long enough for Seyavi to have evolved the philosophy of life which I have set down at the beginning. She had gone beyond learning to do for her son, and learned to believe it worth while.

In our kind of society, when a woman ceases to alter the fashion of her hair, you guess that she has passed the crisis of her experience. If she goes on crimping and uncrimping with the changing mode, it is safe to suppose she has never come up against anything too big for her. The Indian woman gets nearly the same personal note in the pattern of her baskets. Not that she does not make all kinds, carriers, water-bottles, and cradles,– these are kitchen ware,–but her works of art are all of the same piece. Seyavi made flaring, flat-bottomed bowls, cooking pots really, when cooking was done by dropping hot stones into water-tight food baskets, and for decoration a design in colored bark of the procession of plumed crests of the valley quail. In this pattern she had made cooking pots in the golden spring of her wedding year, when the quail went up two and two to their resting places about the foot of Oppapago. In this fashion she made them when, after pillage, it was possible to reinstate the housewifely crafts. Quail ran then in the Black Rock by hundreds,–so you will still find them in fortunate years,–and in the famine time the women cut their long hair to make snares when the flocks came morning and evening to the springs.

Seyavi made baskets for love and sold them for money, in a generation that preferred iron pots for utility. Every Indian woman is an artist,–sees, feels, creates, but does not philosophize about her processes. Seyavi's bowls are wonders of technical precision, insideand out, the palm finds no fault with them, but the subtlest appeal is in the sense that warns us of humanness in the way the design spreads into the flare of the bowl. There used to be an Indian woman at Olancha who made bottle-neck trinket baskets in the rattlesnake pattern, and could accommodate the design to the swelling bowl and flat shoulder of the basket without sensible disproportion, and so cleverly that you might own one a year without thinking how it was done; but Seyavi's baskets had a touch beyond cleverness. The weaver and the warp lived next to the earth and were saturated with the same elements. Twice a year, in the time of white butterflies and again when young quail ran neck and neck in the chaparral, Seyavi cut willows for basketry by the creek where it wound toward the river against the sun and sucking winds. It never quite reached the river except in far-between times of summer flood, but it always tried, and the willows encouraged it as much as they could. You nearly always found them a little farther down than the trickle of eager water. The Paiute fashion of counting time appeals to me more than any other calendar. They have no stamp of heathen gods nor great ones, nor any succession of moons as have red men of the East and North, but count forward and back by the progress of the season; the time of *taboose*, before the trout begin to leap, the end of the piñon harvest, about the beginning of deep snows. So they get nearer the sense of the season, which runs early or late according as the rains are forward or delayed. But whenever Seyavi cut willows for baskets was always a golden time, and the soul of the weather went into the wood. If you had ever owned one of Seyavi's golden russet cooking bowls with the pattern of plumed quail, you would understand all this without saying anything.

Before Seyavi made baskets for the satisfaction of desire,—for that is a house-bred theory of art that makes anything more of it,—she danced and dressed her hair. In those days, when the spring was at flood and the blood pricked to the mating fever, the maids chose their flowers, wreathed themselves, and danced in the twilights, young desire crying out to young desire. They sang what the heart prompted, what the flower expressed, what boded in the mating weather.

"And what flower did you wear, Seyavi?"

"I, ah,—the white flower of twining (clematis), on my body and my hair, and so I sang:—

> "*I am the white flower of twining,*
> *Little white flower by the river,*
> *Oh, flower that twines close by the river;*
> *Oh, trembling flower!*
> *So trembles the maiden heart.*"

So sang Seyavi of the campoodie before she made baskets, and in her later days laid her arms upon her knees and laughed in them at the recollection. But it was not often she would say so much, never understanding the keen hunger I had for bits of lore and the "fool talk" of her people. She had fed her young son with meadowlarks' tongues, to make him quick of speech; but in late years was loath to admit it, though she had come through the period of unfaith in the lore of the clan with a fine appreciation of its beauty and significance.

"What good will your dead get, Seyavi, of the baskets you burn?" said I, coveting them for my own collection.

Thus Seyavi, "As much good as yours of the flowers you strew."

Oppapago looks on Waban, and Waban on Coso and the Bitter Lake, and the campoodie looks on these three; and more, it sees the beginning of winds along the foot of Coso, the gathering of clouds behind the high ridges, the spring flush, the soft spread of wild almond bloom on the mesa. These first, you understand, are the Paiute's walls, the other his furnishings. Not the wattled hut is his home, but the land, the winds, the hill front, the stream. These he cannot duplicate at any furbisher's shop as you who live within doors, who, if your purse allows, may have the same home at Sitka and Samarcand. So you see how it is that the homesickness of an Indian is often unto death, since he gets no relief from it; neither wind nor weed nor sky-line, nor any aspect of the hills of a strange land sufficiently like his own. So it was when the government reached out for the Paiutes, they gathered into the Northern Reservation only such poor tribes as could devise no other end of their affairs. Here, all along the river, and south to Shoshone Land, live the clans who owned the earth, fallen into the deplorable condition of hangers-on. Yet you hear them laughing at the hour when they draw in to the campoodie after labor, when there is a smell of meat and the steam of the cooking pots goes up against the sun. Then the children lie with their toes in the ashes to hear tales; then they are merry, and have the joys of repletion and the nearness of their kind. They have their hills, and though jostled are sufficiently free to get some fortitude for what will come. For now you shall hear of the end of the basket maker.

In her best days Seyavi was most like Deborah, deep bosomed, broad in the hips, quick in counsel, slow of speech, esteemed of her people. This was that Seyavi who reared a man by her own hand, her own wit, and none other. When the townspeople began to take note of her—and it was some years after the war before there began to be any towns—she was then in the quick maturity of primitive women; but when I knew her she seemed already old. Indian women do not often live to great age, though they look incredibly steeped in years. They have the wit to win sustenance from the raw material of life without intervention, but they have not the sleek look of the women whom the social organization conspires to nourish. Seyavi had somehow squeezed out of her daily round a spiritual ichor that kept the skill in her knotted fingers long after the accustomed time, but that also failed. By all counts she would have been about sixty years old when it came her turn to sit in the dust on the sunny side of the wickiup, with little strength left for anything but looking. And in time she paid the toll of the smoky huts and became blind. This is a thing so long expected by the Paiutes that when it comes they find it neither bitter nor sweet, but tolerable because common. There were three other blind women in the campoodie, withered fruit on a bough, but they had memory and speech. By noon of the sun there were never any left in the campoodie but these or some mother of weanlings, and they sat to keep the ashes warm upon the hearth. If it were cold, they burrowed in the blankets of the hut; if it were warm, they followed the shadow of the wickiup around. Stir much out of their places they hardly dared, since one might not help another; but they called, in high, old cracked voices, gossip and reminder across the ash heaps.

Then, if they have your speech or you theirs, and have an hour to spare, there are things to be learned of life not set down in any books, folk tales, famine tales, love and long-suffering and desire, but no whimpering. Now and then one or another of the blind keepers of the camp will come across to where you sit gossiping, tapping her way among the kitchen middens, guided by your voice that carries far in the clearness and stillness of mesa afternoons. But suppose you find Seyavi retired into the privacy of her blanket, you will get nothing for that day. There is no other privacy possible in a campoodie. All the processes of life are carried on out of doors or behind the thin, twig-woven walls of the wickiup, and laughter is the only corrective for behavior. Very early the Indian learns to possess his countenance in impassivity, to cover his head with his blanket. Something to wrap around him is as necessary to the Paiute as to you your closet to pray in.

So in her blanket Seyavi, sometime basket maker, sits by the unlit hearths of her tribe and digests her life, nourishing her spirit against the time of the spirit's need, for she knows in fact quite as much of these matters as you who have a larger hope, though she has none but the certainty that having borne herself courageously to this end she will not be reborn a coyote.

Mary Austin has divided Seyavi's life into three parts: before, during, and after her career as a basketmaker. (See pages 132 and 133.) Describe the corresponding parts of a modern American woman's life as Mary Austin has described Seyavi's.

Mary Austin says that Indian women "have the wit to win sustenance from the raw material of life without intervention but they have not the sleek look of the women whom the social organization conspires to nourish." Contrast the responsibilities and abilities of primitive and civilized women. Do you think each becomes "saturated with the elements" of her existence? How?

Compare and contrast the Paiute's ability of "reducing life to its lowest ebb and yet saving it alive on grasshoppers, lizards, and strange herbs" with Bustopher Jones' dining habits at eight or nine St. James Street clubs.

Compare Seyavi's and Bustopher's philosophy of life. At the end of her life Seyavi knows that because she has borne her life courageously "she will not be reborn a coyote"; Bustopher says, "I shall last out my time."

María Concepción

KATHERINE ANNE PORTER

María Concepción walked carefully, keeping to the middle of the white dusty road, where the maguey thorns and the treacherous curved spines of organ cactus had not gathered so profusely. She would have enjoyed resting for a moment in the dark shade by the roadside, but she had no time to waste drawing cactus needles from her feet. Juan and his chief would be waiting for their food in the damp trenches of the buried city.

She carried about a dozen living fowls slung over her right shoulder, their feet fastened together. Half of them fell upon the flat of her back, the balance dangled uneasily over her breast. They wriggled their benumbed and swollen legs against her neck, they twisted their stupefied eyes and peered into her face inquiringly. She did not see them or think of them. Her left arm was tired with the weight of the food basket, and she was hungry after her long morning's work.

Her straight back outlined itself strongly under her clean bright blue cotton rebozo. Instinctive serenity softened her black eyes, shaped like almonds, set far apart, and tilted a bit endwise. She walked with the free, natural, guarded ease of the primitive woman carrying an unborn child. The shape of her body was easy, the swelling life was not a distortion, but the right inevitable proportions of a woman. She was entirely contented. Her husband was at work and she was on her way to market to sell her fowls.

Her small house sat half-way up a shallow hill, under a clump of pep-per-trees, a wall of organ cactus enclosing it on the side nearest to the road. Now she came down into the valley, divided by the narrow spring, and crossed a bridge of loose stones near the hut where María Rosa the beekeeper lived with her old godmother, Lupe the medicine woman. María Concepción had no faith in the charred owl bones, the singed rabbit fur, the cat entrails, the messes and ointments sold by Lupe to the ailing of the village. She was a good Christian, and drank simple herb teas for head-ache and stomachache, or bought her remedies bottled, with printed direc-tions that she could not read, at the drugstore near the city market, where she went almost daily. But she often bought a jar of honey from young María Rosa, a pretty, shy child only fifteen years old.

María Concepción and her husband, Juan Villegas, were each a little past their eighteenth year. She had a good reputation with the neighbors as an energetic religious woman who could drive a bargain to the end. It was commonly known that if she wished to buy a new rebozo for herself or a shirt for Juan, she could bring out a sack of hard silver coins for the purpose.

She had paid for the license, nearly a year ago, the potent bit of stamped paper which permits people to be married in the church. She had given money to the priest before she and Juan walked together up to the altar the Monday after Holy Week. It had been the adventure of the villa-gers to go, three Sundays one after another, to hear the banns called by the priest for Juan de Dios Villegas and María Concepción Manríquez, who were actually getting married in the church, instead of behind it, which was the usual custom, less expensive, and as binding as any other cere-mony. But María Concepción was always as proud as if she owned a ha-cienda.

She paused on the bridge and dabbled her feet in the water, her eyes resting themselves from the sun-rays in a fixed gaze to the far-off moun-tains, deeply blue under their hanging drift of clouds. It came to her that she would like a fresh crust of honey. The delicious aroma of bees, their slow thrilling hum, awakened a pleasant desire for a flake of sweetness in her mouth.

"If I do not eat it now, I shall mark my child," she thought, peering through the crevices in the thick hedge of cactus that sheered up nakedly, like bared knife blades set protectingly around the small clearing. The place was so silent she doubted if María Rosa and Lupe were at home.

The leaning jacal of dried rush-withes and corn sheaves, bound to tall saplings thrust into the earth, roofed with yellow maguey leaves flattened and overlapping like shingles, hunched drowsy and fragrant in the warmth of noonday. The hives, similarly made, were scattered towards the back of the clearing, like small mounds of clean vegetable refuse. Over each mound there hung a dusty golden shimmer of bees.

A light gay scream of laughter rose from behind the hut; a man's short laugh joined in. "Ah, hahahaha!" went the voices together high and low, like a song.

"So María Rosa has a man!" María Concepción stopped short, smiling, shifted her burden slightly, and bent forward shading her eyes to see more clearly through the spaces of the hedge.

María Rosa ran, dodging between beehives, parting two stunted jasmine bushes as she came, lifting her knees in swift leaps, looking over her shoulder and laughing in a quivering, excited way. A heavy jar, swung to her wrist by the handle, knocked against her thighs as she ran. Her toes pushed up sudden spurts of dust, her half-raveled braids showered around her shoulders in long crinkled wisps.

Juan Villegas ran after her, also laughing strangely, his teeth set, both rows gleaming behind the small soft black beard growing sparsely on his lips, his chin, leaving his brown cheeks girl-smooth. When he seized her, he clenched so hard her chemise gave way and ripped from her shoulder. She stopped laughing at this, pushed him away and stood silent, trying to pull up the torn sleeve with one hand. Her pointed chin and dark red mouth moved in an uncertain way, as if she wished to laugh again; her long black lashes flickered with the quick-moving lights in her hidden eyes.

María Concepción did not stir nor breathe for some seconds. Her forehead was cold, and yet boiling water seemed to be pouring slowly along her spine. An unaccountable pain was in her knees, as if they were broken. She was afraid Juan and María Rosa would feel her eyes fixed upon them and would find her there, unable to move, spying upon them. But they did not pass beyond the enclosure, nor even glance towards the gap in the wall opening upon the road.

Juan lifted one of María Rosa's loosened braids and slapped her neck with it playfully. She smiled softly, consentingly. Together they moved back through the hives of honey-comb. María Rosa balanced her jar on one hip and swung her long full petticoats with every step. Juan flourished his wide hat back and forth, walking proudly as a game-cock.

María Concepción came out of the heavy cloud which enwrapped her head and bound her throat, and found herself walking onward, keeping the road without knowing it, feeling her way delicately, her ears strumming as if all María Rosa's bees had hived in them. Her careful sense of duty kept her moving toward the buried city where Juan's chief, the American archeologist, was taking his midday rest, waiting for his food.

Juan and María Rosa! She burned all over now, as if a layer of tiny fig-cactus bristles, as cruel as spun glass, had crawled under her skin. She wished to sit down quietly and wait for her death, but not until she had cut the throats of her man and that girl who were laughing and kissing under the cornstalks. Once when she was a young girl she had come back from market to find her jacal burned to a pile of ash and her few silver coins gone. A dark empty feeling had filled her; she kept moving about the place, not believing her eyes, expecting it all to take shape again before her. But it was gone, and though she knew an enemy had done it, she could not find out who it was, and could only curse and threaten the air. Now here was a worse thing, but she knew her enemy. María Rosa, that sinful girl, shameless! She heard herself saying a harsh, true word about María Rosa, saying it aloud as if she expected someone to agree with her: "Yes, she is a whore! She has no right to live."

At this moment the gray untidy head of Givens appeared over the edges of the newest trench he had caused to be dug in his field of excavations. The long deep crevasses, in which a man might stand without being seen, lay crisscrossed like orderly gashes of a giant scalpel. Nearly all of the men of the community worked for Givens, helping him to uncover the lost city of their ancestors. They worked all the year through and prospered, digging every day for those small clay heads and bits of pottery and fragments of painted walls for which there was no good use on earth, being all broken and encrusted with clay. They themselves could make better ones, perfectly stout and new, which they took to town and peddled to foreigners for real money. But the unearthly delight of the chief in finding these worn-out things was an endless puzzle. He would fairly roar for joy at times, waving a shattered pot or a human skull above his head, shouting for his photographer to come and make a picture of this!

Now he emerged, and his young enthusiast's eyes welcomed María Concepción from his old-man face, covered with hard wrinkles and burned to the color of red earth. "I hope you've brought me a nice fat one." He selected a fowl from the bunch dangling nearest him as María Concepción, wordless, leaned over the trench. "Dress it for me, there's a good girl. I'll broil it."

María Concepción took the fowl by the head, and silently, swiftly drew her knife across its throat, twisting the head off with the casual firmness she might use with the top of a beet.

"Good God, woman, you do have nerve," said Givens, watching her. "I can't do that. It gives me the creeps."

"My home country is Guadalajara," exclaimed María Concepción, without bravado, as she picked and gutted the fowl.

She stood and regarded Givens condescendingly, that diverting white man who had no woman of his own to cook for him, and moreover appeared not to feel any loss of dignity in preparing his own food. He squatted now, eyes squinted, nose wrinkled to avoid the smoke, turning the roasting fowl busily on a stick. A mysterious man, undoubtedly rich, and Juan's chief, therefore to be respected, to be placated.

"The tortillas are fresh and hot, señor," she murmured gently. "With your permission I will now go to market."

"Yes, yes, run along; bring me another of these tomorrow." Givens turned his head to look at her again. Her grand manner sometimes reminded him of royalty in exile. He noticed her unnatural paleness. "The sun is too hot, eh?" he asked.

"Yes, sir. Pardon me, but Juan will be here soon?"

"He ought to be here now. Leave his food. The others will eat it."

She moved away; the blue of her rebozo became a dancing spot in the heat waves that rose from the gray-red soil. Givens liked his Indians best when he could feel a fatherly indulgence for their primitive childish ways. He told comic stories of Juan's escapades, of how often he had saved him, in the past five years, from going to jail, and even from being shot, for his varied and always unexpected misdeeds.

"I am never a minute too soon to get him out of one pickle or another," he would say. "Well, he's a good worker, and I know how to manage him."

After Juan was married, he used to twit him, with exactly the right shade of condescension, on his many infidelities to María Concepción. "She'll catch you yet, and God help you!" he was fond of saying, and Juan would laugh with immense pleasure.

It did not occur to María Concepción to tell Juan she had found him out. During the day her anger against him died, and her anger against María Rosa grew. She kept saying to herself, "When I was a young girl like María Rosa, if a man had caught hold of me so, I would have broken my jar over his head." She forgot completely that she had not resisted even so much as María Rosa, on the day that Juan had first taken hold of her. Besides she had married him afterwards in the church, and that was a very different thing.

Juan did not come home that night, but went away to war and María Rosa went with him. Juan had a rifle at his shoulder and two pistols at his belt. María Rosa wore a rifle also, slung on her back along with the blankets and the cooking pots. They joined the nearest detachment of troops in the field, and María Rosa marched ahead with the battalion of experienced women of war, which went over the crops like locusts, gathering provisions for the army. She cooked with them, and ate with them what was left after the men had eaten. After battles she went out on the field with the others to salvage clothing and ammunition and guns from the slain before they should begin to swell in the heat. Sometimes they would encounter the women from the other army, and a second battle as grim as the first would take place.

There was no particular scandal in the village. People grinned, shrugged. It was far better that they were gone. The neighbors went around saying that María Rosa was safer in the army than she would be in the same village with María Concepción.

María Concepción did not weep when Juan left her; and when the baby was born, and died within four days, she did not weep. "She is mere stone," said old Lupe, who went over and offered charms to preserve the baby.

"May you rot in hell with your charms," said María Concepción.

If she had not gone so regularly to church, lighting candles before the saints, kneeling with her arms spread in the form of a cross for hours at a time, and receiving holy communion every month, there might have been talk of her being devil-possessed, her face was so changed and blind-looking. But this was impossible when, after all, she had been married by the priest. It must be, they reasoned, that she was being punished for her pride. They decided that this was the true cause for everything: she was altogether too proud. So they pitied her.

During the year that Juan and María Rosa were gone María Concepción sold her fowls and looked after her garden and her sack of hard coins grew. Lupe had no talent for bees, and the hives did not prosper. She began to blame María Rosa for running away, and to praise María Concepción for her behavior. She used to see María Concepción at the market or at church, and she always said that no one could tell by looking at her now that she was a woman who had such a heavy grief.

"I pray God everything goes well with María Concepción from this out," she would say, "for she has had her share of trouble."

When some idle person repeated this to the deserted woman, she went down to Lupe's house and stood within the clearing and called to the medicine woman, who sat in her doorway stirring a mess of her infallible cure for sores: "Keep your prayers to yourself, Lupe, or offer them for others who need them. I will ask God for what I want in this world."

"And will you get it, you think, María Concepción?" asked Lupe, tittering cruelly and smelling the wooden mixing spoon. "Did you pray for what you have now?"

Afterward everyone noticed that María Concepción went oftener to church, and even seldomer to the village to talk with the other women as they sat along the curb, nursing their babies and eating fruit, at the end of the market-day.

"She is wrong to take us for enemies," said old Soledad, who was a thinker and a peace-maker. "All women have these troubles. Well, we should suffer together."

But María Concepción lived alone. She was gaunt, as if something were gnawing her away inside, her eyes were sunken, and she would not speak a word if she could help it. She worked harder than ever, and her butchering knife was scarely ever out of her hand.

Juan and María Rosa, disgusted with military life, came home one day without asking permission of anyone. The field of war had unrolled itself, a long scroll of vexations, until the end had frayed out within twenty miles of Juan's village. So he and María Rosa, now lean as a wolf, burdened with a child daily expected, set out with no farewells to the regiment and walked home.

They arrived one morning about daybreak. Juan was picked up on sight by a group of military police from the small barracks on the edge of town, and taken to prison, where the officer in charge told him with impersonal cheerfulness that he would add one to a catch of ten waiting to be shot as deserters the next morning.

María Rosa, screaming and falling on her face in the road, was taken under the armpits by two guards and helped briskly to her jacal, now sadly run down. She was received with professional importance by Lupe, who helped the baby to be born at once.

Limping with foot soreness, a layer of dust concealing his fine new clothes got mysteriously from somewhere, Juan appeared before the captain at the barracks. The captain recognized him as head digger for his good friend Givens, and dispatched a note to Givens saying: "I am holding the person of Juan Villegas awaiting your further disposition."

When Givens showed up Juan was delivered to him with the urgent request that nothing be made public about so humane and sensible an operation on the part of military authority.

Juan walked out of the rather stifling atmosphere of the drumhead court, a definite air of swagger about him. His hat, of unreasonable dimensions and embroidered with silver thread, hung over one eyebrow, secured at the back by a cord of silver dripping with bright blue tassels. His shirt was of a checkerboard pattern in green and black, his white cotton trousers were bound by a belt of yellow leather tooled in red. His feet were bare, full of stone bruises, and sadly ragged as to toenails. He removed his cigarette from the corner of his full-lipped wide mouth. He removed the splendid hat. His black dusty hair, pressed moistly to his forehead, sprang up suddenly in a cloudly thatch on his crown. He bowed to the officer, who appeared to be gazing at a vacuum. He swung his arm wide in a free circle upsoaring towards the prison window, where forlorn heads poked over the window sill, hot eyes following after the lucky departing one. Two or three of the heads nodded, and a half dozen hands were flipped at him in an effort to imitate his own casual and heady manner.

Juan kept up this insufferable pantomime until they rounded the first clump of fig-cactus. Then he seized Givens' hand and burst into oratory. "Blessed be the day your servant Juan Villegas first came under your eyes. From this day my life is yours without condition, ten thousand thanks with all my heart!" ·

"For God's sake stop playing the fool," said Givens irritably. "Some day I'm going to be five minutes too late."

"Well, it is nothing much to be shot, my chief—certainly you know I was not afraid—but to be shot in a drove of deserters, against a cold wall, just in the moment of my home-coming, by order of that . . ."

Glittering epithets tumbled over one another like explosions of a rocket. All the scandalous analogies from the animal and vegetable worlds were applied in a vivid, unique and personal way to the life, loves, and family history of the officer who had just set him free. When he had quite cursed himself dry, and his nerves were soothed, he added: "With your permission, my chief!"

"What will María Concepción say to all this?" asked Givens. "You are very informal, Juan, for a man who was married in the church."

Juan put on his hat.

"Oh, María Concepción! That's nothing. Look, my chief, to be married in the church is a great misfortune for a man. After that he is not himself any more. How can that woman complain when I do not drink even at fiestas enough to be really drunk? I do not beat her; never, never. We were always at peace. I say to her, Come here, and she comes straight. I say, Go there, and she goes quickly. Yet sometimes I looked at her and thought, Now I am married to that woman in the church, and I felt a sinking inside, as if something were lying heavy on my stomach. With María Rosa it is all different. She is not silent; she talks. When she talks too much, I slap her and say, Silence, thou simpleton! and she weeps. She is just a girl with whom I do as I please. You know how she used to keep those clean little bees in their hives? She is like their honey to me. I swear it. I would not harm María Concepción because I am married to her in the church; but also, my chief, I will not leave María Rosa, because she pleases me more than any other woman."

"Let me tell you, Juan, things haven't been going as well as you think. You be careful. Some day María Concepción will just take your head off with that carving knife of hers. You keep that in mind."

Juan's expression was the proper blend of masculine triumph and sentimental melancholy. It was pleasant to see himself in the role of hero to two such desirable women. He had just escaped from the threat of a disagreeable end. His clothes were new and handsome, and they had cost him just nothing. María Rosa had collected them for him here and there after battles. He was walking in the early sunshine, smelling the good smells of ripening cactus-figs, peaches, and melons, of pungent berries dangling from the pepper-trees, and the smoke of his cigarette under his nose. He was on his way to civilian life with his patient chief. His situation was ineffably perfect, and he swallowed it whole.

"My chief," he addressed Givens handsomely, as one man of the world to another, "women are good things, but not at this moment. With your permission, I will now go to the village and eat. My God, *how* I shall eat! Tomorrow morning very early I will come to the buried city and work like seven men. Let us forget María Concepción and María Rosa. Each one in her place. I will manage them when the time comes."

News of Juan's adventure soon got abroad, and Juan found many friends about him during the morning. They frankly commended his way of leaving the army. It was in itself the act of a hero. The new hero ate a great deal and drank somewhat, the occasion being better than a feastday. It was almost noon before he returned to visit María Rosa.

He found her sitting on a clean straw mat, rubbing fat on her three-hour-old son. Before this felicitous vision Juan's emotions so twisted him that he returned to the village and invited every man in the "Death and Resurrection" pulque shop to drink with him.

Having thus taken leave of his balance, he started back to María Rosa, and found himself unaccountably in his own house, attempting to beat María Concepción by way of re-establishing himself in his legal household.

María Concepción, knowing all the events of that unhappy day, was not in a yielding mood, and refused to be beaten. She did not scream nor implore; she stood her ground and resisted; she even struck at him. Juan, amazed, hardly knowing what he did, stepped back and gazed at her inquiringly through a leisurely whirling film which seemed to have lodged behind his eyes. Certainly he had not even thought of touching her. Oh, well, no harm done. He gave up, turned away, half-asleep on his feet. He dropped amiably in a shadowed corner and began to snore.

María Concepción, seeing that he was quiet, began to bind the legs of her fowls. It was market-day and she was late. She fumbled and tangled the bits of cord in her haste, and set off across the plowed fields instead of taking the accustomed road. She ran with a crazy panic in her head, her stumbling legs. Now and then she would stop and look about her, trying to place herself, then go on a few steps, until she realized that she was not going towards the market.

At once she came to her senses completely, recognized the thing that troubled her so terribly, was certain of what she wanted. She sat down quietly under a sheltering thorny bush and gave herself over to her long devouring sorrow. The thing which had for so long squeezed her whole body into a tight dumb knot of suffering suddenly broke with shocking violence. She jerked with the involuntary recoil of one who receives a blow, and the sweat poured from her skin as if the wounds of her whole life were shedding their salt ichor. Drawing her rebozo over her head, she bowed her forehead on her updrawn knees, and sat there in deadly silence and immobility. From time to time she lifted her head where the sweat formed steadily and poured down her face, drenching the front of her chemise, and her mouth had the shape of crying, but there were no tears and no sound. All her being was a dark confused memory of grief burning in her at night, of deadly baffled anger eating at her by day, until her very tongue tasted bitter, and her feet were as heavy as if she were mired in the muddy roads during the time of rains.

After a great while she stood up and threw the rebozo off her face, and set out walking again.

Juan awakened slowly, with long yawns and grumblings, alternated with short relapses into sleep full of visions and clamors. A blur of orange light seared his eyeballs when he tried to unseal his lids. There came from somewhere a low voice weeping without tears, saying meaningless phrases over and over. He began to listen. He tugged at the leash of his stupor, he strained to grasp those words which terrified him even though he could not quite hear them. Then he came awake with frightening suddenness, sitting up and staring at the long sharpened streak of light piercing the corn-husk walls from the level disappearing sun.

María Concepción stood in the doorway, looming colossally tall to his betrayed eyes. She was talking quickly, and calling his name. Then he saw her clearly.

"God's name!" said Juan, frozen to the marrow, "here I am facing my death!" for the long knife she wore habitually at her belt was in her hand. But instead, she threw it away, clear from her, and got down on her knees, crawling toward him as he had seen her crawl many times toward the shrine at Guadalupe Villa. He watched her approach with such horror that the hair of his head seemed to be lifting itself away from him. Falling forward upon her face, she huddled over him, lips moving in a ghostly whisper. Her words became clear, and Juan understood them all.

For a second he could not move nor speak. Then he took her head between both his hands, and supported her in this way, saying swiftly, anxiously reassuring, almost in a babble:

"Oh, thou poor creature! Oh, madwoman! Oh, my María Concepción, unfortunate! Listen. . . . Don't be afraid. Listen to me! I will hide thee away, I thy own man will protect thee! Quiet! Not a sound!"

Trying to collect himself, he held her and cursed under his breath for a few moments in the gathering darkness. María Concepción bent over, face almost on the ground, her feet folded under her, as if she would hide behind him. For the first time in his life Juan was aware of danger. This was danger. María Concepción would be dragged away between two gendarmes, with him following helpless and unarmed, to spend the rest of her days in Belén Prison, maybe. Danger! The night swarmed with threats. He stood up and dragged her up with him. She was silent and perfectly rigid, holding to him with resistless strength, her hands stiffened on his arms.

"Get me the knife," he told her in a whisper. She obeyed, her feet slipping along the hard earth floor, her shoulders straight, her arms close to her side. He lighted a candle. María Concepción held the knife out to him. It was stained and dark even to the handle with drying blood.

He frowned at her harshly, noting the same stains on her chemise and hands.

"Take off thy clothes and wash thy hands," he ordered. He washed the knife carefully, and threw the water wide of the doorway. She watched him and did likewise with the bowl in which she had bathed.

"Light the brasero and cook food for me," he told her in the same peremptory tone. He took her garments and went out. When he returned, she was wearing an old soiled dress, and was fanning the fire in the charcoal burner. Seating himself cross-legged near her, he stared at her as at a creature unknown to him, who bewildered him utterly, for whom there was no possible explanation. She did not turn her head, but kept silent and still, except for the movements of her strong hands fanning the blaze which cast sparks and small jets of white smoke, flaring and dying rhythmically with the motion of the fan lighting her face and darkening it by turns.

Juan's voice barely disturbed the silence: "Listen to me carefully, and tell me the truth, and when the gendarmes come here for us, thou shalt have nothing to fear. But there will be something for us to settle between us afterward."

The light from the charcoal burner shone in her eyes; a yellow phosphorescence glimmered behind the dark iris.

"For me everything is settled now," she answered, in a tone so tender, so grave, so heavy with suffering, that Juan felt his vitals contract. He wished to repent openly, not as a man, but as a very small child. He could not fathom her, nor himself, nor the mysterious fortunes of life grown so instantly confused where all had seemed so gay and simple. He felt too that she had become invaluable, a woman without equal among a million women, and he could not tell why. He drew an enormous sigh that rattled in his chest.

"Yes, yes, it is all settled. I shall not go away again. We must stay here together."

Whispering, he questioned her and she answered whispering, and he instructed her over and over until she had her lesson by heart. The hostile darkness of the night encroached upon them, flowing over the narrow threshold, invading their hearts. It brought with it sighs and murmurs, the pad of secretive feet in the near-by road, the sharp staccato whimper of wind through the cactus leaves. All these familiar, once friendly cadences were now invested with sinister terrors; a dread, formless and uncontrollable, took hold of them both.

"Light another candle," said Juan, loudly, in too resolute, too sharp a tone. "Let us eat now."

They sat facing each other and ate from the same dish, after their old habit. Neither tasted what they ate. With food half-way to his mouth, Juan listened. The sound of voices rose, spread, widened at the turn of the road along the cactus wall. A spray of lantern light shot through the hedge, a single voice slashed the blackness, ripped the fragile layer of silence suspended above the hut.

"Juan Villegas!"

"Pass, friends!" Juan roared back cheerfully.

They stood in the doorway, simple cautious gendarmes from the village, mixed-bloods themselves with Indian sympathies, well known to all the community. They flashed their lanterns almost apologetically upon the pleasant, harmless scene of a man eating supper with his wife.

"Pardon, brother," said the leader. "Someone has killed the woman María Rosa, and we must question her neighbors and friends." He paused, and added with an attempt at severity, "Naturally!"

"Naturally," agreed Juan. "You know that I was a good friend of María Rosa. This is bad news."

They all went away together, the men walking in a group, María Concepción following a few steps in the rear, near Juan. No one spoke.

The two points of candlelight at María Rosa's head fluttered uneasily;

the shadows shifted and dodged on the stained darkened walls. To María Concepción everything in the smothering enclosing room shared an evil restlessness. The watchful faces of those called as witnesses, the faces of old friends, were made alien by the look of speculation in their eyes. The ridges of the rose-colored rebozo thrown over the body varied continually, as though the thing it covered was not perfectly in repose. Her eyes swerved over the body in the open painted coffin, from the candle tips at the head to the feet, jutting up thinly, the small scarred soles protruding, freshly washed, a mass of crooked, half-healed wounds, thornpicks and cuts of sharp stones. Her gaze went back to the candle flame, to Juan's eyes warning her, to the gendarmes talking among themselves. Her eyes would not be controlled.

With a leap that shook her her gaze settled upon the face of María Rosa. Instantly her blood ran smoothly again: there was nothing to fear. Even the restless light could not give a look of life to that fixed countenance. She was dead. María Concepción felt her muscles give way softly; her heart began beating steadily without effort. She knew no more rancor against that pitiable thing, lying indifferently in its blue coffin under the fine silk rebozo. The mouth drooped sharply at the corners in a grimace of weeping arrested half-way. The brows were distressed; the dead flesh could not cast off the shape of its last terror. It was all finished. María Rosa had eaten too much honey and had had too much love. Now she must sit in hell, crying over her sins and her hard death forever and ever.

Old Lupe's cackling voice arose. She had spent the morning helping María Rosa, and it had been hard work. The child had spat blood the moment it was born, a bad sign. She thought then that bad luck would come to the house. Well, about sunset she was in the yard at the back of the house grinding tomatoes and peppers. She had left mother and babe asleep. She heard a strange noise in the house, a choking and smothered calling, like someone wailing in sleep. Well, such a thing is only natural. But there followed a light, quick, thudding sound—

"Like the blows of a fist?" interrupted an officer.

"No, not at all like such a thing."

"How do you know?"

"I am well acquainted with that sound, friends," retorted Lupe. "This was something else."

She was at a loss to describe it exactly. A moment later, there came the sound of pebbles rolling and slipping under feet; the she knew someone had been there and was running away.

"Why did you wait so long before going to see?"

"I am old and hard in the joints," said Lupe. "I cannot run after people. I walked as fast as I could to the cactus hedge, for it is only by this way that anyone can enter. There was no one in the road, sir, no one. Three cows, with a dog driving them; nothing else. When I got to María Rosa, she was lying all tangled up, and from her neck to her middle she was full of knife-holes. It was a sight to move the Blessed Image Himself! Her eyes were—"

"Never mind. Who came oftenest to her house before she went away? Did you know her enemies?"

Lupe's face congealed, closed. Her spongy skin drew into a network of secretive wrinkles. She turned withdrawn and expressionless eyes upon the gendarmes.

"I am an old woman. I do not see well. I cannot hurry on my feet. I know no enemy of María Rosa. I did not see anyone leave the clearing."

"You did not hear splashing in the spring near the bridge?"

"No, sir."

"Why, then, do our dogs follow a scent there and lose it?"

"God only knows, my friend. I am an old wo—"

"Yes. How did the footfalls sound?"

"Like the tread of an evil spirit!" Lupe broke forth in a swelling oracular tone that startled them. The Indians stirred uneasily, glanced at the dead, then at Lupe. They half expected her to produce the evil spirit among them at once.

The gendarme began to lose his temper.

"No, poor unfortunate; I mean, were they heavy or light? The footsteps of a man or of a woman? Was the person shod or barefoot?"

A glance at the listening circle assured Lupe of their thrilled attention. She enjoyed the dangerous importance of her situation. She could have ruined that María Concepción with a word, but it was even sweeter to make fools of these gendarmes who went about spying on honest people. She raised her voice again. What she had not seen she could not describe, thank God! No one could harm her because her knees were stiff and she could not run even to seize a murderer. As for knowing the difference between footfalls, shod or bare, man or woman, nay, between devil and human, who ever heard of such madness?

"My eyes are not ears, gentlemen," she ended grandly, "but upon my heart I swear those footsteps fell as the tread of the spirit of evil!"

"Imbecile!" yapped the leader in a shrill voice. "Take her away, one of you! Now, Juan Villegas, tell me—"

Juan told his story patiently, several times over. He had returned to his wife that day. She had gone to market as usual. He had helped her prepare her fowls. She had returned about mid-afternoon, they had talked, she had cooked, they had eaten, nothing was amiss. Then the gendarmes came with the news about María Rosa. That was all. Yes, María Rosa had run away with him, but there had been no bad blood between him and his wife on this account, nor between his wife and María Rosa. Everybody knew that his wife was a quiet woman.

María Concepción heard her own voice answering without a break. It was true at first she was troubled when her husband went away, but after that she had not worried about him. It was the way of men, she believed. She was a church-married woman and knew her place. Well, he had come home at last. She had gone to market, but had come back early, because now she had her man to cook for. That was all.

Other voices broke in. A toothless old man said: "She is a woman of good reputation among us, and María Rosa was not." A smiling young mother, Anita, baby at breast, said: "If no one thinks so, how can you accuse her? It was the loss of her child and not of her husband that changed her so." Another: "María Rosa had a strange life, apart from us. How do we know who might have come from another place to do her evil?" And old Soledad spoke up boldly: "When I saw María Concepción in the market today, I said, 'Good luck to you, María Concepción, this is a happy day for you!' " and she gave María Concepción a long easy stare, and the smile of a born wise-woman.

María Concepción suddenly felt herself guarded, surrounded, upborne by her faithful friends. They were around her, speaking for her, defending her, the forces of life were ranged invincibly with her against the beaten dead. María Rosa had thrown away her share of strength in them, she lay forfeited among them. María Concepción looked from one to the other of the circling, intent faces. Their eyes gave back reassurance, under-standing, a secret and mighty sympathy.

The gendarmes were at a loss. They, too, felt that sheltering wall cast impenetrably around her. They were certain she had done it, and yet they could not accuse her. Nobody could be accused; there was not a shred of true evidence. They shrugged their shoulders and snapped their fingers and shuffled their feet. Well, then, good night to everybody. Many pardons for having intruded. Good health!

A small bundle lying against the wall at the head of the coffin squirmed like an eel. A wail, a mere sliver of sound, issued. María Con-cepción took the son of María Rosa in her arms.

"He is mine," she said clearly, "I will take him with me."

No one assented in words, but an approving nod, a bare breath of com-plete agreement, stirred among them as they made way for her.

María Concepción, carrying the child, followed Juan from the clear-ing. The hut was left with its lighted candles and a crowd of old women who would sit up all night, drinking coffee and smoking and telling ghost stories.

Juan's exaltation had burned out. There was not an ember of excite-ment left in him. He was tired. The perilous adventure was over. María Rosa had vanished, to come no more forever. Their days of marching, of eating, of quarreling and making love between battles, were all over. To-morrow he would go back to dull and endless labor, he must descend into the trenches of the buried city as María Rosa must go into her grave. He felt his veins fill up with bitterness, with black unendurable melancholy. Oh, Jesus! what bad luck overtakes a man!

Well, there was no way out of it now. For the moment he craved only to sleep. He was so drowsy he could scarcely guide his feet. The occasional light touch of the woman at his elbow was as unreal, as ghostly as the brushing of a leaf against his face. He did not know why he had fought to save her, and now he forgot her. There was nothing in him except a vast blind hurt like a covered wound.

He entered the jacal, and without waiting to light a candle, threw off his clothing, sitting just within the door. He moved with lagging, half-awake hands, to strip his body of its heavy finery. With a long groaning sigh of relief he fell straight back on the floor, almost instantly asleep, his arms flung up and outward.

María Concepción, a small clay jar in her hand, approached the gentle little mother goat tethered to a sapling, which gave and yielded as she pulled at the rope's end after the farthest reaches of grass about her. The kid, tied up a few feet away, rose bleating, its feathery fleece shivering in the fresh wind. Sitting on her heels, holding his tether, she allowed him to suckle a few moments. Afterward—all her movements very deliberate and even—she drew a supply of milk for the child.

She sat against the wall of her house, near the doorway. The child, fed and asleep, was cradled in the hollow of her crossed legs. The silence overfilled the world, the skies flowed down evenly to the rim of the valley, the stealthy moon crept slantwise to the shelter of the mountains. She felt soft and warm all over; she dreamed that the newly born child was her own, and she was resting deliciously.

María Concepción could hear Juan's breathing. The sound vapored from the low doorway, calmly; the house seemed to be resting after a burdensome day. She breathed, too, very slowly and quietly, each inspiration saturating her with repose. The child's light, faint breath was a mere shadowy moth of sound in the silver air. The night, the earth under her, seemed to swell and recede together with a limitless, unhurried, benign breathing. She drooped and closed her eyes, feeling the slow rise and fall within her own body. She did not know what it was, but it eased her all through. Even as she was falling asleep, head bowed over the child, she was still aware of a strange, wakeful happiness.

How would people in a large civilized city like Mexico City or Los Angeles or New York view María Rosa's murder? Compare the "civilized" and the "primitive" response to love, marriage, work, birth, death, crime.

Givens, Juan Villegas' boss, feels a "fatherly indulgence" for the Indians' "primitive childish ways." What does Givens' attitude reveal about him? How much does he really know about these Indians?

Discuss the character of María Concepción. Is she a woman who could "do very well" without a man? Compare her with Seyavi. (See p. 130.)

Read the description of Juan Villegas when he leaves court (pp. 139–40). Using this passage as a model, write a description of your own about some person you know. (See Unit 11: Writing Description, p. 115.)

CONSCIOUSNESS

AND 5

REVERIE

UNIT 13
PREWRITING

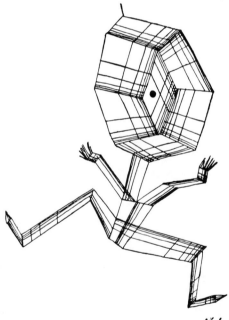

66 This journey downward, whether it is called dream, idea, fancy . . . [these] curiosities become realities, the realities . . . which make life a little wider than it ordinarily seems to be. 99

PAUL KLEE

Paul Klee, *About to Take a Trip.*

You live in two worlds, in a world of things and a world of thoughts. You live with the realities of everyday life, with visible objects you can touch—like rocks, flowers, rivers, mountains, and mud puddles; potatoes and mushrooms and Agassiz's fish that we talked about in the preceding chapter; with chairs, cars, and shoes; and with people.

And you live also in another world that you cannot touch, in the world of your thoughts, mental images, ideas, opinions, reveries, and dreams.

In Chapter 4 we asked you to write about things you can see. In this chapter we ask you to write about what you can't see. We ask you to write, not about the world around you, but about the world within you. Here also are realities to write about—as real as that dead fish in the pan.

But thoughts are more difficult to observe than dead fish—they do not lie still, are constantly changing shape, and you can't see them with your physical eye. Things and thoughts are different, and observing them calls for different abilities. Since you were five years old you have probably known that a thing and a thought are not the same.

> ❝I remember reading that it was a great day in a child's mental development when he learnt to tell a deliberate lie, for this meant the implicit understanding that thought was different from things and could be dealt with separately. ❞
>
> JOANNA FIELD

But if your thoughts are not the same as the things you see around you, they are, if you are sane, based on what you do see around you. A few people even have the ability to reproduce in their mind's eye almost exactly what they see with their physical eyes.

❝A ten-year-old boy was asked to examine this picture for nine seconds. Later, looking at an empty white screen, he was able to glean details of the picture as though it were still present. He could count the number of cans on the milk cart. When asked about the sign on top of the door he deciphered it with difficulty: "That's hard to read . . . it says 'Number' then an 8 or 9. . . ." He could also make out the name of the shop owner and the drawing of a cow beneath the word *Milchhandlung*. ❞

RUDOLPH ARNHEIM

Of course, the mental image this ten-year-old boy had in his head was not the same thing as the picture on the page, even though it was very like it. Now try an experiment with this phenomenon yourself:

- Look at a person, a picture, or an object in the room.
- Shut your eyes and see with your mind's eye what you have just seen with your physical eyes.
- With your eyes still shut, formulate some thought or opinion about the person or thing.

You probably noticed that with your eyes open, you received direct impressions of the touchable object in the external world. With your eyes shut, you were able to "see" within you a form of the image left by the impression you received through your physical eyes. And you know that your thoughts and opinions about the object arose from your mental impression of that object.

CONNECTING EXERCISES

▶A. Watch people walking along the street, riding a bus, sitting in a class. Try imagining what is going on in their heads as they are doing these things. To what extent do you imagine they are thinking about the immediate physical world around them, the one they can see, hear, touch? To what extent do you think they are in a reverie about something somewhere else at some other time?

While you are walking or sitting in a classroom, be conscious of your thoughts.

▶B. In a television show, movie, or book discover one way in which you, the viewer or reader, are allowed an insight into another person's thoughts. Can you find some point of opposition between what is actually happening around the person and his thoughts?

DISCUSSION

Read the following poem and discuss the apparent ironic discrepancy between Cory's external, physical world and his inner, emotional world.

Richard Cory

Whenever Richard Cory went down town,
We people on the pavement looked at him:
He was a gentleman from sole to crown,
Clean favored and imperially slim.

And he was always quietly arrayed,
And he was always human when he talked;
But still he fluttered pulses when he said,
"Good-morning," and he glittered when he walked.

And he was rich—yes, richer than a king—
And admirably schooled in every grace:
In fine, we thought that he was everything
To make us wish that we were in his place.

So on we worked, and waited for the light,
And went without the meat and cursed the bread;
And Richard Cory, one calm summer night,
Went home and put a bullet through his head.

EDWIN ARLINGTON ROBINSON

About a man Richard Cory who killed himself with a bullet. While everyone thought he had everything

UNIT 14
WRITING REVERIE

Just as close observation of our environment increases our awareness of life around us, studying the operations of our minds may increase our consciousness of the life within us. James Harvey Robinson, in *Mind in the Making* (quoted in Unit 15), says that "we do not think enough about thinking." The reverie, Professor Robinson believes, forms "the chief index to our fundamental character."

When you write your reverie paper you will be giving your reader a glimpse into the workings of your mind. But before you will be able to give your reader that glimpse, you will need to see those workings yourself. And it is more difficult to see one of your reveries than it is a buzzing fly. Not only is the mind's flight erratic and capricious, but its silent activity may conceal its very existence. Yet your mind is active—constantly.

> " The most ordinary movement in the world, such as sitting down at a table and pulling the inkstand toward one, may agitate a thousand odd, disconnected fragments, now bright, now dim, hanging and bobbing and dipping and flaunting, like the under-linen of a family of fourteen on a line in a gale of wind. "
>
> VIRGINIA WOOLF

There are ways to make the difficult job of observing your reveries less difficult. One method you may use is to concentrate on one subject and to note

155

Andrew Wyeth, *Christina's World.* (1948) Collection, The Museum of Modern Art, New York.

whenever your mind is not on that subject. Mark Twain provides an example of what we mean in this dramatic presentation of a man trying to concentrate his mind and emotions on a subject appropriate to the Sabbath day:

> 66This is the day set apart by a benignant Creator for rest—for repose from the wearying toils of the week, and for calm and serious (Brown's dog has commenced to howl again—I wonder why Brown persists in keeping that dog chained up?) meditation upon those tremendous subjects pertaining to our future existence. How thankful we ought to be (There goes that rooster, now.) for this sweet respite; how fervently we ought to lift up our voice and (Confound that old hen—lays an egg every forty minutes, and then cackles until she lays the next one.) testify our gratitude. How sadly, how soothingly the music of that deep-toned bell floats up from the distant church! How gratefully we murmur (Scat!—that old gray tomcat is always bully-ragging that other one—got him down, now, and digging the hair out of him by the handful.) thanksgiving for these Sabbath blessings. 99

Psychologist Joanna Field used another device to catch a glimpse of her reveries. She said she realized "the importance of making thought see itself" but that she usually felt "a strong disinclination" to make the necessary effort. To help herself trace a train of thought back from any particular moment Field would ask herself, "What am I thinking about?" And then, "What was the thought that came before that and the one before that? And so on."

WRITING EXERCISES

Do one of the following, keeping in mind that you are gathering material for a reverie paper.

▶ A. Set a watch and a notebook before you.
For 10 minutes look at the second hand of the watch and try to think only about the watch.
Continually ask yourself "What am I thinking about?"
Record all thoughts that are not directly connected with your observation of the watch.

▶ B. During a 20-minute walk, attempt to be aware only of your immediate environment.
Continually ask yourself "What am I thinking about?"
Record all thoughts not directly concerned with the physical world around you.

▶ C. For a week make frequent efforts to trace a train of thought back from one particular moment.
At the end of each day record in a notebook examples of what you have noticed. Try to find examples of inner *monologue*, including self-justification (You tell yourself you were right to have done or failed to do something about which you feel uneasy. What are the reasons you give yourself?); complaints (Someone you know has acted badly or has an irritating personality. What are your complaints?); recognition of weakness (You felt embarrassed, that you failed in some way. How are you resolving to improve your character?). Try to find examples of inner *dialogue*, including a conversation and an argument. (What do you say? What does the other person say?)

Using notes on one of your reveries (above) as a basis, write a paper that communicates to your readers thoughts that have passed through your head during one short period of time.

Read your paper in class or exchange observations with other members of the class about the results of the exercises described above. How successful were you in recognizing your thoughts? What method did you use? Did you feel a "strong disinclination" to observe your thoughts? What did your reveries tell you about yourself?

Following is a student paper that developed from notes taken while doing Exercise B (p. 157). While walking to class, the student attempted to hold his mind on only the objects around him. The sight of a passing girl, however, shifted his thoughts to events that had taken place years before and hundreds of miles away.

MARSHA

Marsha! See her everywhere—classroom, cafeteria, library and it's never her. She's not here. How long will this go on? I can't blame her. The bitch! We had so little. Poor? I've never known such poverty. The days of french toast and milk, all on credit from the milkman. Scraping together enough money to buy Holly an ice cream when we took our favorite walk around the block past the house with the broken windows where the ghost lived all alone. Her hand tightening around my fingers as we passed.

If I just hadn't gone. Oh, how I wanted to go! Afraid the war would be over before I finished school. It wasn't. Four years ago or yesterday? Posing for snapshots in my tropical uniform and freezing in the Colorado winter. More excited about going that morning than sad about leaving. Looking more like I was going to a parade than a war. The glamour! My head bursting with march music and medals waiting to be won. Boots and brass shining in the early sun. I had to go! Why was she crying?

The bitter loneliness. Unanswered letters. God! How I miss her. The warm yellow glow of her hair. That godawful space between her two front teeth, given to both children like an heirloom to be kept in the family. And the love, oh, the love. That first night. Nervous. Stalling for time in the bathroom. That moment. We stayed in the room so long the maid finally knocked and giggled as we screamed in protest.

Long hours at school and work. Accusations of infidelity. First this woman then another. Telling the truth only to be called a liar. Or was it true?

```
     Still see her, every day in a dozen different women.
The wisp of a smile dispelling all wrongs and all
anger.   The soft brown eyes that brought solace to my
mind racing with thoughts of illness and death.  Why do
I look for her?  It's over.  I'm torn apart.  I must
start again.  I must begin again.  I can't.

                              Walter Lander
```

This paper contains many nonsentences, word groups that are incomplete in form. Subjects and verbs may be missing, yet the word group is punctuated as a sentence: "Long hours at school and work. Accusations of infidelity. First this woman then another. Telling the truth only to be called a liar." From the context readers are required to fill in missing words and understand what is meant. The writer has written this way to reflect the way his mind worked as he had the reverie.

WRITING HINT: USE CONTRARIES TO GIVE INNER TENSION TO YOUR WRITING.

Reveries are rich in oppositions because they arise from unsettled emotions and thoughts. In the reverie given above, the writer has become aware of both sides of his emotion. Without making the contrast rigid or overly obvious, he has brought antagonists together, creating a push-and-pull activity within the circle of his controlling idea: I'm torn apart.

tension

[I] see her ⟷ it's never her

I can't blame her ⟷ the bitch!

If I just hadn't gone ⟷ Oh, how I wanted to go

The warm yellow glow ⟷ That godawful space
of her hair   between her two
                               front teeth

I look for her ⟷ it's over

  I must begin again ⟷ I can't

The conflict within the speaker is also shown in the way he has formed some of his sentences:

More *excited* about *going* . . . than *sad* about *leaving.*

Looking more like I was going to a *parade* . . . than a *war.*

CLASS EXERCISES

▶A. To reinforce your notion of opposition, write three sentences, each with different content but all in the same form as this one:

if *attacked,*	the dragon *bellows;*
if *ignored,*	he *preens* his scales.

Remember that one way you can generate interest and tension in your writing is to let a conflict develop between one feeling and another, or between one thought and another, or between one word and another.

▶B. Analyze the following two reveries for opposition:

Husband worried about wife in child birth "if she should die" (going back and forth)

66 "It is very dangerous." The nurse went into the room and shut the door. . . . I did not think. I could not think. I knew she was going to die . . . She won't die. People don't die in childbirth nowadays. That was what all husbands thought. Yes, but what if she should die? She won't die. She's just having a bad time. The initial labour is usually protracted. She's only having a bad time. Afterward we'd say what a bad time, and Catherine would say it wasn't really so bad. But what if she should die? She can't die. Yes, but what if she should die? She can't . . . Don't be a fool. It's just a bad time. It's just nature giving her hell. It's only the first labour, which is almost always protracted. Yes, but what if she should die? She can't die. Why should she die? What reason is there for her to die? There's just a child that has to be born, the by-product of good nights in Milan. It makes trouble and is born and then you look after it and get fond of

it maybe. But what if she should die? She won't die. But what if she should die? She can't die. But what if she should die? Hey, what about that? What if she should die? **"**

ERNEST HEMINGWAY

" He went to the mantelpiece, glared at a colored photograph of Eliot there. The picture had been taken at the end of the Second World War. It showed a much-decorated captain of the Infantry. "So clean, so tall, so purposeful—so clean, so clean!" He gnashed his crockery teeth. "What a noble mind is here o'erthrown!"

He scratched himself, though he did not itch. "How puffy and pasty he looks these days. I've seen healthier complexions on rhubarb pies! Sleeps in his underwear, eats a balanced diet of potato chips, Southern Comfort, and Rosewater Golden Lager Ambrosia Beer." He rattled his fingernails against the photograph. "Him! Him! Captain Eliot Rosewater—Silver Star, Bronze Star, Soldier's Medal, and Purple Heart with Cluster! Sailing champion! Ski champion! Him! Him! My God—the number of times life has said, 'Yes, yes, yes,' to him! Millions of dollars, hundreds of significant friends, the most beautiful, intelligent, talented, affectionate wife imaginable! A splendid education, an elegant mind in a big clean body—and what is his reply when life says nothing but, 'Yes, yes, yes'?

"'No, no, no.'

"Why? Will someone tell me why?" **"**

KURT VONNEGUT, JR.

UNIT 15

SELECTIONS

Walter Erben says of Chagall:

Marc Chagall was born on July 7, 1887 in Vitebsk, the district capital of the province of the same name on the Russo-Polish border. . . . [For Chagall] Vitebsk and all the lived and dreamed reality contained in it, were of overwhelming significance. For Chagall Vitebsk was not only his place of origin, but also his present and his goal.

[Chagall] is suspicious of words like "fairy tale, fantasy" and "symbolism." "Our whole inner world is reality, perhaps more so than the visible world. If we describe everything that appears to us illogical as 'fantastic,' a 'fairy tale' or a 'figment of the imagination,' we are admitting that we do not understand nature." On being asked about the continual recurrence of certain motifs and figures in his pictures, he replied:

"That I have made the cows, girls, cocks and houses of provincial Russia my fundamental forms is explained by the fact that they belong to the milieu from which I originated and they have undoubtedly left the deepest imprint on my visual memory. However vitally and variously a painter may react to the atmosphere and influences of his later surroundings, a certain 'aroma' of his birthplace will always remain attached to his work. . . . Thus I hope I have preserved the influences of my childhood in more than merely their material aspect."

Marc Chagall, *I and the Village*. (1911) Collection, The Museum of Modern Art, New York.

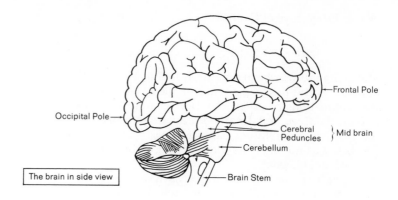

The brain in side view

Mind in the Making

JAMES HARVEY ROBINSON

Formerly philosphers thought of mind as having to do exclusively with conscious thought. It was that within man which perceived, remembered, judged, reasoned, understood, believed, willed. But of late it has been shown that we are unaware of a great part of what we perceive, remember, will, and infer; and that a great part of the thinking of which we are aware is determined by that of which we are not conscious. It has indeed been demonstrated that our unconscious psychic life far outruns our conscious. This seems perfectly natural to anyone who considers the following facts:

The sharp distinction between the mind and the body is, as we shall find, a very ancient and spontaneous uncritical savage prepossession. What we think of as "mind" is so intimately associated with what we call "body" that we are coming to realize that the one cannot be understood without the other. Every thought reverberates through the body, and, on the other hand, alterations in our physical condition affect our whole attitude of mind. The insufficient elimination of the foul and decaying products of digestion may plunge us into deep melancholy, whereas a few whiffs of nitrous monoxide may exalt us to the seventh heaven of supernal knowledge and godlike complacency. And *vice versa*, a sudden word or thought may cause our heart to jump, check our breathing, or make our knees as water. There is a whole new literature growing up which studies the effects of our bodily secretions and our muscular tensions and their relation to our emotions and our thinking.

Then there are hidden impulses and desires and secret longings of which we can only with the greatest difficulty take account. They influence our conscious thought in the most bewildering fashion. Many of these unconscious influences appear to originate in our very early years. The older philosophers seem to have forgotten that even they were infants and children at their most impressionable age and never could by any possibility get over it. . . .

We do not think enough about thinking, and much of our confusion is the result of current illusions in regard to it. Let us forget for the moment any impressions we may have derived from the philosophers, and see what seems to happen in ourselves. The first thing that we notice is that our thought moves with such incredible rapidity that it is almost impossible to arrest any specimen of it long enough to have a look at it. When we are offered a penny for our thoughts we always find that we have recently had so many things in mind that we can easily make a selection which will not compromise us too nakedly. On inspection we shall find that even if we are not downright ashamed of a great part of our spontaneous thinking it is far too intimate, personal, ignoble or trivial to permit us to reveal more than a small part of it. I believe this must be true of everyone. We do not, of course, know what goes on in other people's heads. They tell us very little and we tell them very little. The spigot of speech, rarely fully opened, could never emit more than driblets of the ever renewed hogshead of thought—*noch grösser wie's Heidelberger Fass.* We find it hard to believe that other people's thoughts are as silly as our own, but they probably are.

We all appear to ourselves to be thinking all the time during our waking hours, and most of us are aware that we go on thinking while we are asleep, even more foolishly than when awake. When uninterrupted by some practical issue we are engaged in what is now known as a *reverie.* This is our spontaneous and favorite kind of thinking. We allow our ideas to take their own course and this course is determined by our hopes and fears, our spontaneous desires, their fulfillment or frustration; by our likes and dislikes, our loves and hates and resentments. There is nothing else anything like so interesting to ourselves as ourselves. All thought that is not more or less laboriously controlled and directed will inevitably circle about the beloved Ego. It is amusing and pathetic to observe this tendency in ourselves and in others. We learn politely and generously to overlook this truth, but if we dare to think of it, it blazes forth like the noontide sun.

The reverie or "free association of ideas" has of late become the subject of scientific research. While investigators are not yet agreed on the results, or at least on the proper interpretation to be given to them, there can be no doubt that our reveries form the chief index to our fundamental character. They are a reflection of our nature as modified by often hidden and forgotten experiences. We need not go into the matter further here, for it is only necessary to observe that the reverie is at all times a potent and in many cases an omnipotent rival to every other kind of thinking. It doubtless influences all our speculations in its persistent tendency to self-magnification and self-justification, which are its chief preoccupations, but it is the last thing to make directly or indirectly for honest increase of knowledge.* Philosophers usually talk as if such thinking did not exist or were in some way negligible. This is what makes their speculations so unreal and often worthless. . . .

The reverie is a reflection of our longings, exultations, and complacencies, our fears, suspicions, and disappointments. We are chiefly engaged in struggling to maintain our self-respect and in asserting that supremacy which we all crave and which seems to us our natural prerogative. It is not strange, but rather quite inevitable, that our beliefs about what is true and false, good and bad, right and wrong, should be mixed up with the reverie and be influenced by the same considerations which determine its character and course. We resent criticisms of our views exactly as we do of anything else connected with ourselves. Our notions of life and its ideals seem to us to be *our own* and as such necessarily true and right, to be defended at all costs.

---

*The poet-clergyman, John Donne, who lived in the time of James I, has given a beautifully honest picture of the doings of a saint's mind: "I throw myself down in my chamber and call in and invite God and His angels thither, and when they are there I neglect God and His angels for the noise of a fly, for the rattling of a coach, for the whining of a door. I talk on in the same posture of praying, eyes lifted up, knees bowed down, as though I prayed to God, and if God or His angels should ask me when I thought last of God in that prayer I cannot tell. Sometimes I find that I had forgot what I was about, but when I began to forget it I cannot tell. A memory of yesterday's pleasures, a fear of to-morrow's dangers, a straw under my knee, a noise in mine ear, a light in mine eye, an anything, a nothing, a fancy, a chimera in my brain troubles me in my prayer."–Quoted by ROBERT LYND, *The Art of Letters*, pp. 46-47.

Find examples in yourself of bodily states and corresponding mental states. When you are feeling buoyant, what is the position of your body? How does it change when you are depressed or angry?

Find examples of "self-magnification and self-justification" in yourself. Do you find anything in yourself that contradicts Robinson's statement that "we are chiefly engaged in struggling to maintain our self-respect"?

Have any of the exercises suggested in Unit 14 given you experiences similar to John Donne's (described in the footnote above)?

from **Ulysses** theme of *paternity*.

JAMES JOYCE (molly's mono logue)

. . . O Lord it was rotten cold too that winter when I was only about ten was I yes I had the big doll with all the funny clothes dressing her up and undressing that icy wind skeeting across from those mountains the something Nevada sierra nevada standing at the fire with the little bit of a short shift I had up to heat myself I loved dancing about in it then make a race back into bed Im sure that fellow opposite used to be there the whole time watching with the lights out in the summer and I in my skin hopping around I used to love myself then stripped at the washstand dabbing and creaming only when it came to the chamber performance I put out the light too so then there were 2 of us Goodbye to my sleep for this night anyhow I hope hes not going to get in with those medicals leading him astray to imagine hes young again coming in at 4 in the morning it must be if not more still he had the manners not to wake me what do they find to gabber about all night squandering money and getting drunker and drunker couldnt they drink water when he starts giving us his orders for eggs and tea Findon haddy and hot buttered toast I suppose well have him sitting up like the king of the country pumping the wrong end of the spoon up and down in his egg wherever he learned that from and I love to hear him falling up the stairs of a morning with the cups rattling on the tray and then play with the cat she rubs up against you for her own sake I wonder has she fleas shes as bad as a woman always licking and lecking but I hate their claws I wonder do they see anything that we cant staring like that when she sits at the top of the stairs so long and listening as I wait always what a robber too that lovely fresh plaice I bought I think Ill get a bit of fish tomorrow or today is it Friday yes I will with some blancmange with black currant jam like long ago not those 2-lb pots of mixed plum and apple from the London and Newcastle Williams and Woods goes twice as far only for the bones I hate those eels cod yes Ill get a nice piece of cod Im aways getting enough for 3 forgetting anyway Im sick of that everlasting butchers meat from Buckleys loin chops and leg beef and rib steak and scrag of mutton and calfs pluck the very name is enough or a picnic suppose we all gave 5/- each and or let him pay and invite some other woman for him who Mrs Fleming and drive out to the furry glen or the strawberry beds wed have him examining all the horses toenails first like he does with the letters no not with Boylan there yes with some cold veal and ham mixed sandwiches there are little houses down at the bottom of the banks there on purpose but its as hot as blazes he says not a bank holiday anyhow I hate those ruck of Mary Ann coalboxes out for the day Whit Monday is a cursed day too no wonder that bee bit him better the seaside but Id never again in this life get into a boat with him after him at Bray telling the boatmen he knew how to row if anyone asked could he ride the steeplechase for the gold cup hed say yes then it came on to get rough the old thing crookeding about and the weight all down my side telling me to pull the right reins now pull the left and the tide all swamping in floods in through the bottom and his oar slipping out of the stirrup its a mercy we werent all drowned he can swim of course me no theres no danger whatsoever keep yourself calm in his flannel trousers Id like to have tattered them down off him before all the people and give him what that one calls flagellate till he was black and blue do him all the good in the world only for that longnosed chap I dont know who he is with that other beauty Burke out of the City Arms hotel was there spying around as usual on the slip always where he wasnt wanted if there was a row on you vomit a better face there was no love lost between us thats 1 consolation I wonder what kind is that book he brought me Sweets of Sin

Try to divide Molly Bloom's reverie into parts. Her reverie begins, for example, when she is reminded of a time in her past when she was cold as she is in the present. Try to decide what causes each of her changes in subject.

Does Molly Bloom's reverie involve any of the "self-magnification or self-justification" described by James Harvey Robinson in this unit (pages 165–66)? Does her reverie support Robinson's assertion (page 165) that the reverie "will inevitably circle about the beloved Ego"?

Do you have reveries similar to Molly Bloom's? How are yours similar; how different?

Soliloquy of the Spanish Cloister

ROBERT BROWNING

I

Gr-r-r—there go, my heart's abhorrences!
  Water your damned flower-pots, do!
If hate killed men, Brother Lawrence,
  God's blood, would not mine kill you!
What? your myrtle-bush wants trimming?
  Oh, that rose has prior claims—
Needs its leaden vase filled brimming?
  Hell dry you up with its flames!

II

At the meal we sit together:
   Salve tibi! I must hear
Wise talk of the kind of weather,
   Sort of season, time of year:
Not a plenteous cork-crop: scarcely
   Dare we hope oak-galls, I doubt:
What's the Latin name for "parsley"?
   What's the Greek name for Swine's Snout?

III

Whew! We'll have our platter burnished,
   Laid with care on our own shelf!
With a fire-new spoon we're furnished,
   And a goblet for ourself,
Rinsed like something sacrificial
   Ere 'tis fit to touch our chaps—
Marked with L for our initial!
   (He-he! There his lily snaps!)

IV

Saint, forsooth! While brown Dolores
   Squats outside the Convent bank
With Sanchicha, telling stories,
   Steeping tresses in the tank,
Blue-black, lustrous, thick like horsehairs,
   —Can't I see his dead eye glow,
Bright as 'twere a Barbary corsair's?
   (That is, if he'd let it show!)

V

When he finishes refection,
   Knife and fork he never lays
Cross-wise, to my recollection,
   As do I, in Jesu's praise.
I the Trinity illustrate,
   Drinking watered orange-pulp—
In three sips the Arian frustrate;
   While he drains his at one gulp.

VI

Oh, those melons! If he's able
   We're to have a feast! so nice!
One goes to the Abbot's table,
   All of us get each a slice.
How go on your flowers? None double
   Not one fruit-sort can you spy?
Strange!—And I, too, at such trouble,
   Keep them close-nipped on the sly!

VII

There's a great text in Galatians,
  Once you trip on it, entails
Twenty-nine distinct damnations,
  One sure, if another fails:
If I trip him just a-dying,
  Sure of heaven as sure can be,
Spin him round and send him flying
  Off to hell, a Manichee?

VIII

Or, my scrofulous French novel
  On gray paper with blunt type!
Simply glance at it, you grovel
  Hand and foot in Belial's gripe:
If I double down its pages
  At the woful sixteenth print,
When he gathers his greengages,
  Ope a sieve and slip it in't?

IX

Or, there's Satan!—one might venture
  Pledge one's soul to him, yet leave
Such a flaw in the indenture
  As he'd miss till, past retrieve,
Blasted lay that rose-acacia
  We're so proud of! *Hy, Zy, Hine.*
'St, there's Vespers! *Plena gratià,*
  Ave, Virgo! Gr-r-r—you swine!

The speaker of this soliloquy reveals more about himself than he does about Brother Lawrence. What lines in the poem show his hate for Brother Lawrence?

How do you think the speaker feels about "brown Dolores" (Stanza IV) and the "scrofulous French novel" (Stanza VIII)? What does the speaker's imagination of Brother Lawrence's feelings about brown Dolores and the French novel tell us about the speaker?

What is your immediate reaction to this poem? Do you find it amusing, disgusting, sad? What details in this poem make you feel this way?

In Stanza V the speaker compares his behavior to Brother Lawrence's. Observe and record one of your reveries in which you make comparisons between yourself and someone else.

The Secret Life of Walter Mitty

JAMES THURBER

"We're going through!" The Commander's voice was like thin ice breaking. He wore his full-dress uniform, with the heavily braided white cap pulled down rakishly over one cold gray eye. "We can't make it, sir. It's spoiling for a hurricane, if you ask me." "I'm not asking you, Lieutenant Berg," said the Commander. "Throw on the power lights! Rev her up to 8,500! We're going through!" The pounding of the cylinders increased: ta-pocketa-pocketa-pocketa-*pocketa-pocketa*. The Commander stared at the ice forming on the pilot window. He walked over and twisted a row of complicated dials. "Switch on No. 8 auxiliary!" he shouted. "Switch on No. 8 auxiliary!" repeated Lieutenant Berg. "Full strength in No. 3 turret!" shouted the Commander. "Full strength in No. 3 turret!" The crew, bending to their various tasks in the huge, hurtling eight-engined Navy hydroplane, looked at each other and grinned. "The Old Man'll get us through," they said to one another. "The Old Man ain't afraid of Hell!" . . .

[handwritten margin note: A skilled pilot (a commander)]

"Not so fast! You're driving too fast!" said Mrs. Mitty. "What are you driving so fast for?"

"Hmm?" said Walter Mitty. He looked at his wife, in the seat beside him, with shocked astonishment. She seemed grossly unfamiliar, like a strange woman who had yelled at him in a crowd. "You were up to fifty-five," she said. "You know I don't like to go more than forty. You were up to fifty-five." Walter Mitty drove on toward Waterbury in silence, the roaring of the SN202 through the worst storm in twenty years of Navy flying fading in the remote, intimate airways of his mind. "You're tensed up again," said Mrs. Mitty. "It's one of your days. I wish you'd let Dr. Renshaw look you over."

Walter Mitty stopped the car in front of the building where his wife went to have her hair done. "Remember to get those overshoes while I'm having my hair done," she said. "I don't need overshoes," said Mitty. She put her mirror back into her bag. "We've been all through that," she said, getting out of the car. "You're not a young man any longer." He raced the engine a little. "Why don't you wear your gloves? Have you lost your gloves?" Walter Mitty reached in a pocket and brought out the gloves. He put them on, but after she had turned and gone into the building and he had driven on to a red light, he took them off again. "Pick it up, brother!" snapped a cop as the light changed, and Mitty hastily pulled on his gloves and lurched ahead. He drove around the streets aimlessly for a time, and then he drove past the hospital on his way to the parking lot.

. . . "It's the millionaire banker, Wellington McMillan," said the pretty nurse. "Yes?" said Walter Mitty, removing his gloves slowly. "Who has the case?" "Dr. Renshaw and Dr. Benbow, but there are two specialists here, Dr. Remington from New York and Mr. Pritchard-Mitford from London. He flew over." A door opened down a long, cool corridor and Dr. Renshaw came out. He looked distraught and haggard. "Hello, Mitty," he said.

"We're having the devil's own time with McMillan, the millionaire banker and close personal friend of Roosevelt. Obstreosis of the ductal tract. Tertiary. Wish you'd take a look at him." "Glad to," said Mitty.

In the operating room there were whispered introductions: "Dr. Remington, Dr. Mitty. Mr. Pritchard-Mitford, Dr. Mitty." "I've read your book on streptothricosis," said Pritchard-Mitford, shaking hands. "A brilliant performance, sir." "Thank you," said Walter Mitty. "Didn't know you were in the States, Mitty," grumbled Remington. "Coals to Newcastle, bringing Mitford and me here for a tertiary." "You are very kind," said Mitty. A huge, complicated machine, connected to the operating table, with many tubes and wires, began at this moment to go pocketa-pocketa-pocketa. "The new anesthetizer is giving way!" shouted an interne. "There is no one in the East who knows how to fix it!" "Quiet, man!" said Mitty, in a low, cool voice. He sprang to the machine, which was now going pocketa-pocketa-queep-pocketa-queep. He began fingering delicately a row of glistening dials. "Give me a fountain pen!" he snapped. Someone handed him a fountain pen. He pulled a faulty piston out of the machine and inserted the pen in its place. "That will hold for ten minutes," he said. "Get on with the operation." A nurse hurried over and whispered to Renshaw, and Mitty saw the man turn pale. "Coreopsis has set in," said Renshaw nervously. "If you would take over, Mitty?" Mitty looked at him and at the craven figure of Benbow, who drank, and at the grave, uncertain faces of the two great specialists. "If you wish," he said. They slipped a white gown on him; he adjusted a mask and drew on thin gloves; nurses handed him shining. . . .

"Back it up, Mac! Look out for that Buick!" Walter Mitty jammed on the brakes. "Wrong lane, Mac," said the parking-lot attendant, looking at Mitty closely. "Gee. Yeh," muttered Mitty. He began cautiously to back out of the lane marked "Exit Only." "Leave her sit there," said the attendant. "I'll put her away." Mitty got out of the car. "Hey, better leave the key." "Oh," said Mitty, handing the man the ignition key. The attendant vaulted into the car, backed it up with insolent skill, and put it where it belonged.

They're so damn cocky, thought Walter Mitty, walking along Main Street; they think they know everything. Once he had tried to take his chains off, outside New Milford, and he had got them wound around the axles. A man had had to come out in a wrecking car and unwind them, a young, grinning garageman. Since then Mrs. Mitty always made him drive to a garage to have the chains taken off. The next time, he thought, I'll wear my right arm in a sling; they won't grin at me then. I'll have my right arm in a sling and they'll see I couldn't possibly take the chains off myself. He kicked at the slush on the sidewalk. "Overshoes," he said to himself, and he began looking for a shoe store.

When he came out into the street again, with the overshoes in a box under his arm. Walter Mitty began to wonder what the other thing was his wife had told him to get. She had told him twice, before they set out from their house for Waterbury. In a way he hated these weekly trips to town—he was always getting something wrong. Kleenex, he thought, Squibb's, razor blades? No. Toothpaste, toothbrush, bicarbonate, carborundum, initiative and referendum? He gave it up. But she would remember it. "Where's the what's-its-name?" she would ask. "Don't tell me you forgot the what's-its-name?" A newsboy went by shouting something about the Waterbury trial.

. . . "Perhaps this will refresh your memory." The District Attorney suddenly thrust a heavy automatic at the quiet figure on the witness stand. "Have you ever seen this before?" Walter Mitty took the gun and examined it expertly. "This is my Webley-Vickers 50.80," he said calmly. An excited buzz ran around the courtroom. The judge rapped for order. "You are a crack shot with any sort of firearms, I believe?" said the District Attorney, insinuatingly. "Objection!" shouted Mitty's attorney. "We have shown that the defendant could not have fired the shot. We have shown that he wore his right arm in a sling on the night of the fourteenth of July." Walter Mitty raised his hand briefly and the bickering attorneys were stilled. "With any known make of gun," he said evenly, "I could have killed Gregory Fitzhurst at three hundred feet *with my left hand*." Pandemonium broke loose in the courtroom. A woman's scream rose above the bedlam and suddenly a lovely, dark-haired girl was in Walter Mitty's arms. The District Attorney struck at her savagely. Without rising from his chair, Mitty let the man have it on the point of the chin. "You miserable cur!" . . .

a great pistol shooter on trial

"Puppy biscuit," said Walter Mitty. He stopped walking and the buildings of Waterbury rose up out of the misty courtroom and surrounded him again. A woman who was passing laughed. "He said 'Puppy biscuit,'" she said to her companion. "That man said 'Puppy biscuit' to himself." Walter Mitty hurried on. He went into an A. & P., not the first one he came to but a smaller one farther up the street. "I want some biscuit for small, young dogs," he said to the clerk. "Any special brand, sir?" The greatest pistol shot in the world thought a moment. "It says 'Puppies Bark for It' on the box," said Walter Mitty.

His wife would be through at the hairdresser's in fifteen minutes, Mitty saw in looking at his watch, unless they had trouble drying it; sometimes they had trouble drying it. She didn't like to get to the hotel first; she would want him to be there waiting for her as usual. He found a big leather chair in the lobby, facing a window, and he put the overshoes and the puppy biscuit on the floor beside it. He picked up an old copy of *Liberty* and sank down into the chair. "Can Germany Conquer the World Through the Air?" Walter Mitty looked at the pictures of bombing planes and of ruined streets.

. . . "The cannonading has got the wind up in young Raleigh, sir," said the sergeant. Captain Mitty looked up at him through tousled hair. "Get him to bed," he said wearily. "With the others. I'll fly alone." "But you can't, sir," said the sergeant anxiously. "It takes two men to handle that bomber and the Archies are pounding hell out of the air. Von Richtman's circus is between here and Saulier." "Somebody's got to get that ammunition dump," said Mitty. "I'm going over. Spot of brandy?" He poured a drink for the sergeant and one for himself. War thundered and whined around the dugout and battered at the door. There was a rending of wood and splinters flew through the room. "A bit of a near thing," said Captain Mitty carelessly. "The box barrage is closing in," said the sergeant. "We only live once, Sergeant," said Mitty, with his faint, fleeting smile. "Or do we?" He poured another brandy and tossed it off. "I never see a man could hold his brandy like you, sir," said the sergeant. "Begging your pardon, sir." Captain Mitty stood up and strapped on his huge Webley-Vickers automatic. "It's forty kilometers through hell, sir," said the sergeant. Mitty finished one last brandy. "After all," he said softly, "what isn't?" The pounding of the cannon increased; there was the rat-tat-tatting of machine guns, and from somewhere came the menacing pocketa-pocketa-pocketa of the new flame-throwers. Walter Mitty walked to the door of the dugout humming "Auprès de Ma Blonde." He turned and waved to the sergeant. "Cheerio!" he said. . . .

Something struck his shoulder. "I've been looking all over this hotel for you," said Mrs. Mitty. "Why do you have to hide in this old chair? How did you expect me to find you?" "Things close in," said Walter Mitty vaguely. "What?" Mrs. Mitty said. "Did you get the what's-its-name? The puppy biscuit? What's in the box?" "Overshoes," said Mitty. "Couldn't you have put them on in the store?" "I was thinking," said Walter Mitty. "Does it ever occur to you that I am sometimes thinking?" She looked at him. "I'm going to take your temperature when I get you home," she said.

They went out through the revolving doors that made a faintly derisive whistling sound when you pushed them. It was two blocks to the parking lot. At the drugstore on the corner she said, "Wait here for me. I forgot something. I won't be a minute." She was more than a minute. Walter Mitty lighted a cigarette. It began to rain, rain with sleet in it. He stood up against the wall of the drugstore, smoking. . . . He put his shoulders back and his heels together. "To hell with the handkerchief," said Walter Mitty scornfully. He took one last drag on his cigarette and snapped it away. Then, with that faint, fleeting smile playing about his lips, he faced the firing squad; erect and motionless, proud and disdainful, Walter Mitty the Undefeated, inscrutable to the last.

What do Walter Mitty's reveries reveal about his "fundamental character"? (See pages 165–66 for Robinson's remarks concerning the connection between reveries and character.)

Comment on the contrast between Walter Mitty's secret life and his real life.

How has Mitty's real life driven him to create his secret life?

What reveries have you seen in yourself in which you were hero or heroine?

UNIT 16

PREWRITING

Female preference

Male preference

> In seventeen out of eighteen cultures so far tested, women preferred the figures in the left-hand, men those in the right-hand columns . . . the *male* style . . . a preference for the simple, the closed, the direct . . . women . . . more interested in the complex, the open, the undefined.

DAVID S. MC CLELLAND

One of the oldest debates centers on the relationship between males and females. You, no doubt, already have your own notions about differences between the sexes and probably have more than enough material for a paper on the subject. A few introductory comments may help you find a focus for your writing.

Many assertions have been made:

> 66 The man's desire is for the woman; but the woman's desire is rarely other than for the desire of the man. 99
>
> SAMUEL TAYLOR COLERIDGE

> 66 Feminine passion is to masculine as an epic to an epigram. 99
>
> KARL KRAUS

> 66 Nature has given women so much power that the law has very wisely given them little. 99
>
> SAMUEL JOHNSON

> 66 If you're a rooster, crow. If you're a hen, shut up and lay eggs. 99
>
> RUSSIAN PROVERB

> 66 Women have served all these centuries as looking glasses possessing the . . . power of reflecting the figure of man at twice its natural size. 99
>
> VIRGINIA WOOLF

CLASS EXERCISE

▶Write a few one- or two-sentence sayings of your own on the subject of male/female.

If you could be male for awhile and female for awhile—live both sides—perhaps you could judge impartially and write a convincing paper on the subject. But Tiresias had this opportunity and it cost him his sight:

66Jove, they say, was happy
and feeling pretty good (with wine) forgetting
Anxiety and care, and killing time
Joking with Juno. "I maintain," he told her,
"You females get more pleasure out of loving
Than we poor males do, ever." She denied it,
So they decided to refer the question
To wise Tiresias' judgment: he should know
What love was like, from either point of view.
Once he had come upon two serpents mating
In the green woods, and struck them from each
    other,
And thereupon, from man was turned to woman,
And was a woman seven years, and saw
The serpents once again, and once more struck them
Apart, remarking: "If there is such magic
In giving you blows, that man is turned to woman,
It may be woman is turned to man. Worth trying."
And so he was a man again; as umpire,
He took the side of Jove. And Juno
Was a bad loser, and she said that umpires
Were always blind, and made him so forever. 99

OVID

The subject can be a touchy one. But trust your experience and your understanding of it, take a position, and write, knowing your readers will be more tolerant of your opinions than Juno was of Tiresias's. You may find a topic of special interest to you in one of the following discussion questions.

DISCUSSION

66Apart from the crude economic question, the things that most women mean when they speak of "happiness," that is, love and children and the little republic of the home, depend upon the favour of men, and the qualities that win this favour are not in general those that are most useful for other purposes. A girl should not be too intelligent or too good or too highly differentiated in any direction. Like a ready-made garment she should be designed to fit the average man. 99

EMILY JAMES PUTNAM

What do you think most women mean when they speak of happiness? What does happiness mean to you? Have you ever known a woman who designed herself to suit a man's favor? What did she do? What was the man's response?

66 *Lothario:*
It is very strange . . . that men are blamed, for . . . they have placed woman on the highest station she is capable of occupying. And where is there any station higher than the ordering of the house? While the husband has to vex himself with outward matters . . . a reasonable housewife is actually governing in the interior of her family; has the comfort and activity of every person in it to provide for, and make possible. What is the highest happiness of mortals, if not to execute what we consider right and good; to be really masters of the means conducive to our aims: And where should or can our nearest aims be, but in the interior of our home? 99

GOETHE

Do you think men "have placed woman on the highest station she is capable of occupying?"

66 Miss Paola Borboni, an Italian stage and movie star still single at 72, has announced she will marry soon. Her fiance is Brono Vilar, a 30-year-old poet and actor. . . .

Vilar said they have decided to marry because Miss Borboni's mother, Gemma, 102, does not approve of their going together without being married.

Vilar, whose mother is 22 years younger than Miss Borboni, said his love for the actress is spiritual.

"I'm a poet and this is a spiritual union. Our relation is not based on sex." 99

NEWS ITEM

Name various desires that may bring males and females together.

66The trouble with man is that he cannot think as fairly about personal situations as he can about broad humanitarian concepts like freedom of speech or prison reform. . . . All men are built on the same plan. . . . When the logic narrows down to their relations with one woman, they revert to very primitive reactions, selfish and assertive: While Dante was living more or less comfortably with his wife, much of the time he was visiting Beatrice in Paradise; and, though Petrarch's sonnets were inspired by the lady of his affections, he had, I believe, a child by his housekeeper. 99

MARY AUSTIN

Generally speaking, are men often fair about "broad humanitarian concepts" and narrow and selfish about personal ones? Can you give an example?

66If we are going to be liberated," says Dana Densmore, "we must reject the false image that makes men love us, and this will make men cease to love us." But this viewpoint is not acceptable. It assumes that men demand a false image, that all men demand false images. It does not distinguish between one man and another man. 99

JOYCE CAROL OATES

Compare this statement with the one above by Mary Austin.

66 Then wear a gold hat,
If that will please her.
And if you can bounce,
Bounce high too.
Until she cry,
Gold-hatted, high-bouncing lover
I must have you. 99

Thomas Parke D'Invilliers
(F. SCOTT FITZGERALD)

Have you known any "gold-hatted" lovers? Is this what most women want?

CONNECTING EXERCISES

▶ A. Take notes on the way a man is affected by a woman's ideas and personality or the way a woman is affected by a man's. Note habits, opinions, words and phrases borrowed from the other person. What is the man's notion of "woman" (or the woman's of "man") and how is the woman (or the man) affected by it?

▶ B. Assume that "real love" is an emotion one person feels for another person. And "false love" is an emotion directed toward oneself.

Remember or observe someone who is more in love with the excitement of being in love or with himself as lover than with the other person. (Romeo is more in love with love than he is with Juliet.)

Or study a person who is so in love with an image of himself, or herself, that "love" means finding a person to support that image. Take notes on the person's conversation (look both for what is said and what is meant), gestures, facial expressions.

▶ C. One or both of the people in a male/female relationship may be good examples of a type: cavalier, Don Juan, Blue Beard, seductive temptress, bitch, faithful woman.

Take notes on specific things a person does or says that serve to make him or her an example of a type. Record actions, gestures, speech.

UNIT 17
WRITING DEFINITION

I know that
You Believe you
understand what you think I said,
But
I am not sure
You Realize that
what you heard
is not
what I meant.

In previous writing units we said that a successful paper needs an abstract idea supported by concrete facts. But ideas and facts are communicated in words, and words mean different things to different people. To let your reader understand as nearly as possible what you mean, you will often need to define words.

Make it a habit to check words that are central to the meaning of your paper. Ask yourself if your reader might understand these words in a way very different from you. If you think he may, then say what these words mean for you—let your reader know how you are using them. Large abstract words—like "freedom," "love," "uninhibited"—need especially to be defined. You may write "liberated woman" and mean (as Betty Friedan did) "a woman exercising all the privileges and responsibilities . . . of a truly equal partnership with men." But if you do not make this clear, your reader may think you mean a woman who smokes slender cigars, goes without a bra, and uses four-letter words.

One way to let your reader know your meaning is to give him a *formal* or *logical definition* of a word you are using:

> A male chauvinist is a man who is convinced that males are superior to females.

In the formal definition the subject ("male chauvinist") is put into a class ("is a man") and is then differentiated from other members of that class ("who is convinced that males are superior to females"). Two parts are essential to the formal definition: classification and differentiation. "Male chauvinist" falls into the category "man," not bird or machine. Within this class the chauvinist is distinguished from men who do not have an entrenched belief in male supremacy.

Definition by *comparison* is another way you may let your reader know what you mean:

> 66Woman in the "Westerns" was a sawdust doll.99
>
> HUTCHINSON

The writer suggests what "woman" in Western novels was like. He implies she was without individuality and life by comparing her to a lifeless toy that resembles a real person.

Or you may define by *description*, by telling your reader the distinguishing characteristics of something:

> 66 The tags used to depict the character [of women in Westerns] were obvious. . . . If she wore calico or gingham . . . possessed a clear complexion and lustrous eyes, she was good. If she wore tights . . . and walked in a saloon . . . she was bad. . . . Women are not that simple. 99
>
> HUTCHINSON

In these sentences the writer defines by enumerating the physical details of the good women and the bad women.

Another way you may let your reader know what you mean is to give an *example:*

> 66 The "Stocking Game" is a sexual game played between a man and a woman. . . . A woman comes into a strange group and after a very short time raises her leg, exposing herself in a provocative way, and remarks, "Oh my, I have a run in my stocking." This is calculated to arouse the men sexually and to make the other women angry. 99
>
> ERIC BERNE

In this passage the writer first gives a *formal* definition of the "stocking game" (that is, he puts it in the general category "sexual game") and then differentiates it—"a game played between a man and a woman." He then gives an *example* of the game in action, of one way in which it is played. He further defines the game by giving an *interpretation* of the object of it (the game is "calculated to arouse men sexually").

WRITING EXERCISES

▶A. Select one word—love, self-love, male, female . . .
• Define the word by formal definition, by comparison, by description, and by example.
• Write a paper on the word you have selected.
• Exchange definitions in class and note the various ways different people write about the same word.

▶B. What one quality do you believe is most essential for happiness in a male/female relationship—compassion, equality, respect, similar goals in life, sexual desire, spiritual feelings, the ability to enjoy life together, to work together?
  Remember or observe a relationship that exemplifies that one quality and write a paper on how the two people act toward each other, their interests, conversation, desires.

WRITING HINT: USE SIMILES AND METAPHORS TO CLARIFY MEANING.

> 66 Metaphor is the swift illumination of an equiva-
> lence. Two images, or an idea and an image, stand
> equal and opposite; clash together and respond sig-
> nificantly, surprising the reader with sudden light. 99
>
> HERBERT READ

Similes and metaphors are the most common ways of defining by comparison. When you define something you "tell what it is." When you use a simile or metaphor you tell what something is by telling what it is like.

A *simile* makes an explicit comparison by using a connective, usually "like" or "as": **Your heart is like a rose-tree in flower.** A *metaphor* also makes a comparison, but the comparison is implied. No connective such as "like" or "as" is used, and the writer asserts the impossible: **Your heart is a rose-tree in flower.**

When you can find a simile or metaphor that works you will find that your writing comes alive as it can in no other way. And a comparison serves a definite function: it keeps language from vagueness by anchoring the abstract to the concrete, by making an intangible idea tangible.

> 66 Language often tends to lose itself in clouds of va-
> porous abstraction, and simile and metaphor can
> bring it back to concrete solidity. Why such magic
> power should reside in simply saying, or implying,
> that A is like B remains a little mysterious. 99
>
> F. L. LUCAS

Note the successful use of simile in this sentence from Raoul De Roussy De Sales's "Love in America" (given in Unit 18): "The popular American mind likes to be entertained by the idea . . . that love is always wholesome, genuine, uplifting, and fresh, like a glass of Grade A milk." De Sales has made a "swift equivalence" between his subject, love in America, and milk (love in America = a glass of Grade A milk). De Sales saw a similarity between an American's attitude toward love and his attitude toward milk. Though love is one thing and milk another, the American expects the complex, imperfect emotion to be Grade A, like the commercial product.

❝It is not easy to tell true love from false love. You find something similar to true love and imagine it to be the one and only true love. It takes many false loves for a person to realize that life is not just all true love.❞

❝If only one could tell true love from false love as one can tell mushrooms from toadstools. With mushrooms it is so simple—you salt them well, put them aside and have patience. But with love, you have no sooner lighted on anything that bears even the remotest resemblance to it than you are perfectly certain it is not only a genuine specimen, but perhaps *the* only genuine mushroom ungathered. It takes a dreadful number of toadstools to make you realize that life is not one long mushroom.❞

KATHERINE MANSFIELD

CLASS EXERCISES

▶A. Make clear what is compared with what in each of the following comparisons from the abovementioned essay by De Sales.

❝[Love in America] fits in with other advertisements, and one feels tempted to write to the broadcasting station for a free sample. . . .❞

❝[Americans] want to get out of love as much enjoyment, comfort, safety, and general sense of satisfaction, as one gets out of a well-balanced diet or a good plumbing installation.❞

❝. . . truth is an explosive, and it should be handled with care, especially in marital life. It is not necessary to lie, but there is little profit in juggling with hand grenades just to show how brave one is.❞

❝. . . there is now flourishing in America a great crop of books which . . . try to establish sets of little rules and little tricks which will guarantee marital bliss if carefully followed, in the same way that cookbooks guarantee that you will obtain pumpkin pie if you use the proper ingredients properly measured.❞

> ❝ It is not necessarily true that there is but one form of love worth bothering about, and that if you cannot get the de luxe model, with a life guarantee of perfect functioning, nothing else is worthwhile. ❞

Not all comparisons work. You don't want to drop one into a sentence whenever you think of one. *Stale metaphors* and *mixed metaphors* are two kinds of comparison that usually don't work.

Stale metaphors, as George Orwell describes them, are that "huge dump of worn-out metaphors which have lost all evocative power and are merely used because they save people the trouble of inventing phrases for themselves."

Tackle the problem.

We are fishing in troubled waters.

They rode roughshod over their opposition.

Mixed metaphors bring together two incongruous images.

And now, gentlemen, let's sail on to the next item on our agenda and digest it.

By uniting a navigational and a gastronomical image, this speaker confuses his listener. Try seeing yourself sailing off to an item as you would to an island and then digesting it.

If you first picture metaphors in your mind's eye, you won't make the mistake of mixing them.

▶ B. Which of the following comparisons are successful?

When the moon hits your eye like a big pizza pie, that's love.

The Fascist octopus has sung its swan song. (George Orwell's example)

She was as white as a sheet and turned as red as a beet.

Better throw in the sponge; it's a blessing in disguise.

He vanished like a fly in the mouth of a frog.

JAMES THURBER

Her voice was faraway music, and her eyes were candles burning on a tranquil night. She moved across the room like wind in violets.

JAMES THURBER

Language not only can toss a rider but knows a thousand tricks for tossing him, each more gay than the last.

E. B. WHITE

You may not find more than one or two comparisons that you want to use for any one paper you write. But this may be all you need to clarify your thoughts for your reader.

Following is a student paper. Analyze it for its use of definition, simile, and metaphor.

I LIKE THEM DUMB, BABY, YOU SUIT ME JUST FINE

Women are those members of the human race who keep their slips and their brains from showing. If a woman's slip is showing she is not well-groomed and so not attractive and attractive is one of the most important things a woman can be. In fact, attractive is something she must be if she is going to attract anything and the anything is usually a man. Early in life women discover (or do they only intuit?) that men prefer them beautiful and dumb. So they try to be as much like the image Marilyn Monroe created as they can even though it killed her and exhausts them. The female might escape this necessity to be attractive only if she does as chickens do and lets the rooster wear the bright feathers.

If she has any brains, a woman will keep them hidden. For a woman must not only be attractive, but must also hide her intelligence like dust under a bed if she's going to get a man as a partner on top of it. As Emily Putnam says, "A girl should not be too intelligent." Men don't like smart women. Men, unlike women, are notoriously logical and reason that if a woman is smart she must have an excess of male hormones. For if a woman is smart she's like a man. A woman who is like a man is . . . well . . . therefore . . . (an example of masculine logic).

Women are often hysterical. Fortunately women don't
need logic and can use hysterics. A woman's real
job is to hide from a man anything that might threaten
his ego. Such a job requires cunning, not logic. If
all else fails hysteria works. Screaming and crying are
obviously stupid, child-like, unattractive.

A woman, then, is someone who lives in a double-bind
—she must hide her intelligence and her unattractive-
ness and at the same time act as if she had nothing
to hide. That could make a person hysterical. Women
are unusually accommodating.

Dianne Gibney

UNIT 18

SELECTIONS

Love in America

RAOUL DE ROUSSY DE SALES

I

America appears to be the only country in the world where love is a national problem.

Nowhere else can one find a people devoting so much time and so much study to the question of the relationship between men and women. Nowhere else is there such concern about the fact that this relationship does not always make for perfect happiness. The great majority of the Americans of both sexes seem to be in a state of chronic bewilderment in the face of a problem which they are certainly not the first to confront, but which—unlike other people—they still refuse to accept as one of those gifts of the gods which one might just as well take as it is: a mixed blessing at times, and at other times a curse or merely a nuisance.

The prevailing conception of love, in America, is similar to the idea of democracy. It is fine in theory. It is the grandest system ever evolved by man to differentiate him from his ancestors, the poor brutes who lived in caverns, or from the apes. Love is perfect, in fact, and there is nothing better. But, like democracy, it does not work, and the Americans feel that something should be done about it. Their statesmen are intent on making democracy work. Everybody is trying to make love work, too.

In either case the result is not very satisfactory. The probable reason is that democracy and love are products of a long and complicated series of compromises between the desires of the heart and the exactions of reason. They have a peculiar way of crumbling into ashes as soon as one tries too hard to organize them too well.

191

African sculpture. Copyright The Barnes Foundation.

Etruscan Sarcophagus from Caere. Museo Nazionale di Villa Giulia, Rome.

The secret of making a success out of democracy and love in their practical applications is to allow for a fairly wide margin of errors, and not to forget that human beings are absolutely unable to submit to a uniform rule for any length of time. But this does not satisfy a nation that, in spite of its devotion to pragmatism, also believes in perfection.

For a foreigner to speak of the difficulties that the Americans encounter in such an intimate aspect of their mutual relationship may appear as an impertinence. But the truth is that no foreigner would ever think of bringing up such a subject of his own accord. In fact, foreigners who come to these shores are quite unsuspecting of the existence of such a national problem. It is their initial observation that the percentage of good-looking women and handsome men is high on this continent, that they are youthful and healthy in mind and body, and that their outlook on life is rather optimistic.

If the newcomers have seen enough American moving pictures before landing here—and they usually have—they must have gathered the impression that love in America is normally triumphant, and that, in spite of many unfortunate accidents, a love story cannot but end very well indeed. They will have noticed that these love stories which are acted in Hollywood may portray quite regrettable situations at times and that blissful unions get wrecked by all sorts of misfortunes. But they never remain wrecked: even when the happy couple is compelled to divorce, this is not the end of everything. In most cases it is only the beginning. Very soon they will remarry, sometimes with one another, and always—without ever an exception—for love.

The observant foreigner knows, of course, that he cannot trust the movies to give him a really reliable picture of the American attitude to-

Brancusi, *The Kiss.*

Mycerinus and Queen. Egyptian, 4th Dynasty.

wards love, marriage, divorce, and remarriage. But they nevertheless indicate that in such matters the popular mind likes to be entertained by the idea (1) that love is the only reason why a man and a woman should get married; (2) that love is always wholesome, genuine, uplifting, and fresh, like a glass of Grade A milk; (3) that when, for some reason or other, it fails to keep you uplifted, wholesome, and fresh, the only thing to do is to begin all over again with another partner.

Thus forewarned, the foreigner who lands on these shores would be very tactless indeed if he started questioning the validity of these premises. Besides, it is much more likely that he himself will feel thoroughly transformed the moment he takes his first stroll in the streets of New York. His European skepticism will evaporate a little more at each step, and if he considers himself not very young any more he will be immensely gratified to find that maturity and even old age are merely European habits of thought, and that he might just as well adopt the American method, which is to be young and act young for the rest of his life—or at least until the expiration of his visa.

If his hotel room is equipped with a radio, his impression that he has at last reached the land of eternal youth and perfect love will be confirmed at any hour of the day and on any point of the dial. No country in the world consumes such a fabulous amount of love songs. Whether the song is gay or nostalgic, the tune catchy or banal, the verses clever or silly, the theme is always love and nothing but love.

Whenever I have gone back to France and listened to the radio, I have always been surprised to find that so many songs can be written on other subjects. I have no statistics on hand, but I think that a good 75 per cent of the songs one hears on the French radio programs deal with politics. There are love songs, of course, but most of them are far from romantic, and this is quite in keeping with the French point of view that love is very often an exceedingly comical affair.

In America the idea seems to be that love, like so much else, should be sold to the public, because it is a good thing. The very word, when heard indefinitely, becomes an obsession. It penetrates one's subconsciousness like the name of some unguent to cure heartaches or athlete's foot. It fits in with the other advertisements, and one feels tempted to write to the broadcasting station for a free sample of this thing called Love.

Thus the visitor from Europe is rapidly permeated with a delightful atmosphere of romanticism and sweetness. He wonders why Italy and Spain ever acquired their reputation of being the lands of romance. This, he says to himself, is the home of poetry and passion. The Americans are the real heirs of the troubadours, and station WXZQ is their love court.

To discover that all this ballyhoo about love (which is not confined to the radio or the movies) is nothing but an aspect of the national optimistic outlook on life does not take very long. It usually becomes evident when the foreign visitor receives the confidences of one or more of the charming American women he will chance to meet. This normally happens after the first or second cocktail party to which he has been invited.

II

I wish at this point to enter a plea in defense of the foreign visitor, against whom a great many accusations are often made either in print or in conversation. These accusations fall under two heads. If the foreigner seems to have no definite objective in visiting America, he is strongly suspected of trying to marry an heiress. If for any reason he cannot be suspected of this intention, then his alleged motives are considerably more sinister. Many American men, and quite a few women, believe that the art of wrecking a happy home is not indigenous to this continent, and that in Europe it has been perfected to such a point that to practice it has become reflex with the visitors from abroad.

It is very true that some foreign visitors come over here to marry for money in exchange for a title or for some sort of glamour. But there are many more foreigners who marry American women for other reasons besides money, and I know quite a few who have become so Americanized that they actually have married for love and for nothing else.

As for the charge that the Europeans are more expert than the Americans in spoiling someone else's marital happiness, it seems to me an unfair accusation. In most cases the initiative of spoiling whatever it is that remains to be spoiled in a shaky marriage is normally taken by one of the married pair, and the wrecker of happiness does not need any special talent to finish the job.

What is quite true, however, is that the American woman entertains the delightful illusion that there *must* be some man on this earth who can understand her. It seems incredible to her that love, within legal bonds or outside of them, should not work out as advertised. From her earliest years she has been told that success is the ultimate aim of life. Her father and mother made an obvious success of their lives by creating her. Her husband is, or wants to be, a successful business man. Every day 130,000,000 people are panting and sweating to make a success of something or other. Success—the constant effort to make things work perfectly and the conviction that they can be made to—is the great national preoccupation.

And what does one do to make a success?

Well, the answer is very simple: one learns how, or one consults an expert.

That is what her husband does when he wants to invest his money or improve the efficiency of his business. That is what she did herself when she decided to "decorate" her house. In the American way of life there are no insoluble problems. You may not know the answer yourself, but nobody doubts that the answer exists—that there is some method or perhaps some trick by which all riddles can be solved and success achieved.

And so the European visitor is put to the task on the presumption that the accumulation of experience which he brings with him may qualify him as an expert in questions of sentiment.

The American woman does not want to be understood for the mere fun of it. What she actually wishes is to be helped to solve certain difficulties which, in her judgment, impede the successful development of her inner self. She seldom accepts the idea that maladjustments and misunderstandings are not only normal but bearable once you have made up your mind that, whatever may be the ultimate aim of our earthly existence, perfect happiness through love or any other form of expression is not part of the program.

III

One of the greatest moral revolutions that ever happened in America was the popularization of Freud's works.

Up to the time that occurred, as far as I am able to judge, America lived in a blissful state of puritanical repression. Love, as a sentiment, was glorified and sanctified by marriage. There was a general impression that some sort of connection existed between the sexual impulses and the vagaries of the heart, but this connection was not emphasized, and the consensus of opinion was that the less said about it the better. The way certain nations, and particularly the French, correlated the physical manifestations of love and its more spiritual aspects was considered particularly objectionable. Love, in other words—and that was not very long ago—had not changed since the contrary efforts of the puritanically minded and the romantic had finally stabilized it midway between the sublime and the parlor game.

The important point is that up to then (and ever since the first Pilgrims set foot on this continent) love had been set aside in the general scheme of American life as the one thing which could not be made to work better than it did. Each one had to cope with his own difficulties in his own way and solve them as privately as he could. It was not a national problem.

Whether or not people were happier under that system is beside the point. It probably does not matter very much whether we live and die with or without a full set of childish complexes and repressions. My own view is that most people are neither complex nor repressed enough as a rule; I wish sometimes for the coming of the Anti-Freud who will complicate and obscure everything again.

But the fact is that the revelations of psychoanalysis were greeted in America as the one missing link in the general program of universal improvement.

Here was a system, at last, that explained fully why love remained so imperfect. It reduced the whole dilemma of happiness to sexual maladjustments, which in turn were only the result of the mistakes made by one's father, mother, or nurse, at an age when one could certainly not be expected to foresee the consequences. Psychoanalysis integrated human emotions into a set of mechanistic formulas. One learned with great relief that the failure to find happiness was not irreparable. Love, as a sublime communion of souls and bodies, was not a legend, nor the mere fancy of the poets. It was real, and—more important still—practically attainable. Anybody could have it, merely by removing a few obstructions which had been growing within himself since childhood like mushrooms in a dark cellar. Love could be made to work like anything else.

It is true that not many people are interested in psychoanalysis any more. As a fad or a parlor game, it is dead. Modern débutantes will not know what you are talking about if you mention the Œdipus complex or refer to the symbolic meaning of umbrellas and top hats in dreams. Traditions die young these days. But the profound effect of the Freudian revelation has lasted. From its materialistic interpretation of sexual impulses, coupled with the American longing for moral perfection, a new science has been born: the dialectics of love; and also a new urge for the American people—they want to turn out, eventually, a perfect product. They want to get out of love as much enjoyment, comfort, safety, and general sense of satisfaction, as one gets out of a well-balanced diet or a good plumbing installation.

IV

Curiously enough, this fairly new point of view which implies that human relationships are governed by scientific laws has not destroyed the romantic ideal of love. Quite the contrary. Maladjustments, now that they are supposed to be scientifically determined, have become much more unbearable than in the horse-and-buggy age of love. Husbands and wives and lovers have no patience with their troubles. They want to be cured, and when they think they are incurable they become very intolerant. Reformers always are.

Usually, however, various attempts at readjustment are made with devastating candor. Married couples seem to spend many precious hours of the day and night discussing what is wrong with their relationship. The general idea is that—according to the teachings of most modern psychologists and pedagogues—one should face the truth fearlessly. Husbands and wives should be absolutely frank with one another, on the assumption that if love between them is real it will be made stronger and more real still if submitted, at frequent intervals, to the test of complete sincerity on both sides.

This is a fine theory, but it has seldom been practiced without disastrous results. There are several reasons why this should be so. First of all, truth is an explosive, and it should be handled with care, especially in marital life. It is not necessary to lie, but there is little profit in juggling with hand grenades just to show how brave one is. Secondly, the theory of absolute sincerity presupposes that, if love cannot withstand continuous blasting, then it is not worth saving anyway. Some people want their love life to be a permanent battle of Verdun. When the system of defense is destroyed beyond repair, then the clause of hopeless maladjustment is invoked by one side, or by both. The next thing to do is to divorce and find someone else to be recklessly frank with for a season.

Another reason why the method of adjustment through truthtelling is not always wise is that it develops fiendish traits of character which might otherwise remain dormant.

I know a woman whose eyes glitter with virtuous self-satisfaction every time she has had a "real heart-to-heart talk" with her husband, which means that she has spent several hours torturing him, or at best boring him to distraction, with a ruthless exposure of the deplorable status of their mutual relationship to date. She is usually so pleased with herself after these periodical inquests that she tells most of her friends, and also her coiffeur, about it. "Dick and I had such a wonderful time last evening. We made a real effort to find out the real truth about each other— or, at least, I certainly did. I honestly believe we have found a new basis of adjustment for ourselves. What a marvelous feeling that is—don't you think so?"

Dick, of course, if he happens to be present, looks rather nervous or glum, but that is not the point. The point is that Dick's wife feels all aglow because she has done her bit in the general campaign for the improvement of marital happiness through truth. She has been a good girl scout.

A man of my acquaintance, who believes in experimenting outside of wedlock, is unable to understand why his wife would rather ignore his experiments. "If I did not love her and if she did not love me," he argues, "I could accept her point of view. But why can't she see that the very fact that I want her to know everything I do is a proof that I love her? If I have to deceive her or conceal things from her, what is the use of being married to her?"

Be it said, in passing, that this unfortunate husband believes that these extramarital "experiments" are absolutely necessary to prevent him from developing a sense of inferiority, which, if allowed to grow, would destroy not only the love he has for his wife, but also his general ability in his dealings with the outside world.

V

The difference between an American cookbook and a French one is that the former is very accurate and the second exceedingly vague. A French recipe seldom tells you how many ounces of butter to use to make *crêpes Suzette*, or how many spoonfuls of oil should go into a salad dressing. French cookbooks are full of esoteric measurements such as a *pinch* of pepper, a *suspicion* of garlic, or a *generous sprinkling* of brandy. There are constant references to seasoning *to taste,* as if the recipe were merely intended to give a general direction, relying on the experience and innate art of the cook to make the dish turn out right.

American recipes look like doctors' prescriptions. Perfect cooking seems to depend on perfect dosage. Some of these books give you a table of calories and vitamins—as if that had anything to do with the problem of eating well!

In the same way, there is now flourishing in America a great crop of books which offer precise recipes for the things you should do, or avoid doing, in order to achieve happiness and keep the fires of love at a constant temperature. In an issue of *Time* magazine, four such books were reviewed together. Their titles are descriptive enough of the purpose of the authors as well as the state of mind of the readers: *Love and Happiness, So You're Going to Get Married, Marriages Are Made at Home, Getting Along Together.*

I have not read all these books, but, according to the reviewer, they all tend to give practical answers to the same mysterious problem of living with someone of the opposite sex. They try to establish sets of little rules and little tricks which will guarantee marital bliss if carefully followed, in the same way that cookbooks guarantee that you will obtain pumpkin pie if you use the proper ingredients properly measured.

As the publisher of one of these books says on the jacket: "There is nothing in this book about the complicated psychological problems that send men and women to psychoanalysts, but there is a lot in it about the little incidents of daily married life—the things that happen in the parlor, bedroom, and bath—that handled one way enable people to live together happily forever after, and handled another way lead to Reno."

Time's review of these books is very gloomy in its conclusion: "Despite their optimistic tone," it says, "the four volumes give a troubled picture of United States domestic life—a world in which husbands are amorous when wives are not, and vice versa; where conflicts spring up over reading in bed or rumpling the evening paper . . . the whole grim panorama giving the impression that Americans are irritable, aggravated, dissatisfied people for whom marriage is an ordeal that only heroes and heroines can bear."

But I believe that the editors of *Time* would be just as dejected if they were reviewing four volumes about American cooking, and for the same reasons. You cannot possibly feel cheerful when you see the art of love or the art of eating thus reduced to such automatic formulas, even if the experts in these matters are themselves cheerful and optimistic. Good food, the pleasures of love, and those of marriage depend on imponderables, individual taste, and no small amount of luck.

VI

Thus the problem of love in America seems to be the resultant of conflicting and rather unrealistic ways of approaching it. Too many songs, too many stories, too many pictures, and too much romance on the one hand,

and too much practical advice on the other. It is as if the experience of being in love could only be one of two things: a superhuman ecstasy, the way of reaching heaven on earth and in pairs; or a psychopathic condition to be treated by specialists.

Between these two extremes there is little room for compromise. That the relationship between men and women offers a wide scale of variations seldom occurs to the experts. It is not necessarily true that there is but one form of love worth bothering about, and that if you cannot get the de luxe model, with a life guarantee of perfect functioning, nothing else is worth while. It is not true either that you can indefinitely pursue the same quest for perfection, or that if a man and a woman have not found ideal happiness together they will certainly find it with somebody else. Life unfortunately does not begin at forty, and when you reach that age, in America or anywhere else, to go on complaining about your sentimental or physiological maladjustments becomes slightly farcical.

It is not easy, nor perhaps of any use, to draw any conclusion from all this, especially for a European who has lost the fresh point of view of the visitor because he lives here, and who is not quite sure of what it means to be a European any more. I sometimes wonder if there is any real difference between the way men and women get along—or do not get along—together on this side of the Atlantic and on the other. There are probably no more real troubles here than anywhere else. Human nature being quite remarkably stable, why should there be? But there is no doubt that the revolt against this type of human inadequacy is very strong indeed here, especially among the women who imagine that the Europeans have found better ways of managing their hearts and their senses than the Americans.

If this is at all true, I believe the reason is to be found in a more philosophical attitude on the part of the Europeans towards such matters. There are no theories about marital bliss, no recipes to teach you how to solve difficulties which, in the Old World, are accepted as part of the common inheritance.

Men and women naturally want to be happy over there, and, if possible, with the help of one another; but they learn very young that compromise is not synonymous with defeat. Even in school (I am speaking more particularly of France now) they are taught, through the literature of centuries, that love is a phenomenon susceptible of innumerable variations, but that—even under the best circumstances—it is so intertwined with the other experiences of each individual life that to be overromantic or too dogmatic about it is of little practical use. *"La vérité est dans les nuances"* [Truth lies in slight variations], wrote Benjamin Constant, who knew a good deal about such matters.

And, speaking of the truly practical and realistic nature of love, it is a very strange thing that American literature contains no work of any note, not even essays, on love as a psychological phenomenon. I know of no good study of the process of falling in and out of love, no analytical description of jealousy, coquettishness, or the development of tediousness. No classification of the various brands of love such as La Rochefoucauld, Pascal, Stendhal, Proust, and many others have elaborated has been attempted from the American angle. The interesting combinations of such passions as ambition, jealousy, religious fervor, and so forth, with love are only dimly perceived by most people and even by the novelists, who, with very few exceptions, seem to ignore or scorn these complicated patterns. These fine studies have been left to the psychiatrists, the charlatans, or the manufacturers of naïve recipes.

The reason for this neglect on the part of real thinkers and essayists may be that for a long time the standards imposed by the puritanical point of view made the whole study more or less taboo with respectable authors. And then the Freudian wave came along and carried the whole problem out of reach of the amateur observer and the artist. In other words, conditions have been such that there has been no occasion to fill this curious gap in American literature.

Of course, nothing is lost. The field remains open, and there is no reason to suppose that love in America will not cease to be a national problem, a hunting ground for the reformer, and that it will not become, as everywhere else, a personal affair very much worth the effort it takes to examine it as such. All that is necessary is for someone to forget for a while love as Hollywood—or the professor—sees it, and sit down and think about it as an eternally fascinating subject for purely human observation.

What magazine or TV advertisements can you think of that support de Sales's statement: "In America the idea seems to be that love, like so much else, should be sold to the public, because it is a good thing." What general notions arise from these advertisements of the American couple "in love"?

In your opinion, what is the effect on the average American's life of the glorification of love? Of practical advice on how to attain happiness in love?

Do you think candor is "devastating" or therapeutic for a love relationship? Why?

from **Dr. Faustus**

THOMAS MANN

At Merseburg near Constance, toward the end of the fifteenth century, there lived an honest young fellow, Heinz Klöpfgeissel by name and cooper by calling, quite sound and well-built. He loved and was loved by a maiden named Bärbel, only daughter of a widowed sexton, and wished to marry her, but the young couple's desire met with her father's opposition, for Klöpfgeissel was poor, and the sexton insisted on a considerable setting-up in life, and that he should be a master in his trade before he gave him his daughter. But the desires of the young people had proved stronger than their patience and the couple had prematurely become a pair. And every night, when the sexton went to ring the bell, Klöpfgeissel slipped in to his Bärbel and their embraces made each find the other the most glorious thing on earth.

Thus things stood when one day the cooper and some lively companions went to Constance to a church dedication and they had a good day and were a bit beyond themselves, so they decided to go to some women. It was not to Klöpfgeissel's mind, he did not want to go with them. But the others jeered at him for an old maid and egged him on with taunts against his honour and hints that all was not right with him; and as he could not stand that, and had drunk just as much beer as the others besides, he let himself be talked round, said: "Ho-ho, I know better than that," and went up with the others into the stews.

But now it came about that he suffered such frightful chagrin that he did not know what sort of face to put on. For against all expectation things went wrong with him with the slut, a Hungarian woman it was, he could give no account of himself at all, he was just not there, and his fury was unbounded, his fright as well. For the creature not only laughed at him, but shook her head and gave it as her view that there must be something wrong, it certainly had a bad smell, when a fine lusty chap like him all of a sudden was just not up to it, he must be possessed, somebody must have given him something—and so on. He paid her a goodly sum so that she would say nothing, and went home greatly cast down.

As soon as he could, though not without misgiving, he made a rendezvous with his Bärbel, and while the sexton was ringing his bell they had a perfect hour together. He found his manly honour restored and should have been well content. For aside from the one and only he cared for no one, and why should he care about himself save only for her? But he had been uneasy in his mind ever since that one failure; it gnawed at him, he felt he must make another test: just once and never again, play false to his dearest and best. So he sought secretly for a chance to test himself— himself and her too, for he could cherish no misgiving about himself that did not end in slight, even tender, yet anxious suspicion of her upon whom his soul hung.

Now, it so fell out that he had to tighten the hoops of two casks in the wine-cellar of the inn landlord, a sickly pot-belly, and the man's wife, a comely wench, still pretty fresh, went down with him to watch him work. She patted his arm, put hers beside it to compare, and so demeaned herself that it would have been impossible to repulse her, save that his flesh, in all the willingness of his spirit, was entirely unable, and he had to say he was not in the humour, and he was in a hurry, and her husband would be coming downstairs, and then to take to his heels, hearing her scornful laughter behind him and owing her a debt which no stout fellow should ever refuse to pay.

He was deeply injured and bewildered about himself, but about himself not only; for the suspicion that even after the first mishap had lodged in his mind now entirely filled him, and he had no more doubt that he was indeed "possessed." And so, because the healing of a poor soul and the honour of his flesh as well were at stake, he went to the priest and told him everything in his ear through the little grating: how he was bewitched, how he was unable, how he was prevented with everybody but one, and how about all that and had the Church any maternal advice to give against such injury.

Now, at that time and in that locality the pestilence of witchcraft, accompanied by much wantonness, sin, and vice instigated by the enemy of the human race, and abhorrent to the Divine Majesty, had been gravely widespread, and stern watchfulness had been made the duty of all shepherds of souls. The priests, all too familiar with this kind of mischief, and men being tampered with in their best strength, went to the higher authorities with Klöpfgeissel's confession. The sexton's daughter was arrested and examined, and confessed, truly and sincerely, that in the anguish of her heart over the faithfulness of the young man, lest he be filched from her before he was hers before God and man, she had procured from an old bathwoman a specific, a salve, said to be made of the fat of an infant dead unbaptized, with which she had anointed her Heinz on the back while embracing him, tracing a certain figure thereon, only in order to bind him to herself. Next the bathingwoman was interrogated, who denied it stoutly. She had to be brought before the civil authorities for the application of methods of questioning which did not become the Church; and under some pressure the expected came to light. The old woman had in fact a compact with the Devil, who appeared to her in the guise of a monk with goat's feet and persuaded her to deny with frightful curses the Godhead and the Christian faith, in return for which he gave her directions for making not only that love unction but also other shameful panaceas, among them a fat, smeared with which a piece of wood would instantly rise with the sorcerer into the air. The ceremonies by which the Evil One had sealed his pact with the old crone came out bit by bit under repeated pressure, and were hair-raising.

Everything now depended upon the question: how far was the salvation of the deceived one involved by her receiving and using the unholy preparations? Unhappily for the sexton's daughter the old woman deposed that the Dragon had laid upon her to make many converts. For every human being she brought to him by betraying it to the use of his gifts, he would make her somewhat more secure against the everlasting flames; so that after assiduous marshalling of converts she would be armed with an asbestos buckler against the flames of hell.—This was Bärbel's undoing. The need to save her soul from eternal damnation, to tear her from the Devil's claws by yielding her body to the flames, was perfectly apparent. And since on account of the increasing ravages of corruption an example was bitterly needed, the two witches, the old one and the young, were burned at the stake, one beside the other on the open square. Heinz Klöpfgeissel, the bewitched one, stood in the throng of spectators with his head bared, murmuring prayers. The shrieks of his beloved, choked by smoke and unrecognizable with hoarseness, seemed to him like the voice of the Demon, croaking as against his will he issued from her. From that hour the vile inhibition was lifted from him, for no sooner was his love reduced to ashes than he recovered the sinfully alienated free use of his manhood.

I have never forgotten this revolting tale, so characteristic of the tone of Schleppfuss's course, not have I ever been able to be quite cool about it. Among us, between Adrian and me, as well as in discussions in Winfried it was much talked about; but neither in him, who was always taciturn about his teachers and what they said, nor in his theological fellow-students did I succeed in rousing the amount of indignation which would have satisfied my own anger at the anecdote, especially against Klöpfgeissel. Even today in my thoughts I address him breathing vengeance and call him a prize ass in every sense of the word. Why did the donkey have to tell? Why had he to test himself on other women when he had the one he loved, loved obviously so much that it made him cold and "impotent" with others? What does "impotent" mean in this connection, when with the one he loved he had all the potency of love? Love is certainly a kind of noble selectiveness of sexuality, and if it is natural that sexual activity should decline in the absence of love, yet it is nothing less than unnatural if it does so in the presence and face of love. In any case, Bärbel had fixed and "restricted" her Heinz—not by means of any devil's hocuspocus but by the charm she had for him and the will by which she held him as by a spell against other temptations. That this protection in its strength and influence on the youth's nature was psychologically reinforced by the magic salve and the girl's belief in it, I am prepared to accept, though it does seem to me simpler and more correct to look at the matter from his side and to make the selective feeling given by his love responsible for the inhibition over which he was so stupidly upset. But this point of view too includes the recognition of a certain natural wonder-working of the spiritual, its power to affect and modify the organic and corporeal in a decisive way—and this so to speak magic side of the thing it was, of course, that Schleppfuss purposely emphasized in his comments on the Klöpfgeissel case.

He did it in a quasi-humanistic sense, in order to magnify the lofty idea which those supposedly sinister centuries had had of the choice constitution of the human body. They had considered it nobler than all other earthly combinations of matter, and in its power of variation through the spiritual had seen the expression of its aristocracy, its high rank in the hierarchy of bodies. It got cold or hot through fear or anger, thin with affliction; blossomed in joy; a mere feeling of disgust could produce a physiological reaction like that of bad food, the mere sight of a dish of strawberries could make the skin of an allergic person break out; yes, sickness and death could follow purely mental operations. But it was only a step—though a necessary one—from this insight into the power of the mind to alter its own and accompanying physical matter, to the conviction, supported by ample human experience, that mind, whether wilfully or not, was able, that is by magic, to alter another person's physical substance. In other words, the reality of magic, of daemonic influence and bewitchment, was corroborated; and phenomena such as the evil eye, a complex of experience concentrated in the saga of the death-dealing eye of the basilisk, were rescued from the realm of so-called superstition. It would have been culpable inhumanity to deny that an impure soul could produce by a mere look, whether deliberate or not, physically harmful effects in others, for instance in little children, whose tender substance was especially susceptible to the poison of such an eye.

Thus Schleppfuss in his exclusive course—exclusive because it was both intellectual and questionable. Questionable: a capital word, I have always ascribed a high philological value to it. It challenges one both to go in to and to avoid; anyhow to a very cautious going-in; and it stands in the double light of the remarkable and the disreputable, either in a thing—or in a man.

In our bow to Schleppfuss when we met him in the street or in the corridors of the university we expressed all the respect with which the high intellectual plane of his lectures inspired us hour by hour; but he on his side took off his hat with a still deeper flourish than ours and said: "Your humble servant."

What is your answer to the question: "Why did the donkey have to tell?" What do you imagine Bärbel would have done had she been in Heinz' position?

Do you think there is a lack of candor between Heinz and Bärbel? (See de Sales's comments on "candor," pp. 196–97.) How would a modern American couple handle this situation?

Do you agree with the statement: "Love is certainly a kind of noble selectiveness of sexuality"? What connections do you see between impotence and love or lack of love?

Frankie and Johnny

ANONYMOUS

Frankie and Johnny were lovers, O, how that couple could love.
Swore to be true to each other, true as the stars above.
He was her man, but he done her wrong.

Frankie she was his woman, everybody knows.
She spent one hundred dollars for a suit of Johnny's clothes.
He was her man, but he done her wrong.

Frankie and Johnny went walking, Johnny in his bran' new suit,
"O good Lawd," says Frankie, "but don't my Johnnie look cute?"
He was her man, but he done her wrong.

Frankie went down to Memphis; she went on the evening train.
She paid one hundred dollars for Johnny a watch and chain.
He was her man, but he done her wrong.

Frankie went down to the corner, to buy a glass of beer;
She says to the bartender, "Has my loving man been here?
He is my man; he wouldn't do me wrong."

"Ain't going to tell you no story, ain't going to tell you no lie,
I seen your man 'bout an hour ago with a girl named Alice Fry.
If he's your man, he's doing you wrong."

Frankie went back to the hotel, she didn't go there for fun,
Under her long red kimono she toted a forty-four gun.
He was her man, he was doing her wrong.

Frankie went down to the hotel, looked in the window so high,
There was her lovin' Johnny a-lovin' up Alice Fry;
He was her man, he was doing her wrong.

Frankie threw back her kimono; took out the old forty-four;
Roota-toot-toot, three times she shot, right through that hotel door.
She shot her man, 'cause he done her wrong.

Johnny grabbed off his Stetson. "O good Lawd, Frankie, don't shoot."
But Frankie put her finger on the trigger, and the gun went roota-toot-
    toot.
He was her man, but she shot him down.

"Roll me over easy, roll me over slow,
Roll me over easy, boys, 'cause my wounds is hurting me so,
I was her man, but I done her wrong."

With the first shot Johnny staggered; with the second shot he fell;
When the third bullet hit him, there was a new man's face in hell.
He was her man, but he done her wrong.

"Oh, bring on your rubber-tired hearses, bring on your rubber-tired hacks.
They're takin' Johnny to the buryin' groun' but they'll never bring him
    back.
He was my man, but he done me wrong."

What kind of woman is Frankie? What kind of man is Johnny? How do their actions define their characters?

Compare and contrast the lovers in this poem with Heinz and Bärbel. (See selection from *Doctor Faustus*, pp. 200–04.)

Do you think Johnny done Frankie wrong? Why or why not?

The Short Happy Life of Francis Macomber

ERNEST HEMINGWAY

It was now lunch time and they were all sitting under the double green fly of the dining tent pretending that nothing had happened.

"Will you have lime juice or lemon squash?" Macomber asked.

"I'll have a gimlet," Robert Wilson told him.

"I'll have a gimlet too. I need something," Macomber's wife said.

"I suppose it's the thing to do," Macomber agreed. "Tell him to make three gimlets."

The mess boy had started them already, lifting the bottles out of the canvas cooling bags that sweated wet in the wind that blew through the trees that shaded the tents.

"What had I ought to give them?" Macomber asked.

"A quid would be plenty," Wilson told him. "You don't want to spoil them."

"Will the headman distribute it?"

"Absolutely."

Francis Macomber had, half an hour before, been carried to his tent from the edge of the camp in triumph on the arms and shoulders of the cook, the personal boys, the skinner and the porters. The gun-bearers had taken no part in the demonstration. When the native boys put him down at the door of his tent, he had shaken all their hands, received their congratulations, and then gone into the tent and sat on the bed until his wife came in. She did not speak to him when she came in and he left the tent at once to wash his face and hands in the portable wash basin outside and go over to the dining tent to sit in a comfortable canvas chair in the breeze and the shade.

"You've got your lion," Robert Wilson said to him, "and a damned fine one too."

Mrs. Macomber looked at Wilson quickly. She was an extremely handsome and well-kept woman of the beauty and social position which had, five years before, commanded five thousand dollars as the price of endorsing, with photographs, a beauty product which she had never used. She had been married to Francis Macomber for eleven years.

"He is a good lion, isn't he?" Macomber said. His wife looked at him now. She looked at both these men as though she had never seen them before.

One, Wilson, the white hunter, she knew she had never truly seen before. He was about middle height with sandy hair, a stubby mustache, a very red face and extremely cold blue eyes with faint white wrinkles at the corners that grooved merrily when he smiled. He smiled at her now and she looked away from his face at the way his shoulders sloped in the loose tunic he wore with the four big cartridges held in loops where the left breast pocket should have been, at his big brown hands, his old slacks, his very dirty boots and back to his red face again. She noticed where the baked red of his face stopped in a white line that marked the circle left by his Stetson hat that hung now from one of the pegs of the tent pole.

"Well, here's to the lion," Robert Wilson said. He smiled at her again and, not smiling, she looked curiously at her husband.

Francis Macomber was very tall, very well built if you did not mind that length of bone, dark, his hair cropped like an oarsman, rather thin-lipped, and was considered handsome. He was dressed in the same sort of safari clothes that Wilson wore except that his were new, he was thirty-five years old, kept himself very fit, was good at court games, had a number of big-game fishing records, and had just shown himself, very publicly, to be a coward.

"Here's to the lion," he said. "I can't ever thank you for what you did."

Margaret, his wife, looked away from him and back to Wilson.

"Let's not talk about the lion," she said.

Wilson looked over at her without smiling and now she smiled at him.

"It's been a very strange day," she said. "Hadn't you ought to put your hat on even under the canvas at noon? You told me that, you know."

"Might put it on," said Wilson.

"You know you have a very red face, Mr. Wilson," she told him and smiled again.

"Drink," said Wilson.

"I don't think so," she said. "Francis drinks a great deal, but his face is never red."

"It's red today," Macomber tried a joke.

"No," said Margaret. "It's mine that's red today. But Mr. Wilson's is always red."

"Must be racial," said Wilson. "I say, you wouldn't like to drop my beauty as a topic, would you?"

"I've just started on it."

"Let's chuck it," said Wilson.

"Conversation is going to be so difficult," Margaret said.

"Don't be silly, Margot," her husband said.

"No difficulty," Wilson said. "Got a damn fine lion."

Margot looked at them both and they both saw that she was going to cry. Wilson had seen it coming for a long time and he dreaded it. Macomber was past dreading it.

"I wish it hadn't happened. Oh, I wish it hadn't happened," she said and started for her tent. She made no noise of crying but they could see that her shoulders were shaking under the rose-colored, sun-proofed shirt she wore.

"Women upset," said Wilson to the tall man. "Amounts to nothing. Strain on the nerves and one thing'n another."

"No," said Macomber. "I suppose that I rate that for the rest of my life now."

"Nonsense. Let's have a spot of giant killer," said Wilson. "Forget the whole thing. Nothing to it anyway."

"We might try," said Macomber. "I won't forget what you did for me though."

"Nothing," said Wilson. "All nonsense."

So they sat there in the shade where the camp was pitched under some wide-topped acacia trees with a boulder-strewn cliff behind them, and a stretch of grass that ran to the bank of a boulder-filled stream in front with forest beyond it, and drank their just-cool lime drinks and avoided one another's eyes while the boys set the table for lunch. Wilson could tell that the boys all knew about it now and when he saw Macomber's personal boy looking curiously at his master while he was putting dishes on the table he snapped at him in Swahili. The boy turned away with his face blank.

"What were you telling him?" Macomber asked.

"Nothing. Told him to look alive or I'd see he got about fifteen of the best."

"What's that? Lashes?"

"It's quite illegal," Wilson said. "You're supposed to fine them."

"Do you still have them whipped?"

"Oh, yes. They could raise a row if they chose to complain. But they don't. They prefer it to the fines."

"How strange!" said Macomber.

"Not strange, really," Wilson said. "Which would you rather do? Take a good birching or lose your pay?"

Then he felt embarrassed at asking it and before Macomber could answer he went on, "We all take a beating every day, you know, one way or another."

This was no better. "Good God," he thought. "I am a diplomat, aren't I?"

"Yes, we take a beating," said Macomber, still not looking at him. "I'm awfully sorry about that lion business. It doesn't have to go any further, does it? I mean no one will hear about it, will they?"

"You mean will I tell it at the Mathaiga Club?" Wilson looked at him now coldly. He had not expected this. So he's a bloody four-letter man as well as a bloody coward, he thought. I rather liked him too until today. But how is one to know about an American?

"No," said Wilson. "I'm a professional hunter. We never talk about our clients. You can be quite easy on that. It's supposed to be bad form to ask us not to talk though."

He had decided now that to break would be much easier. He would eat, then, by himself and could read a book with his meals. They would eat by themselves. He would see them through the safari on a very formal basis—what was it the French called it? Distinguished consideration—and it would be a damn sight easier than having to go through this emotional trash. He'd insult him and make a good clean break. Then he could read a book with his meals and he'd still be drinking their whisky. That was the phrase for it when a safari went bad. You ran into another white hunter and you asked, "How is everything going?" and he answered, "Oh, I'm still drinking their whisky," and you knew everything had gone to pot.

"I'm sorry," Macomber said and looked at him with his American face that would stay adolescent until it became middle-aged, and Wilson noted his crew-cropped hair, fine eyes only faintly shifty, good nose, thin lips and handsome jaw. "I'm sorry I didn't realize that. There are lots of things I don't know."

So what could he do, Wilson thought. He was all ready to break it off quickly and neatly and here the beggar was apologizing after he had just insulted him. He made one more attempt. "Don't worry about me talking," he said. "I have a living to make. You know in Africa no woman ever misses her lion and no white man ever bolts."

"I bolted like a rabbit," Macomber said.

Now what in hell were you going to do about a man who talked like that, Wilson wondered.

Wilson looked at Macomber with his flat, blue, machine-gunner's eyes and the other smiled back at him. He had a pleasant smile if you did not notice how his eyes showed when he was hurt.

"Maybe I can fix it up on Buffalo," he said. "We're after them next, aren't we?"

"In the morning if you like," Wilson told him. Perhaps he had been wrong. This was certainly the way to take it. You most certainly could not tell a damned thing about an American. He was all for Macomber again. If you could forget the morning. But, of course, you couldn't. The morning had been about as bad as they come.

"Here comes the Memsahib," he said. She was walking over from her tent looking refreshed and cheerful and quite lovely. She had a very perfect oval face, so perfect that you expected her to be stupid. But she wasn't stupid, Wilson thought, no, not stupid.

"How is the beautiful red-faced Mr. Wilson? Are you feeling better, Francis, my pearl?"

"Oh, much," said Macomber.

"I've dropped the whole thing," she said, sitting down at the table. "What importance is there to whether Francis is any good at killing lions? That's not his trade. That's Mr. Wilson's trade. Mr. Wilson is really very impressive killing anything. You do kill anything, don't you?"

"Oh, anything," said Wilson. "Simply anything." They are, he thought, the hardest in the world; the hardest, the cruelest, the most predatory and the most attractive and their men have softened or gone to pieces nervously as they have hardened. Or is it that they pick men they can handle? They can't know that much at the age they marry, he thought. He was grateful that he had gone through his education on American women before now because this was a very attractive one.

"We're going after buff in the morning," he told her.

"I'm coming," she said.

"No, you're not."

"Oh, yes, I am. Mayn't I, Francis?"

"Why not stay in camp?"

"Not for anything," she said. "I wouldn't miss something like today for anything."

When she left, Wilson was thinking, when she went off to cry, she seemed a hell of a fine woman. She seemed to understand, to realize, to be hurt for him and for herself and to know how things really stood. She is away for twenty minutes and now she is back, simply enamelled in that American female cruelty. They are the damnedest women. Really the damnedest.

"We'll put on another show for you tomorrow," Francis Macomber said.

"You're not coming," Wilson said.

"You're very mistaken," she told him. "And I want *so* to see you perform again. You were lovely this morning. That is if blowing things' heads off is lovely."

"Here's the lunch," said Wilson. "You're very merry, aren't you?"

"Why not? I didn't come out here to be dull."

"Well, it hasn't been dull," Wilson said. He could see the boulders in the river and the high bank beyond with the trees and he remembered the morning.

"Oh, no," she said. "It's been charming. And tomorrow. You don't know how I look forward to tomorrow."

"That's eland he's offering you," Wilson said.

"They're the big cowy things that jump like hares, aren't they?"

"I suppose that describes them," Wilson said.

"It's very good meat," Macomber said.

"Did you shoot it, Francis?" she asked.

"Yes."

"They're not dangerous, are they?"

"Only if they fall on you," Wilson told her.

"I'm so glad."

"Why not let up on the bitchery just a little, Margot," Macomber said, cutting the eland steak and putting some mashed potato, gravy and carrot on the down-turned fork that tined through the piece of meat.

"I suppose I could," she said, "since you put it so prettily."

"Tonight we'll have champagne for the lion," Wilson said. "It's a bit too hot at noon."

"Oh, the lion," Margot said. "I'd forgotten the lion!"

So, Robert Wilson thought to himself, she *is* giving him a ride, isn't she? Or do you suppose that's her idea of putting up a good show? How should a woman act when she discovers her husband is a bloody coward? She's damn cruel but they're all cruel. They govern, of course, and to govern one has to be cruel sometimes. Still, I've seen enough of their damn terrorism.

"Have some more eland," he said to her politely.

That afternoon, late, Wilson and Macomber went out in the motor car with the native driver and the two gun-bearers. Mrs. Macomber stayed in the camp. It was too hot to go out, she said, and she was going with them in the early morning. As they drove off Wilson saw her standing under the big tree, looking pretty rather than beautiful in her faintly rosy khaki, her dark hair drawn back off her forehead and gathered in a knot low on her neck, her face as fresh, he thought, as though she were in England. She waved to them as the car went off through the swale of high grass and curved around through the trees into the small hills of orchard bush.

In the orchard bush they found a herd of impala, and leaving the car they stalked one old ram with long, wide-spread horns and Macomber killed it with a very creditable shot that knocked the buck down at a good two hundred yards and sent the herd off bounding wildly and leaping over one another's backs in long, leg-drawn-up leaps as unbelievable and as floating as those one makes sometimes in dreams.

"That was a good shot," Wilson said. "They're a small target."

"Is it a worth-while head?" Macomber asked.

"It's excellent," Wilson told him. "You shoot like that and you'll have no trouble."

"Do you think we'll find buffalo tomorrow?"

"There's a good chance of it. They feed out early in the morning and with luck we may catch them in the open."

"I'd like to clear away that lion business," Macomber said. "It's not very pleasant to have your wife see you do something like that."

I should think it would be even more unpleasant to do it, Wilson thought, wife or no wife, or to talk about it having done it. But he said, "I wouldn't think about that any more. Any one could be upset by his first lion. That's all over."

But that night after dinner and a whisky and soda by the fire before going to bed, as Francis Macomber lay on his cot with the mosquito bar over him and listened to the night noises it was not all over. It was neither all over nor was it beginning. It was there exactly as it happened with some parts of it indelibly emphasized and he was miserably ashamed at it. But more than shame he felt cold, hollow fear in him. The fear was still there like a cold slimy hollow in all the emptiness where once his confidence had been and it made him feel sick. It was still there with him now.

It had started the night before when he had wakened and heard the lion roaring somewhere up along the river. It was a deep sound and at the end there were sort of coughing grunts that made him seem just outside the tent, and when Francis Macomber woke in the night to hear it he was afraid. He could hear his wife breathing quietly, asleep. There was no one to tell he was afraid, nor to be afraid with him, and, lying alone, he did not know the Somali proverb that says a brave man is always frightened three times by a lion; when he first sees his track, when he first hears him roar and when he first confronts him. Then while they were eating breakfast by lantern light out in the dining tent, before the sun was up, the lion roared again and Francis thought he was just at the edge of camp.

"Sounds like an old-timer," Robert Wilson said, looking up from his kippers and coffee. "Listen to him cough."

"Is he very close?"

"A mile or so up the stream."

"Will we see him?"

"We'll have a look."

"Does his roaring carry that far? It sounds as though he were right in camp."

"Carries a hell of a long way," said Robert Wilson. "It's strange the way it carries. Hope he's a shootable cat. The boys said there was a very big one about here."

"If I get a shot, where should I hit him," Macomber asked, "to stop him?"

"In the shoulders," Wilson said. "In the neck if you can make it. Shoot for bone. Break him down."

"I hope I can place it properly," Macomber said.

"You shoot very well," Wilson told him. "Take your time. Make sure of him. The first one in is the one that counts."

"What range will it be?"

"Can't tell. Lion has something to say about that. Don't shoot unless it's close enough so you can make sure."

"At under a hundred yards?" Macomber asked.

Wilson looked at him quickly.

"Hundred's about right. Might have to take him a bit under. Shouldn't chance a shot at much over that. A hundred's a decent range. You can hit him wherever you want at that. Here comes the Memsahib."

"Good morning," she said. "Are we going after that lion?"

"As soon as you deal with your breakfast," Wilson said. "How are you feeling?"

"Marvellous," she said. "I'm very excited."

"I'll just go and see that everything is ready," Wilson went off. As he left the lion roared again.

"Noisy beggar," Wilson said. "We'll put a stop to that."

"What's the matter, Francis?" his wife asked him.

"Nothing," Macomber said.

"Yes, there is," she said. "What are you upset about?"

"Nothing," he said.

"Tell me," she looked at him. "Don't you feel well?"

"It's that damned roaring," he said. "It's been going on all night, you know."

"Why didn't you wake me," she said. "I'd love to have heard it."

"I've got to kill the damned thing," Macomber said, miserably.

"Well, that's what you're out here for, isn't it?"

"Yes. But I'm nervous. Hearing the thing roar gets on my nerves."

"Well then, as Wilson said, kill him and stop his roaring."

"Yes, darling," said Francis Macomber. "It sounds easy, doesn't it?"

"You're not afraid, are you?"

"Of course not. But I'm nervous from hearing him roar all night."

"You'll kill him marvellously," she said. "I know you will. I'm awfully anxious to see it."

"Finish your breakfast and we'll be starting."

"It's not light yet," she said. "This is a ridiculous hour."

Just then the lion roared in a deep-chested moaning, suddenly guttural, ascending vibration that seemed to shake the air and ended in a sigh and a heavy, deep-chested grunt.

"He sounds almost here," Macomber's wife said.

"My God," said Macomber. "I hate that damned noise."

"It's very impressive."

"Impressive. It's frightful."

Robert Wilson came up then carrying his short, ugly, shockingly big-bored .505 Gibbs and grinning.

"Come on," he said. "Your gun-bearer has your Springfield and the big gun. Everything's in the car. Have you solids?"

"Yes."

"I'm ready," Mrs. Macomber said.

"Must make him stop that racket," Wilson said. "You get in front. The Memsahib can sit back here with me."

They climbed into the motor car and, in the gray first daylight, moved off up the river through the trees. Macomber opened the breech of his rifle and saw he had metal-cased bullets, shut the bolt and put the rifle on safety. He saw his hand was trembling. He felt in his pocket for more cartridges and moved his fingers over the cartridges in the loops of his tunic front. He turned back to where Wilson sat in the rear seat of the doorless, box-bodied motor car beside his wife, them both grinning with excitement, and Wilson leaned forward and whispered.

"See the birds dropping. Means the old boy has left his kill."

On the far bank of the stream Macomber could see, above the trees, vultures circling and plummeting down.

"Chances are he'll come to drink along here," Wilson whispered. "Before he goes to lay up. Keep an eye out."

They were driving slowly along the high bank of the stream which here cut deeply to its boulder-filled bed, and they wound in and out through big trees as they drove. Macomber was watching the opposite bank when he felt Wilson take hold of his arm. The car stopped.

"There he is," he heard the whisper. "Ahead and to the right. Get out and take him. He's a marvellous lion."

Macomber saw the lion now. He was standing alone almost broadside, his great head up and turned toward them. The early morning breeze that blew toward them was just stirring his dark mane, and the lion looked huge, silhouetted on the rise of bank in the gray morning light, his shoulders heavy, his barrel of a body bulking smoothly.

"How far is he?" asked Macomber, raising his rifle.

"About seventy-five. Get out and take him."

"Why not shoot from where I am?"

"You don't shoot them from cars," he heard Wilson saying in his ear. "Get out. He's not going to stay there all day."

Macomber stepped out of the curved opening at the side of the front seat, onto the step and down onto the ground. The lion still stood looking majestically and coolly toward this object that his eyes showed only in silhouette, bulking like some super-rhino. There was no man smell carried toward him and he watched the object, moving his great head a little from side to side. Then watching the object, not afraid, but hesitating before going down the bank to drink with such a thing opposite him, he saw a man figure detach itself from it and he turned his heavy head and swung away toward the cover of the trees as he heard a cracking crash and felt the slam of a .30-06 220-grain solid bullet that bit his flank and ripped in sudden hot scalding nausea through his stomach. He trotted, heavy, big-footed, swinging wounded full-bellied, through the trees toward the tall grass and cover, and the crash came again to go past him ripping the air apart. Then it crashed again and he felt the blow as it hit his lower ribs and ripped on through, blood sudden hot and frothy in his mouth, and he galloped toward the high grass where he could crouch and not be seen and make them bring the crashing thing close enough so he could make a rush and get the man that held it.

Macomber had not thought how the lion felt as he got out of the car. He only knew his hands were shaking and as he walked away from the car it was almost impossible for him to make his legs move. They were stiff in the thighs, but he could feel the muscles fluttering. He raised the rifle, sighted on the junction of the lion's head and shoulders and pulled the trigger. Nothing happened though he pulled until he thought his finger would break. Then he knew he had the safety on and as he lowered the rifle to move the safety over he moved another frozen pace forward, and the lion seeing his silhouette now clear of the silhouette of the car, turned and started off at a trot, and, as Macomber fired, he heard a whunk that meant that the bullet was home; but the lion kept on going. Macomber shot again and every one saw the bullet throw a spout of dirt beyond the trotting lion. He shot again, remembering to lower his aim, and they all heard the bullet hit, and the lion went into a gallop and was in the tall grass before he had the bolt pushed forward.

Macomber stood there feeling sick at his stomach, his hands that held the Springfield still cocked, shaking, and his wife and Robert Wilson were standing by him. Beside him too were the two gun-bearers chattering in Wakamba.

"I hit him," Macomber said. "I hit him twice."

"You gut-shot him and you hit him somewhere forward," Wilson said without enthusiasm. The gun-bearers looked very grave. They were silent now.

"You may have killed him," Wilson went on. "We'll have to wait a while before we go in to find out."

"What do you mean?"

"Let him get sick before we follow him up."

"Oh," said Macomber.

"He's a hell of a fine lion," Wilson said cheerfully. "He's gotten into a bad place though."

"Why is it bad?"

"Can't see him until you're on him."

"Oh," said Macomber.

"Come on," said Wilson. "The Memsahib can stay here in the car. We'll go to have a look at the blood spoor."

"Stay here, Margot," Macomber said to his wife. His mouth was very dry and it was hard for him to talk.

"Why?" she asked.

"Wilson says so."

"We're going to have a look," Wilson said. "You stay here. You can see even better from here."

"All right."

Wilson spoke in Swahili to the driver. He nodded and said, "Yes, Bwana."

Then they went down the steep bank and across the stream, climbing over and around the boulders and up the other bank, pulling up by some projecting roots, and along it until they found where the lion had been trotting when Macomber first shot. There was dark blood on the short grass that the gun-bearers pointed out with grass stems, and that ran away behind the river bank trees.

"What do we do?" asked Macomber.

"Not much choice," said Wilson. "We can't bring the car over. Bank's too steep. We'll let him stiffen up a bit and then you and I'll go in and have a look for him."

"Can't we set the grass on fire?" Macomber asked.

"Too green."

"Can't we send beaters?"

Wilson looked at him appraisingly. "Of course we can," he said. "But it's just a touch murderous. You see we know the lion's wounded. You can drive an unwounded lion—he'll move on ahead of a noise—but a wounded lion's going to charge. You can't see him until you're right on him. He'll make himself perfectly flat in cover you wouldn't think would hide a hare. You can't very well send boys in there to that sort of a show. Somebody bound to get mauled."

"What about the gun-bearers?"

"Oh, they'll go with us. It's their *shauri*. You see, they signed on for it. They don't look too happy though, do they?"

"I don't want to go in there," said Macomber. It was out before he knew he'd said it.

"Neither do I," said Wilson very cheerily. "Really no choice though." Then, as an afterthought, he glanced at Macomber and saw suddenly how he was trembling and the pitiful look on his face.

"You don't have to go in, of course," he said. "That's what I'm hired for, you know. That's why I'm so expensive."

"You mean, you'd go in by yourself? Why not leave him there?"

Robert Wilson, whose entire occupation had been with the lion and the problem he presented, and who had not been thinking about Macomber except to note that he was rather windy, suddenly felt as though he had opened the wrong door in a hotel and seen something shameful.

"What do you mean?"

"Why not just leave him?"

"You mean pretend to ourselves he hasn't been hit?"

"No. Just drop it."

"It isn't done."

"Why not?"

"For one thing, he's certain to be suffering. For another, some one else might run onto him."

"I see."

"But you don't have to have anything to do with it."

"I'd like to," Macomber said. "I'm just scared, you know."

"I'll go ahead when we go in," Wilson said, "with Kongoni tracking. You keep behind me and a little to one side. Chances are we'll hear him growl. If we see him we'll both shoot. Don't worry about anything. I'll keep you backed up. As a matter of fact, you know, perhaps you'd better not go. It might be much better. Why don't you go over and join the Memsahib while I just get it over with?"

"No, I want to go."

"All right," said Wilson. "But don't go in if you don't want to. This is my *shauri* now, you know."

"I want to go," said Macomber.

They sat under a tree and smoked.

"Want to go back and speak to the Memsahib while we're waiting?" Wilson asked.

"No."

"I'll just step back and tell her to be patient."

"Good," said Macomber. He sat there, sweating under his arms, his mouth dry, his stomach hollow feeling, wanting to find courage to tell Wilson to go on and finish off the lion without him. He could not know that Wilson was furious because he had not noticed the state he was in earlier and sent him back to his wife. While he sat there Wilson came up. "I have your big gun," he said. "Take it. We've given him time, I think. Come on."

Macomber took the big gun and Wilson said:

"Keep behind me and about five yards to the right and do exactly as I tell you." Then he spoke in Swahili to the two gun-bearers who looked the picture of gloom.

"Let's go," he said.

"Could I have a drink of water?" Macomber asked. Wilson spoke to the older gun-bearer, who wore a canteen on his belt, and the man unbuckled it, unscrewed the top and handed it to Macomber, who took it noticing how heavy it seemed and how hairy and shoddy the felt covering was in his hand. He raised it to drink and looked ahead at the high grass with the flat-topped trees behind it. A breeze was blowing toward them and the grass rippled gently in the wind. He looked at the gun-bearer and he could see the gun-bearer was suffering too with fear.

Thirty-five yards into the grass the big lion lay flattened out along the ground. His ears were back and his only movement was a slight twitching up and down of his long, black-tufted tail. He had turned at bay as soon as he had reached this cover and he was sick with the wound through his full belly, and weakening with the wound through his lungs that brought a thin foamy red to his mouth each time he breathed. His flanks were wet and hot and flies were on the little openings the solid bullets had made in his tawny hide, and his big yellow eyes, narrowed with hate, looked straight ahead, only blinking when the pain came as he breathed, and his claws dug in the soft baked earth. All of him, pain, sickness, hatred and all of his remaining strength, was tightening into an absolute concentration for a rush. He could hear the men talking and he waited, gathering all of himself into this preparation for a charge as soon as the men would come into the grass. As he heard their voices his tail stiffened to twitch up and down, and, as they came into the edge of the grass, he made a coughing grunt and charged.

Kongoni, the old gun-bearer, in the lead watching the blood spoor, Wilson watching the grass for any movement, his big gun ready, the second gun-bearer looking ahead and listening, Macomber close to Wilson, his rifle cocked, they had just moved into the grass when Macomber heard the blood-choked coughing grunt, and saw the swishing rush in the grass. The next thing he knew he was running; running wildly, in panic in the open, running toward the stream.

He heard the *ca-ra-wong!* of Wilson's rifle, and again in a second crashing *carawong!* and turning saw the lion, horrible-looking now, with half his head seeming to be gone, crawling toward Wilson in the edge of the tall grass while the red-faced man worked the bolt on the short ugly rifle and aimed carefully as another blasting *carawong!* came from the muzzle, and the crawling, heavy, yellow bulk of the lion stiffened and the huge, mutilated head slid forward and Macomber, standing by himself in the clearing where he had run, holding a loaded rifle, while two black men and a white man looked back at him in contempt, knew the lion was dead. He came toward Wilson, his tallness all seeming a naked reproach, and Wilson looked at him and said:

"Want to take pictures?"

"No," he said.

That was all any one had said until they reached the motor car. Then Wilson had said:

"Hell of a fine lion. Boys will skin him out. We might as well stay here in the shade."

Macomber's wife had not looked at him nor he at her and he had sat by her in the back seat with Wilson sitting in the front seat. Once he had reached over and taken his wife's hand without looking at her and she had removed her hand from his. Looking across the stream to where the gun-bearers were skinning out the lion he could see that she had been able to see the whole thing. While they sat there his wife had reached forward and put her hand on Wilson's shoulder. He turned and she had leaned forward over the low seat and kissed him on the mouth.

"Oh, I say," said Wilson, going redder than his natural baked color.

"Mr. Robert Wilson," she said. "The beautiful red-faced Mr. Robert Wilson."

Then she sat down beside Macomber again, and looked away across the stream to where the lion lay, with uplifted, white-muscled, tendon-marked naked forearms, and white bloating belly, as the black men fleshed away the skin. Finally the gun-bearers brought the skin over, wet and heavy, and climbed in behind with it, rolling it up before they got in, and the motor car started. No one said anything more until they were back in camp.

That was the story of the lion. Macomber did not know how the lion had felt before he started his rush, nor during it when the unbelievable smash of the .505 with a muzzle velocity of two tons had hit him in the mouth, nor what kept him coming after that, when the second dripping crash had smashed his hind quarters and he had come crawling on toward the crashing, blasting thing that had destroyed him. Wilson knew something about it and only expressed it by saying, "Damned fine lion," but Macomber did not know how Wilson felt about things either. He did not know how his wife felt except that she was through with him.

His wife had been through with him before but it never lasted. He was very wealthy, and would be much wealthier, and he knew she would not leave him ever now. That was one of the few things that he really knew. He knew about that, about motorcycles—that was earliest—about motor cars, about duck-shooting, about fishing, trout, salmon and big-sea, about sex in books, many books, too many books, about all court games, about dogs, not much about horses, about hanging on to his money, about most of the other things his world dealt in, and about his wife not leaving him. His wife had been a great beauty and she was still a great beauty in Africa, but she was not a great enough beauty any more at home to be able to leave him and better herself and she knew it and he knew it. She had missed the chance to leave him and he knew it. If he had been better with women she would probably have started to worry about him getting another new, beautiful wife; but she knew too much about him to worry about him either. Also, he had always had a great tolerance which seemed the nicest thing about him if it were not the most sinister.

All in all they were known as a comparatively happily married couple, one of those whose disruption is often rumored but never occurs, and as the society columnist put it, they were adding more than a spice of *adventure* to their much envied and ever-enduring *Romance* by a *Safari* in what was known as *Darkest Africa* until the Martin Johnsons lighted it on so many silver screens where they were pursuing *Old Simba* the lion, the buffalo, *Temba* the elephant and as well collecting specimens for the Museum of Natural History. This same columnist had reported them *on the verge* at least three times in the past and they had been. But they always made it up. They had a sound basis of union. Margot was too beautiful for Macomber to divorce her and Macomber had too much money for Margot ever to leave him.

It was now about three o'clock in the morning and Francis Macomber, who had been asleep a little while after he had stopped thinking about the lion, wakened and then slept again, woke suddenly, frightened in a dream of the bloody-headed lion standing over him, and listening while his heart pounded, he realized that his wife was not in the other cot in the tent. He lay awake with that knowledge for two hours.

At the end of that time his wife came into the tent, lifted her mosquito bar and crawled cozily into bed.

"Where have you been?" Macomber asked in the darkness.

"Hello," she said. "Are you awake?"

"Where have you been?"

"I just went out to get a breath of air."

"You did, like hell."

"What do you want me to say, darling?"

"Where have you been?"

"Out to get a breath of air."

"That's a new name for it. You *are* a bitch."

"Well, you're a coward."

"All right," he said. "What of it?"

"Nothing as far as I'm concerned. But please let's not talk, darling, because I'm very sleepy."

"You think that I'll take anything."

"I know you will, sweet."

"Well, I won't."

"Please, darling, let's not talk. I'm so very sleepy."

"There wasn't going to be any of that. You promised there wouldn't be."

"Well, there is now," she said sweetly.

"You said if we made this trip that there would be none of that. You promised."

"Yes, darling. That's the way I meant it to be. But the trip was spoiled yesterday. We don't have to talk about it, do we?"

"You don't wait long when you have an advantage, do you?"

"Please let's not talk. I'm so sleepy, darling."

"I'm going to talk."

"Don't mind me then, because I'm going to sleep." And she did.

At breakfast they were all three at the table before daylight and Francis Macomber found that, of all the men that he had hated, he hated Robert Wilson the most.

"Sleep well?" Wilson asked in his throaty voice, filling a pipe.

"Did you?"

"Topping," the white hunter told him.

You bastard, thought Macomber, you insolent bastard.

So she woke him when she came in, Wilson thought, looking at them both with his flat, cold eyes. Well, why doesn't he keep his wife where she belongs? What does he think I am, a bloody plaster saint? Let him keep her where she belongs. It's his own fault.

"Do you think we'll find buffalo?" Margot asked, pushing away a dish of apricots.

"Chance of it," Wilson said and smiled at her. "Why don't you stay in camp?"

"Not for anything," she told him.

"Why not order her to stay in camp?" Wilson said to Macomber.

"You order her," said Macomber coldly.

"Let's not have any ordering, nor," turning to Macomber, "any silliness, Francis," Margot said quite pleasantly.

"Are you ready to start?" Macomber asked.

"Any time," Wilson told him. "Do you want the Memsahib to go?"

"Does it make any difference whether I do or not?"

The hell with it, thought Robert Wilson. The utter complete hell with it. So this is what it's going to be like. Well, this is what it's going to be like, then.

"Makes no difference," he said.

"You're sure you wouldn't like to stay in camp with her yourself and let me go out and hunt the buffalo?" Macomber asked.

"Can't do that," said Wilson. "Wouldn't talk rot if I were you."

"I'm not talking rot. I'm disgusted."

"Bad word, disgusted."

"Francis, will you please try to speak sensibly?" his wife asked.

"I speak too damned sensibly," Macomber said. "Did you ever eat such filthy food?"

"Something wrong with the food?" asked Wilson quietly.

"No more than with everything else."

"I'd pull yourself together, laddybuck," Wilson said very quietly. "There's a boy waits at table that understands a little English."

"The hell with him."

Wilson stood up and puffing on his pipe strolled away, speaking a few words in Swahili to one of the gun-bearers who was standing waiting for him. Macomber and his wife sat on at the table. He was staring at his coffee cup.

"If you make a scene I'll leave you, darling," Margot said quietly.

"No, you won't."

"You can try it and see."

"You won't leave me."

"No," she said. "I won't leave you and you'll behave yourself."

"Behave myself? That's a way to talk. Behave myself."

"Yes. Behave yourself."

"Why don't *you* try behaving?"

"I've tried it so long. So very long."

"I hate that red-faced swine," Macomber said. "I loathe the sight of him."

"He's really *very* nice."

"Oh, *shut up,*" Macomber almost shouted. Just then the car came up and stopped in front of the dining tent and the driver and the two gun-bearers got out. Wilson walked over and looked at the husband and wife sitting there at the table.

"Going shooting?" he asked.

"Yes," said Macomber, standing up. "Yes."

"Better bring a woolly. It will be cool in the car," Wilson said.

"I'll get my leather jacket," Margot said.

"The boy has it," Wilson told her. He climbed into the front with the driver and Francis Macomber and his wife sat, not speaking, in the back seat.

Hope the silly beggar doesn't take a notion to blow the back of my head off, Wilson thought to himself. Women *are* a nuisance on safari.

The car was grinding down to cross the river at a pebbly ford in the gray daylight and then climbed, angling up the steep bank, where Wilson had ordered a way shovelled out the day before so they could reach the parklike wooded rolling country on the far side.

It was a good morning, Wilson thought. There was a heavy dew and as the wheels went through the grass and low bushes he could smell the odor of the crushed fronds. It was an odor like verbena and he liked this early morning smell of the dew, the crushed bracken and the look of the tree trunks showing black through the early morning mist, as the car made its way through the untracked, parklike country. He had put the two in the back seat out of his mind now and was thinking about buffalo. The buffalo that he was after stayed in the daytime in a thick swamp where it was impossible to get a shot, but in the night they fed out into an open stretch of country and if he could come between them and their swamp with the car, Macomber would have a good chance at them in the open. He did not want to hunt buff with Macomber in thick cover. He did not want to hunt buff or anything else with Macomber at all, but he was a professional hunter and he had hunted with some rare ones in his time. If they got buff today there would only be rhino to come and the poor man would have gone through his dangerous game and things might pick up. He'd have nothing more to do with the woman and Macomber would get over that too. He must have gone through plenty of that before by the look of things. Poor beggar. He must have a way of getting over it. Well, it was the poor sod's own bloody fault.

He, Robert Wilson, carried a double size cot on safari to accommodate any windfalls he might receive. He had hunted for a certain clientele, the international, fast, sporting set, where the women did not feel they were getting their money's worth unless they had shared that cot with the white hunter. He despised them when he was away from them although he liked some of them well enough at the time, but he made his living by them; and their standards were his standards as long as they were hiring him.

They were his standards in all except the shooting. He had his own standards about the killing and they could live up to them or get some one else to hunt them. He knew, too, that they all respected him for this. This Macomber was an odd one though. Damned if he wasn't. Now the wife. Well, the wife. Yes, the wife. Hm, the wife. Well he'd dropped all that. He looked around at them. Macomber sat grim and furious. Margot smiled at him. She looked younger today, more innocent and fresher and not so professionally beautiful. What's in her heart God knows, Wilson thought. She hadn't talked much last night. At that it was a pleasure to see her.

The motor car climbed up a slight rise and went on through the trees and then out into a grassy prairie-like opening and kept in the shelter of the trees along the edge, the driver going slowly and Wilson looking carefully out across the prairie and all along its far side. He stopped the car and studied the opening with his field glasses. Then he motioned to the driver to go on and the car moved slowly along, the driver avoiding wart-hog holes and driving around the mud castles ants had built. Then, looking across the opening, Wilson suddenly turned and said,

"By God, there they are!"

And looking where he pointed, while the car jumped forward and Wilson spoke in rapid Swahili to the driver, Macomber saw three huge, black animals looking almost cylindrical in their long heaviness, like big black tank cars, moving at a gallop across the far edge of the open prairie. They moved at a stiff-necked, stiff bodied gallop and he could see the up-swept wide black horns on their heads as they galloped heads out; the heads not moving.

"They're three old bulls," Wilson said. "We'll cut them off before they get to the swamp."

The car was going a wild forty-five miles an hour across the open and as Macomber watched, the buffalo got bigger and bigger until he could see the gray, hairless, scabby look of one huge bull and how his neck was a part of his shoulders and the shiny black of his horns as he galloped a little behind the others that were strung out in that steady plunging gait; and then, the car swaying as though it had just jumped a road, they drew up close and he could see the plunging hugeness of the bull, and the dust in his sparsely haired hide, the wide boss of horn and his outstretched, wide-nostrilled muzzle, and he was raising his rifle when Wilson shouted, "Not from the car, you fool!" and he had no fear, only hatred, of Wilson, while the brakes clamped on and the car skidded, plowing sideways to an almost stop and Wilson was out on one side and he on the other, stumbling as his feet hit the still speeding-by of the earth, and then he was shooting at the bull as he moved away, hearing the bullets whunk into him, emptying his rifle at him as he moved steadily away, finally remembering to get his shots forward into the shoulder, and as he fumbled to re-load, he saw the bull was down. Down on his knees, his big head tossing, and seeing the other two still galloping he shot at the leader and hit him. He shot again and missed and he heard the *carawonging* roar as Wilson shot and saw the leading bull slide forward onto his nose.

"Get that other," Wilson said. "Now you're shooting!"

But the other bull was moving steadily at the same gallop and he missed, throwing a spout of dirt, and Wilson missed and the dust rose in a cloud and Wilson shouted, "Come on. He's too far!" and grabbed his arm and they were in the car again, Macomber and Wilson hanging on the sides and rocketing swayingly over the uneven ground, drawing up on the steady, plunging, heavy-necked, straight-moving gallop of the bull.

They were behind him and Macomber was filling his rifle, dropping shells onto the ground, jamming it, clearing the jam, then they were almost up with the bull when Wilson yelled "Stop," and the car skidded so that it almost swung over and Macomber fell forward onto his feet, slammed his bolt forward and fired as far forward as he could aim into the galloping, rounded black back, aimed and shot again, then again, then again and the bullets, all of them hitting, had no effect on the buffalo that he could see. Then Wilson shot, the roar deafening him, and he could see the bull stagger. Macomber shot again, aiming carefully, and down he came, onto his knees.

"All right," Wilson said. "Nice work. That's the three."

Macomber felt a drunken elation.

"How many times did you shoot?" he asked.

"Just three," Wilson said. "You killed the first bull. The biggest one. I helped you finish the other two. Afraid they might have got into cover. You had them killed. I was just mopping up a little. You shot damn well."

"Let's go to the car," said Macomber. "I want a drink."

"Got to finish off that buff first," Wilson told him. The buffalo was on his knees and he jerked his head furiously and bellowed in pig-eyed, roaring rage as they came toward him.

"Watch he doesn't get up," Wilson said. Then, "Get a little broadside and take him in the neck just behind the ear."

Macomber aimed carefully at the center of the huge, jerking, rage-driven neck and shot. At the shot the head dropped forward.

"That does it," said Wilson. "Got the spine. They're a hell of a looking thing, aren't they?"

"Let's get the drink," said Macomber. In his life he had never felt so good.

In the car Macomber's wife sat very white faced. "You were marvellous, darling," she said to Macomber. "What a ride."

"Was it rough?" Wilson asked.

"It was frightful. I've never been more frightened in my life."

"Let's all have a drink," Macomber said.

"By all means," said Wilson. "Give it to the Memsahib." She drank the neat whisky from the flask and shuddered a little when she swallowed. She handed the flask to Macomber who handed it to Wilson.

"It was frightfully exciting," she said. "It's given me a dreadful headache. I didn't know you were allowed to shoot them from cars though."

"No one shot from cars," said Wilson coldly.

"I mean chase them."

"Wouldn't ordinarily," Wilson said. "Seemed sporting enough to me while we were doing it. Taking more chance driving that way across the plain full of holes and one thing and another than hunting on foot. Buffalo could have charged us each time we shot if he liked. Gave him every chance. Wouldn't mention it to any one though. It's illegal if that's what you mean."

"It seemed very unfair to me," Margot said, "chasing those big helpless things in a motor car."

"Did it?" said Wilson.

"What would happen if they heard about it in Nairobi?"

"I'd lose my license for one thing. Other unpleasantnesses," Wilson said, taking a drink from the flask. "I'd be out of business."

"Really?"

"Yes, really."

"Well," said Macomber, and he smiled for the first time all day. "Now she has something on you."

"You have such a pretty way of putting things, Francis," Margot Macomber said. Wilson looked at them both. If a four-letter man marries a five-letter woman, he was thinking, what number of letters would their children be? What he said was, "We lost a gun-bearer. Did you notice it?"

"My God, no," Macomber said.

"Here he comes," Wilson said. "He's all right. He must have fallen off when we left the first bull."

Approaching them was the middle-aged gun-bearer, limping along in his knitted cap, khaki tunic, shorts and rubber sandals, gloomy-faced and disgusted looking. As he came up he called out to Wilson in Swahili and they all saw the change in the white hunter's face.

"What does he say?" asked Margot.

"He says the first bull got up and went into the bush," Wilson said with no expression in his voice.

"Oh," said Macomber blankly.

"Then it's going to be just like the lion," said Margot, full of anticipation.

"It's not going to be a damned bit like the lion," Wilson told her. "Did you want another drink, Macomber?"

"Thanks, yes," Macomber said. He expected the feeling he had had about the lion to come back but it did not. For the first time in his life he really felt wholly without fear. Instead of fear he had a feeling of definite elation.

"We'll go and have a look at the second bull," Wilson said. "I'll tell the driver to put the car in the shade."

"What are you going to do?" asked Margot Macomber.

"Take a look at the buff," Wilson said.

"I'll come."

"Come along."

The three of them walked over to where the second buffalo bulked blackly in the open, head forward on the grass, the massive horns swung wide.

"He's a very good head," Wilson said. "That's close to a fifty-inch spread."

Macomber was looking at him with delight.

"He's hateful looking," said Margot. "Can't we go into the shade?"

"Of course," Wilson said. "Look," he said to Macomber, and pointed. "See that patch of bush?"

"Yes."

"That's where the first bull went in. The gun-bearer said when he fell off the bull was down. He was watching us helling along and the other two buff galloping. When he looked up there was the bull up and looking at him. Gun-bearer ran like hell and the bull went off slowly into that bush."

"Can we go in after him now?" asked Macomber eagerly.

Wilson looked at him appraisingly. Damned if this isn't a strange one, he thought. Yesterday he's scared sick and today he's a ruddy fire-eater.

"No, we'll give him a while."

"Let's please go into the shade," Margot said. Her face was white, and she looked ill.

They made their way to the car where it stood under a single, wide-spreading tree and all climbed in.

"Chances are he's dead in there," Wilson remarked. "After a little we'll have a look."

Macomber felt a wild unreasonable happiness that he had never known before.

"By God, that was a chase," he said. "I've never felt any such feeling. Wasn't it marvellous, Margot?"

"I hated it."

"Why?"

"I hated it," she said bitterly. "I loathed it."

"You know I don't think I'd ever be afraid of anything again," Macomber said to Wilson. "Something happened in me after we first saw the buff and started after him. Like a dam bursting. It was pure excitement."

"Cleans out your liver," said Wilson. "Damn funny things happen to people."

Macomber's face was shining. "You know something did happen to me," he said. "I feel absolutely different."

His wife said nothing and eyed him strangely. She was sitting far back in the seat and Macomber was sitting forward talking to Wilson who turned sideways talking over the back of the front seat.

"You know, I'd like to try another lion," Macomber said. "I'm really not afraid of them now. After all, what can they do to you?"

"That's it," said Wilson. "Worst one can do is kill you. How does it go? Shakespeare. Damned good. See if I can remember. Oh, damned good. Used to quote it to myself at one time. Let's see. 'By my troth, I care not; a man can die but once; we owe God a death and let it go which way it will he that dies this year is quit for the next.' Damned fine, eh?"

He was very embarrassed, having brought out this thing he had lived by, but he had seen men come of age before and it always moved him. It was not a matter of their twenty-first birthday.

It had taken a strange chance of hunting, a sudden precipitation into action without opportunity for worrying beforehand, to bring this about with Macomber, but regardless of how it had happened it had most certainly happened. Look at the beggar now, Wilson thought. It's that some of them stay little boys so long, Wilson thought. Sometimes all their lives. Their figures stay boyish when they're fifty. The great American boy-men. Damned strange people. But he liked this Macomber now. Damned strange fellow. Probably meant the end of cuckoldry too. Well, that would be a damned good thing. Damned good thing. Beggar had probably been afraid all his life. Don't know what started it. But over now. Hadn't had time to be afraid with the buff. That and being angry too. Motor car too. Motor cars made it familiar. Be a damn fire eater now. He'd seen it in the war work the same way. More of a change than any loss of virginity. Fear gone like an operation. Something else grew in its place. Main thing a man had. Made him into a man. Women knew it too. No bloody fear.

From the far corner of the seat Margot Macomber looked at the two of them. There was no change in Wilson. She saw Wilson as she had seen him the day before when she had first realized what his great talent was. But she saw the change in Francis Macomber now.

"Do you have that feeling of happiness about what's going to happen?" Macomber asked, still exploring his new wealth.

"You're not supposed to mention it," Wilson said, looking in the other's face. "Much more fashionable to say you're scared. Mind you, you'll be scared too, plenty of times."

"But you *have* a feeling of happiness about action to come?"

"Yes," said Wilson. "There's that. Doesn't do to talk too much about all this. Talk the whole thing away. No pleasure in anything if you mouth it up too much."

"You're both talking rot," said Margot. "Just because you've chased some helpless animals in a motor car you talk like heroes."

"Sorry," said Wilson. "I have been gassing too much." She's worried about it already, he thought.

"If you don't know what we're talking about why not keep out of it?" Macomber asked his wife.

"You've gotten awfully brave, awfully suddenly," his wife said contemptuously, but her contempt was not secure. She was very afraid of something.

Macomber laughed, a very natural hearty laugh. "You know I *have*," he said. "I really have."

"Isn't it sort of late?" Margot said bitterly. Because she had done the best she could for many years back and the way they were together now was no one person's fault.

"Not for me," said Macomber.

Margot said nothing but sat back in the corner of the seat.

"Do you think we've given him time enough?" Macomber asked Wilson cheerfully.

"We might have a look," Wilson said. "Have you any solids left?"

"The gun-bearer has some."

Wilson called in Swahili and the older gun-bearer, who was skinning out one of the heads, straightened up, pulled a box of solids out of his pocket and brought them over to Macomber, who filled his magazine and put the remaining shells in his pocket.

"You might as well shoot the Springfield," Wilson said. "You're used to it. We'll leave the Mannlicher in the car with the Memsahib. Your gun-bearer can carry your heavy gun. I've this damned cannon. Now let me tell you about them." He had saved this until the last because he did not want to worry Macomber. "When a buff comes he comes with his head high and thrust straight out. The boss of the horns covers any sort of a brain shot. The only shot is straight into the nose. The only other shot is into his chest or, if you're to one side, into the neck or the shoulders. After they've been hit once they take a hell of a lot of killing. Don't try anything fancy. Take the easiest shot there is. They've finished skinning out that head now. Should we get started?"

He called to the gun-bearers, who came up wiping their hands, and the older one got into the back.

"I'll only take Kongoni," Wilson said. "The other can watch to keep the birds away."

As the car moved slowly across the open space toward the island of brushy trees that ran in a tongue of foliage along a dry water course that cut the open swale, Macomber felt his heart pounding and his mouth was dry again, but it was excitement, not fear.

"Here's where he went in," Wilson said. Then to the gun-bearer in Swahili, "Take the blood spoor."

The car was parallel to the patch of bush. Macomber, Wilson and the gun-bearer got down. Macomber, looking back, saw his wife, with the rifle by her side, looking at him. He waved to her and she did not wave back.

The brush was very thick ahead and the ground was dry. The middle-aged gun-bearer was sweating heavily and Wilson had his hat down over his eyes and his red neck showed just ahead of Macomber. Suddenly the gun-bearer said something in Swahili to Wilson and ran forward.

"He's dead in there," Wilson said. "Good work," and he turned to grip Macomber's hand and as they shook hands, grinning at each other, the gun-bearer shouted wildly and they saw him coming out of the bush sideways, fast as a crab, and the bull coming, nose out, mouth tight closed, blood dripping, massive head straight out, coming in a charge, his little pig eyes bloodshot as he looked at them. Wilson, who was ahead, was kneeling shooting, and Macomber, as he fired, unhearing his shot in the roaring of Wilson's gun, saw fragments like slate burst from the huge boss of the horns, and the head jerked, he shot again at the wide nostrils and saw the horn jolt again and fragments fly, and he did not see Wilson now and, aiming carefully, shot again with the buffalo's huge bulk almost on him and his rifle almost level with the on-coming head, nose out, and he could see the little wicked eyes and the head started to lower and he felt a sudden white-hot, blinding flash explode inside his head and that was all he ever felt.

Wilson had ducked to one side to get in a shoulder shot. Macomber had stood solid and shot for the nose, shooting a touch high each time and hitting the heavy horns, splintering and chipping them like hitting a slate roof, and Mrs. Macomber, in the car, had shot at the buffalo with the 6.5 Mannlicher as it seemed about to gore Macomber and had hit her husband about two inches up and a little to one side of the base of his skull.

Francis Macomber lay now, face down, not two yards from where the buffalo lay on his side and his wife knelt over him with Wilson beside her.

"I wouldn't turn him over," Wilson said.

The woman was crying hysterically.

"I'd get back in the car," Wilson said. "Where's the rifle?"

She shook her head, her face contorted. The gun-bearer picked up the rifle.

"Leave it as it is," said Wilson. Then, "Go get Abdulla so that he may witness the manner of the accident."

He knelt down, took a handkerchief from his pocket, and spread it over Francis Macomber's crew-cropped head where it lay. The blood sank into the dry, loose earth.

Wilson stood up and saw the buffalo on his side, his legs out, his thinly haired belly crawling with ticks. "Hell of a good bull," his brain registered automatically. "A good fifty inches, or better. Better." He called to the driver and told him to spread a blanket over the body and stay by it. Then he walked over to the motor car where the woman sat crying in the corner.

"That was a pretty thing to do," he said in a toneless voice. "He *would* have left you too."

"Stop it," she said.

"Of course it's an accident," he said. "I know that."

"Stop it," she said.

"Don't worry," he said. "There will be a certain amount of unpleasantness but I will have some photographs taken that will be very useful at the inquest. There's the testimony of the gun-bearers and the driver too. You're perfectly all right."

"Stop it," she said.

"There's a hell of a lot to be done," he said. "And I'll have to send a truck off to the lake to wireless for a plane to take the three of us into Nairobi. Why didn't you poison him? That's what they do in England."

"Stop it. Stop it. Stop it," the woman cried.

Wilson looked at her with his flat blue eyes.

"I'm through now," he said. "I was a little angry. I'd begun to like your husband."

"Oh, please stop it," she said. "Please, please stop it."

"That's better," Wilson said. "Please is much better. Now I'll stop."

Would you classify Margot as a bitch? Do you think Margot was a bitch before she married Francis? "How should a woman act when she discovers that her husband is a bloody coward?"

What does the narrator, Wilson, mean when he speaks of that "damn terrorism" women govern with? How does Margot control Francis? In what specific ways is her control determined by Francis' character? "Well, why doesn't he keep his wife where she belongs?"

Wilson describes American women as "the hardest in the world; the hardest, the cruelest, the most predatory and the most attractive and their men have softened or gone to pieces nervously as they have hardened." Compare this statement with de Sales's portrait of the American woman. Do you agree with either of these views?

When Wilson says that there is "no choice" but to go into the bush after the wounded lion, Francis says, "Why not leave him there?" Wilson then feels "as though he had opened the wrong door in a hotel and seen something shameful." Discuss how this simile works within the story.

INDIVIDUAL

7 AND

MASS

UNIT 19

PREWRITING

Henry Moore, *Reclining Figure*.

"Our novels are increasingly concerned with the figure of the faceless and anonymous hero, who is at once everyman and nobody . . . our sculpture [shows us] cryptic human figures . . . full of holes or gaps."

WILLIAM BARRETT

What is it that distinguishes, or fails to distinguish a person from the mass? For many writers, the essential distinction lies in the "act of choice." Either a man makes his own life choices or he allows forces outside him to make them for him. A man develops an "authentic," a genuine self when he exercises his freedom of choice; a "bogus" or false self when society, family, or friends control his decisions.

> 66 It is in the tiny quiet chamber of decision that the human being makes himself truly human. 99
>
> VAN CLEVE MORRIS

In this chapter we ask you to look at yourself and people around you and to observe when you, or they, actually make decisions or when forces from outside determine thoughts and actions. How does a person make efforts to develop an "authentic" self? In what ways are people controlled by forces opposed to their real desires? When are your desires your own and when are they not?

DISCUSSION

> 66 He who lets the world, or his own portion of it, choose his plan of life for him has no need of any other faculty than the apelike one of imitation. . . . One whose desires and impulses are not his own, has no character, no more than a steam engine has a character. . . . He who chooses his plan for himself employs all his faculties. 99
>
> JOHN STUART MILL

Recall a time when you let someone choose your course of action for you. Remember a time when you followed your own impulses.

> 66 [The] basic analogy is that of the human being to the atom. Just as the atom is controlled by the "field" or the surrounding atomic mass, so the human being is "attracted" by masses of energy, or "forces," in society around him and is controlled by them in the main lines of his . . . behaviour. 99
>
> GEORGE HOCHFIELD

What are some of the ways you are controlled by the society that surrounds you?

> 66 One finds oneself in a situation which one did not make for oneself, but given that situation one can choose various ways of behaving in it. . . . Man is free, beyond certain limits, to choose what he is to be and do. 99
>
> EDMUND WILSON

Some people even resent the fact that their freedom is limited by the law of gravity. What are a few other inescapable forces that restrict our freedom? Within these restrictions what freedoms are open to us?

> 66 The central doctrine [of existentialism] is that man is what he makes of himself: he is not predestined by a God, or by society, or by biology. He has a free will, and the responsibility which goes with it. If he refuses to choose or lets outside forces determine him, he is contemptible. 99
>
> WILLIAM FLINT THRALL, ADISON HIBBARD, and C. HUGH HOLMAN

Have you ever felt contemptible when you have not exercised your will? When you have exercised it?

> 66 *Hall:* Then even if I feel free, I'm still being controlled?
> *Skinner:* Absolutely; we're all controlled all the time. That's one thing I think we simply must recognize. You are controlling me, I am controlling you, parents control their children, children control their parents, employers control workers, workers control employers. We are controlled by the physical environment we live in. We are controlled by the social environment. The literature of freedom does not prepare us to deal with this. 99
>
> B. F. SKINNER in an interview with Elizabeth Hall

Give an example of a parent controlling his child; of a child controlling his parent. Do you think we are "all controlled all the time" and that our general notions of freedom do not prepare us to deal with this fact?

❝_Cogito, ergo sum._ (I think, therefore I am.)**❞**

RENÉ DESCARTES

❝_In dem ich wahle, bin ich._ (I choose, therefore I am.)**❞**

KARL JASPERS

How do you understand these quotations? Which seems more correct?

What do you make of this graffito? Try using the quotation that follows it or one of the preceding quotations to interpret it.

❝The Crowd is an abstraction and has no hands, but each individual has . . . two hands.**❞**

SÖREN KIERKEGAARD

❝Man lives in society. How are the supreme claims of the individual and the supreme claims of the collectivity to be reconciled? Aspects of this problem are innumerable. There is the voice of duty that says: "Become what thou art" and the voice of duty that says: "Obey the laws of the tribe. . . . Do as the neighbours think you should." There are the self-regarding claims of the ego-centred individual and the tyranny of the totalitarian state. How to find a right balance between freedom and authority, how to combine liberty with order, how to enable the individual to develop freely and at the same time achieve the greatest good of the greatest number: these are amongst the perennial questions, both of the personal and the public life.

P. W. MARTIN

From your experience give an example of the "self-regarding claims of the ego-centred individual"; of the "tyranny of the totalitarian state."

Giacometti, *Head.*

How do you understand this piece of sculpture?

CONNECTING EXERCISES

▶ A. Ask yourself: "Can I decide to act differently from the way I habitually do and then act that way?"

- Choose to change one small habitual reaction (the way you say hello to someone, the way you say goodby, the way you agree or disagree, or remain passive in conversation with friends).
- Write out how you plan to *be* in the situation. Indicate exactly how you choose to act, what you will say, and how you will feel.
- The following day, read over your notes and carry out your plan.
- Write what happened.

(One of the student themes at the end of this unit developed from this experiment. In it the writer plans to change her usually compliant relation to salesmen. In a shoe store she demands a pair of shoes too small for her feet.)

▶ B. In a TV show, advertisement, movie, book, or political event find an example of a person blindly obeying the laws of the tribe. Or find an example of a person satisfying ego-centered desires at the expense of the rights of others.

UNIT 20

WRITING EXAMPLE

An example or two can make your writing come alive. Use an example to clarify meaning, create interest, and to let your reader know there is a living human being at the other end of the line. You communicate with your reader not only with opinions and ideas but with your experience. Let him know not only what you believe but what you have done, heard, seen, or read.

The following passage illustrates the successful combination of opinion and example. Arguing that the uneducated sometimes write better than the educated, Professor F. L. Lucas says:

> "In language, as in life, it is possible to be perfectly correct—and yet perfectly tedious, or odious. "

And then he immediately follows this opinion with examples:

> " The illiterate last letter of the doomed Vanzetti was more moving than most professional orators; 18th Century ladies, who should have been spanked for their spelling, could yet write far better letters than most professors of English; and the talk of Synge's Irish peasants seems to me vastly more vivid than the later style of Henry James. Yet Synge averred that his characters owed far less of their eloquence to what he invented for them than to what he had overheard in the cottages of Wicklow and Kerry:

> *"Christy.* 'It's little you'll think if my love's a
> poacher's, or an earl's itself, when you'll feel my
> hands stretched around you, and I squeezing kisses
> on your puckered lips, till I'd feel a kind of pity for
> the Lord God in all ages sitting lonesome in His
> golden chair.'
>
> *"Pegeen.* 'That'll be right fun, Christy Mahon, and
> any girl would walk her heart out before she'd meet
> a young man was your like for eloquence, or talk at
> all.' "

We know what Lucas means. We know how he understands his opinion. We feel his presence and hear his voice through the examples he uses to make his point. If, when you write, you give examples, you will get something of the same effect.

After writing the first draft of a paper try reading it through to see if you have given your reader examples of what you mean. If you haven't, include an account of a *personal experience,* an *anecdote,* or a *first-hand observation* and then see if your paper doesn't read better.

In the following passage Daniel O'Leary gives a personal account of what he thought and did one night as he watched a poorly acted stage play:

> "Suddenly this thought came into my head: What
> would happen if I were to take off my boots, and fling
> one at Mr. . . . and one at Miss . . .? Could I give my fu-
> ture life such settled purpose that the act would take
> its place, not among whims, but among forms of in-
> tensity? I ran through my life from childhood and
> decided I could. 'You have not the courage,' I said,
> speaking in a low voice. 'I have,' said I, and began
> unlacing my boots."
>
> WILLIAM BUTLER YEATS

O'Leary gives us his experience. We see him unlacing his boots, and we know what he means.

Another way to give your reader an example of what you mean is to tell him what someone else said or did. In the following passage Martin Buber uses an anecdote to illustrate and support his idea:

> Every person born into this world represents
> something new, something that never existed before,
> something original and unique. It is the duty of every
> person . . . to know and consider that he is unique in
> the world in his particular character and that there
> has never been anyone like him in the world. . . .

> Every single man is a new thing in the world, and is called upon to fulfil his particularity in the world. . . . Every man's foremost task is the actualization of his unique, unprecedented and never-recurring potentialities, and not the repetition of something that another, and be it even the greatest, has already achieved.
>
> Zusya . . . said, a short while before his death: "In the world to come I shall not be asked: 'Why were you not Moses?' I shall be asked: 'Why were you not Zusya?' "

The anecdote given in the second paragraph of this passage anchors the abstraction given in the first. After we have forgotten the abstract words of the first paragraph we may remember Zusya and the words he spoke—and through this, remember Buber's idea.

Look for anecdotes in your reading. Listen for them in conversations. When you use an anecdote, make sure it fits the idea of your paper. An anecdote that doesn't clarify or support is worse than none.

One of the most convincing ways you can give your reader an example of what you mean is to observe and describe in detail some part of your subject: If you say that in some cases society has now gotten the better of the individual, go out and observe and then describe such an individual. You think the egocentric personality is in some ways harmful to the development of society: Show the reader an example of what you mean. You believe the white population fails to see the individual black or vice versa: Record an observation. Note the following use of example:

> Let us consider this waiter in the cafe. His movement is quick and forward, a little too precise, a little too rapid. He comes toward the patrons with a step a little too quick. He bends forward a little too eagerly; his voice, his eyes express an interest a little too solicitous for the order of the customer. Finally there he returns, trying to imitate in his walk the inflexible stiffness of some kind of automation while carrying his tray with the recklessness of a tight-rope walker by putting it in a perpetually unstable, perpetually broken equilibrium which he perpetually reestablishes by a light movement of the arm and hand. All his behavior seems to us a game. He applies himself to chaining his movements as if they were mechanisms, the one regulating the other; his gestures and even his voice seem to be mechanisms; he gives himself the quickness and pitiless rapidity of things. He is playing, he is amusing himself. But what is he playing? We need not watch long before

we can explain it: he is playing at being a waiter in a cafe. There is nothing here to surprise us.... This obligation is not different from that which is imposed on all tradesmen. Their condition is wholly one of ceremony. The public demands of them that they realize it as a ceremony; there is the dance of the grocer, of the tailor, of the auctioneer, by which they endeavor to persuade their clientele that they are nothing but a grocer, an auctioneer, a tailor. A grocer who dreams is offensive to the buyer, because such a grocer is not wholly a grocer. Society demands that he limit himself to his function as a grocer. **99**

JEAN-PAUL SARTRE

Sartre begins by bringing the waiter before our eyes ("carrying his tray with the recklessness of a tight-rope walker"). Next he interprets what he has shown us (the waiter "playing at being a waiter in a café"). Then he extends the implications of this one example by saying that the waiter is like other workmen. And then Sartre concludes with his idea ("Society demands that [the individual worker] limit himself to his function."). This general idea Sartre shows us through his description of the actions of one waiter.

If you go out with pencil and note pad to record a first-hand observation, try to avoid distorting what you see to make it fit your idea. Once you have seen the facts you may find that you have to alter your idea.

WRITING EXERCISES

▶ A. Reread the Martin Buber passage on pages 237–38.
- Ask yourself: "What is my 'particularity'?" "In what way am I different?"
- Ask yourself what life choices you will need to make to give your "particularity" a chance to develop—what kind of work, marriage, interests, activities will you need to choose?
- Write a paper about one of these choices—what the decision is, how you will make it, what results you expect.

▶ B. Ask yourself: "Does society mold the individual in a form?" Or, "In what ways does an individual avoid being cast in a mold?"
- Observe the actions of a student, a teacher, an administrator, an athlete, a member of any particular group.
- Record their actions.
- Can you generalize about one group on the basis of your observations?
- Write a pro and con paper using something you have recorded or something you have read as an example to support your position.

WRITING HINT:
USE CONCRETE SUBJECTS, ACTIVE VERBS.

There are no absolute guidelines for writing good sentences, only general suggestions for avoiding bad ones. The following suggestions may help you spot weak sentences in your compositions and help you revise them into stronger ones:

(1) *Almost always use a single, concrete word as subject, rather than a string of words headed by an abstract noun.*

Compare the following sentences. (The "original" is from the rough draft and the "revised" from the final draft of the student theme concluding this unit.

Original

The fact that the clerk puckered his mouth to keep from laughing is what made me almost lose control.

Revised

The clerk puckered his mouth to keep from laughing and I nearly lost control.

In the rough draft the writer chose the abstract word "fact" as the grammatical subject of her sentence. And once she did, she committed herself to say something about it. But "the fact" is not her real subject and it leads her into using a long string of words for the subject and *is* for the verb. As a result, the sentence is subject-heavy and verb-weak. In the revised sentence the writer broke her idea into two parts and made the subjects concrete and the verbs active:

The clerk		puckered
I	nearly	lost

The revision is clearer and more direct. Here the writer communicates with the reader immediately.

Look in your writing for sentences headed by groups of words like:

The *idea* which was discussed in class about choice is . . .
The *intention* of this theme is . . .
The *need* that I feel to do nothing is . . .
The *fact* being that I can make decisions is . . .
The *reason* for my not being able to decide on a career is . . .

If your sentences do not say clearly and directly what you want them to say, rewrite. If possible make what you are talking about the actor of your sentence—and whenever possible use a concrete word as subject.

❝One of the hardest things to learn in learning to write well is how to keep the noun phrases short. ❞

FRANCIS CHRISTENSEN

(2) *When the subject warrants it, use vigorous, active verbs rather than a form of the verb "to be."* "Is," "was," and "are" do little more than indicate a state of being (or function as an equal-sign) and lack the vitality of verbs like "jump," "clutch," and "throw," whose subjects perform an action.

You should not, however, always try to avoid the verb "to be" when your subject calls for one. If you are describing, defining, or explaining, some form of "to be" is often appropriate. In the Jean-Paul Sartre passage above (pages 238–39) note that "to be" is the verb used when the writer explains the example:

This *obligation* is not different . . .
Their *condition* is wholly one of ceremony. . . .

But note too that when the writer gives the example itself, most of the verbs indicate an action:

He [the waiter] comes toward the patron . . .
He   bends forward . . .
his *voice,* his *eyes* express an interest . . .

If nearly all the verbs in a piece of your writing are forms of "to be," try recasting some of your sentences to make the subject the actor. Or give an example of what you mean by letting something or someone do or say something; concrete subjects and active verbs should then come naturally. Your overall objective should be to communicate with your reader directly in straightforward prose.

❝I have something to tell you that I, for some reason, think is worth telling, and so I want to tell it as clearly and purely and simply as I can. ❞

KATHERINE ANNE PORTER

CLASS EXERCISE

▶A. Exchange papers or go through your own paper. Look for weak sentences. Revise.

▶B. Mark and discuss the subjects and verbs in the following theme. Note that the paper is one long example used to illustrate an abstract idea. This paper is based on notes taken for the Connecting Exercise on page 235.

Usually I buy what salesmen want to sell me instead of
what I ask for. I always act compliant, sweet, and
accepting. Last Friday I decided on an experiment: I
planned to go to two downtown shoestores the next
afternoon. In both stores I planned to ask for a size
3A pump in bright purple with a three-inch heel. (I
wear a size 8A.) I also planned to be outraged when the
shoe didn't fit and then leave the store in a huff. In
this way I hoped to change my usual passive attitude
into an aggressive one.

On Saturday at 2:20 p.m. I walked into Frank More
Shoes. There were three clerks, but no customers.
I sat down and a middle-aged man wearing a bright orange
tie waited on me. I asked for a purple pump in size
3A and said I had worn that size since I was fifteen.
The clerk changed his formerly sour expression, looked
surprised, and smiled slightly. "Size 3A?" he said
doubtfully. He tried to look at my shoe which I had
taken off, but I withheld it. He went to the stockroom
and returned with a silver pump in size 8A and explained
that they had no pumps in my size in purple. He was
amused and indulgent but polite. I did not contradict
him. I was unable to carry out this part of my plan. I
said thank you and left the store.

From Frank More Shoes I went to Penney's, sat down,
and asked for a purple pump size 3A to go with a
purple satin evening gown. The young man who waited
on me was dubious. He said, "Are you sure you want size
3A?" I replied, "I have a very small foot, as you can
see. My sister wore these shoes I have on and stretched
them out." He smiled halfheartedly as if to say,
"Why do I always get all the kooks?" He ran his hand
through his hair, shook his head, and went to the back
of the store. I could hear him talking and laughing
with another clerk. The other clerk appeared, a short,
stern-looking man who asked what I wanted. I repeated
my request. "We have no shoes of such description
and size," he said. I didn't know what to say and
thought to myself, "This is a silly thing to be doing."
Again I did not act outraged and left the store quietly.

I was able to exert some self-control and act
perfectly natural when I requested shoes five sizes too
small. But I had a shaky moment in Penney's after

saying my sister had stretched out my shoes and that I
had a very small foot. The clerk puckered his mouth to
keep from laughing and I nearly lost control.
    I didn't get angry. I did not want to cause a
scene. I am just too afraid to make myself conspicuous
in any situation. I guess I won't be able to change
my compliant attitude toward salesmen but I'll remember
this experiment for a long time to come. If I hadn't
tried it I would have thought anyone could change any
particular habit he wanted. Now I know that changing a
deeply ingrained behaviour is a challenge, if not an
impossibility.

Catherine Finnegan

▶ C. The following student paper was written from notes taken for Writing
Exercise B (page 239). What examples does the writer use to support her argument? Where has she gotten these arguments?

LIVING JUST ANYHOW

Few of us think for ourselves because most of us don't
question the basic assumptions held by our society. We
are all like the woman who always cut the ends from
a ham before baking it. When her husband asked her why,
she replied that her mother had always done so. When
she asked her mother why, her mother said that's the way
her mother had baked ham. When the woman asked her
grandmother why she had cut the ends from the ham, her
grandmother said that the pan she had was too small and
only by cutting off the ends would the ham fit. If
no one had questioned this process this particular
family could have wasted a lot of ham.
    As children we imitate our parents. In many ways
such imitation is not harmful but often we are unaware
that we are not really ourselves but an imitation of
others. We imitate our parents who have imitated their
parents who have imitated . . .
    Parents are only one influence. Social pressures
and ideas also determine how we act and think. Most of
the time we don't know what's happening. During World
War II, my sociology text says, many American men
went to Europe to fight. The United States Government

provided day care centers and public opinion condoned mothers working in factories and leaving their children in these centers. As soon as men returned from the war, women were no longer needed (or wanted) in the fac- tories. Suddenly the media barraged women with infor- mation about what would happen if mothers worked outside the home. The same debate is going on today, under different circumstances, of course, but with the same lack of individual thinking.

We probably don't realize how much our society decides our life. I was reading in National Geographic the other day that in Abkhazia, a region in the Soviet Republic of Georgia, people expect to live to be at least 100 years old. Most do. In the United States we program our lives to a shorter existence. It's possible that our society even influences the length of our lives as well as what we do during this length.

Unless we make the effort to think for ourselves, we will live just anyhow and anyhow usually means as grandmother did or as society wants us to.

Georginna Fujii

SELECTIONS

Stranger in the Village

JAMES BALDWIN

From all available evidence no black man had ever set foot in this tiny Swiss village before I came. I was told before arriving that I would probably be a "sight" for the village; I took this to mean that people of my complexion were rarely seen in Switzerland, and also that city people are always something of a "sight" outside of the city. It did not occur to me—possibly because I am an American—that there could be people anywhere who had never seen a Negro.

It is a fact that cannot be explained on the basis of the inaccessibility of the village. The village is very high, but it is only four hours from Milan and three hours from Lausanne. It is true that it is virtually unknown. Few people making plans for a holiday would elect to come here. On the other hand, the villagers are able, presumably, to come and go as they please—which they do: to another town at the foot of the mountain, with a population of approximately five thousand, the nearest place to see a movie or go to the bank. In the village there is no movie house, no bank, no library, no theater; very few radios, one jeep, one station wagon; and at the moment, one typewriter, mine, an invention which the woman next door to me here had never seen. There are about six hundred people living here, all Catholic—I conclude this from the fact that the Catholic church is open all year round, whereas the Protestant chapel, set off on a hill a little removed from the village, is open only in the summertime when the tourists arrive. There are four or five hotels, all closed now, and four or five *bistros*, of which, however, only two do any business during the winter.

"100 Boots at the Market" is part of a series of photographs by Los Angeles artist Eleanor Antin. Other pictures in the series—"100 Boots on the Way to Church," "100 Boots Parking"—reflect the same theme. What impression does this photograph give you?

These two do not do a great deal, for life in the village seems to end around nine or ten o'clock. There are a few stores, butcher, baker, *épicerie,* a hardware store, and a money-changer—who cannot change travelers' checks, but must send them down to the bank, an operation which takes two or three days. There is something called the *Ballet Haus,* closed in the winter and used for God knows what, certainly not ballet, during the summer. There seems to be only one schoolhouse in the village, and this for the quite young children; I suppose this to mean that their older brothers and sisters at some point descend from these mountains in order to complete their education—possibly, again, to the town just below. The landscape is absolutely forbidding, mountains towering on all four sides, ice and snow as far as the eye can reach. In this white wilderness, men and women and children move all day, carrying washing, wood, buckets of milk or water, sometimes skiing on Sunday afternoons. All week long boys and young men are to be seen shoveling snow off the rooftops, or dragging wood down from the forest in sleds.

The village's only real attraction, which explains the tourist season, is the hot spring water. A disquietingly high proportion of these tourists are cripples, or semi-cripples, who come year after year—from other parts of Switzerland, usually—to take the waters. This lends the village, at the height of the season, a rather terrifying air of sanctity, as though it were a lesser Lourdes. There is often something beautiful, there is always some-

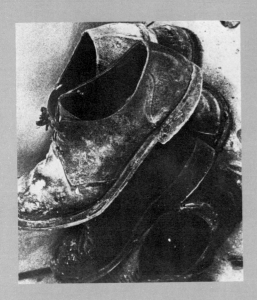

The shoes in this photograph belong to sculptor Henry Moore, whose work *Reclining Figure* opens this chapter. Compare the "100 Boots" with Henry Moore's shoes—in terms of their use, their individuality, their owners.

thing awful, in the spectacle of a person who has lost one of his faculties, a faculty he never questioned until it was gone, and who struggles to recover it. Yet people remain people, on crutches or indeed on deathbeds; and wherever I passed, the first summer I was here, among the native villagers or among the lame, a wind passed with me—of astonishment, curiosity, amusement, and outrage. That first summer I stayed two weeks and never intended to return. But I did return in the winter, to work; the village offers, obviously, no distractions whatever and has the further advantage of being extremely cheap. Now it is winter again, a year later, and I am here again. Everyone in the village knows my name, though they scarcely ever use it, knows that I come from America—though, this, apparently, they will never really believe: black men come from Africa—and everyone knows that I am the friend of the son of a woman who was born here, and that I am staying in their chalet. But I remain as much a stranger today as I was the first day I arrived, and the children shout *Neger! Neger!* as I walk along the streets.

It must be admitted that in the beginning I was far too shocked to have any real reaction. In so far as I reacted at all, I reacted by trying to be pleasant—it being a great part of the American Negro's education (long before he goes to school) that he must make people "like" him. This smile-and-the-world-smiles-with-you routine worked about as well in this situation as it had in the situation for which it was designed, which is to say that it did not work at all. No one, after all, can be liked whose human weight and complexity cannot be, or has not been, admitted. My smile was simply another unheard-of phenomenon which allowed them to see my teeth—they did not, really, see my smile and I began to think that, should I take to snarling, no one would notice any difference. All of the physical characteristics of the Negro which had caused me, in America, a very different and almost forgotten pain were nothing less than miraculous—or infernal—in the eyes of the village people. Some thought my hair was the color of tar, that it had the texture of wire, or the texture of cotton. It was jocularly suggested that I might let it all grow long and make myself a winter coat. If I sat in the sun for more than five minutes some daring creature was certain to come along and gingerly put his fingers on my hair, as though he were afraid of an electric shock, or put his hand on my hand, astonished that the color did not rub off. In all of this, in which it must be conceded there was the charm of genuine wonder and in which there were certainly no elements of intentional unkindness, there was yet no suggestion that I was human: I was simply a living wonder.

I knew that they did not mean to be unkind, and I know it now; it is necessary, nevertheless, for me to repeat this to myself each time that I walk out of the chalet. The children who shout *Neger!* have no way of knowing the echoes this sound raises in me. They are brimming with good humor and the more daring swell with pride when I stop to speak with them. Just the same, there are days when I cannot pause and smile, when I have no heart to play with them; when, indeed, I mutter sourly to myself, exactly as I muttered on the streets of a city these children have never seen, when I was no bigger than these children are now: *Your* mother *was a nigger.* Joyce is right about history being a nightmare—but it may be the nightmare from which no one *can* awaken. People are trapped in history and history is trapped in them.

There is a custom in the village—I am told it is repeated in many villages—of "buying" African natives for the purpose of converting them to Christianity. There stands in the church all year round a small box with a slot for money, decorated with a black figurine, and into this box the villagers drop their francs. During the *carnaval* which precedes Lent, two village children have their faces blackened—out of which bloodless darkness their blue eyes shine like ice—and fantastic horsehair wigs are placed on their blond heads; thus disguised, they solicit among the villagers for money for the missionaries in Africa. Between the box in the church and the blackened children, the village "bought" last year six or eight African natives. This was reported to me with pride by the wife of one of the *bistro* owners and I was careful to express astonishment and pleasure at the solicitude shown by the village for the souls of black folks. The *bistro* owner's wife beamed with a pleasure far more genuine than my own and seemed to feel that I might now breathe more easily concerning the souls of at least six of my kinsmen.

I tried not to think of these so lately baptized kinsmen, of the price paid for them, or the peculiar price they themselves would pay, and said nothing about my father, who having taken his own conversion too literally never, at bottom, forgave the white world (which he described as heathen) for having saddled him with a Christ in whom, to judge at least from their treatment of him, they themselves no longer believed. I thought of white men arriving for the first time in an African village, strangers there, as I am a stranger here, and tried to imagine the astounded populace touching their hair and marveling at the color of their skin. But there is a great difference between being the first white man to be seen by Africans and being the first black man to be seen by whites. The white man takes the astonishment as tribute, for he arrives to conquer and to convert the natives, whose inferiority in relation to himself is not even to be questioned; whereas I, without a thought of conquest, find myself among a people whose culture controls me, has even, in a sense, created me, people who have cost me more in anguish and rage than they will ever know, who yet do not even know of my existence. The astonishment with which I might have greeted them, should they have stumbled into my African village a few hundred years ago, might have rejoiced their hearts. But the astonishment with which they greet me today can only poison mine.

And this is so despite everything I may do to feel differently, despite my friendly conversations with the *bistro* owner's wife, despite their three-year-old son who has at last become my friend, despite the *saluts* and *bonsoirs* which I exchange with people as I walk, despite the fact that I know that no individual can be taken to task for what history is doing, or has done. I say that the culture of these people controls me—but they can scarcely be held responsible for European culture. America comes out of Europe, but these people have never seen America, nor have most of them seen more of Europe than the hamlet at the foot of their mountain. Yet they move with an authority which I shall never have; and they regard me, quite rightly, not only as a stranger in their village but as a suspect latecomer, bearing no credentials, to everything they have—however unconsciously—inherited.

For this village, even were it incomparably more remote and incredibly more primitive, is the West, the West onto which I have been so strangely grafted. These people cannot be, from the point of view of power, strangers anywhere in the world; they have made the modern world, in effect, even if they do not know it. The most illiterate among them is related, in a way that I am not, to Dante, Shakespeare, Michelangelo, Aeschylus, Da Vinci, Rembrandt, and Racine; the cathedral at Chartres says something to them which it cannot say to me, as indeed would New York's Empire State Building, should anyone here ever see it. Out of their hymns and dances come Beethoven and Bach. Go back a few centuries and they are in their full glory—but I am in Africa, watching the conquerors arrive.

The rage of the disesteemed is personally fruitless, but it is also absolutely inevitable; this rage, so generally discounted, so little understood even among the people whose daily bread it is, is one of the things that makes history. Rage can only with difficulty, and never entirely, be brought under the domination of the intelligence and is therefore not susceptible to any arguments whatever. This is a fact which ordinary representatives of the *Herrenvolk*, having never felt this rage and being unable to imagine, quite fail to understand. Also, rage cannot be hidden, it can only be dissembled. This dissembling deludes the thoughtless, and strengthens rage and adds, to rage, contempt. There are, no doubt, as many ways of coping with the resulting complex of tensions as there are black men in the world, but no black man can hope ever to be entirely liberated from this internal warfare—rage, dissembling, and contempt having inevitably accompanied his first realization of the power of white men. What is crucial here is that, since white men represent in the black man's world so heavy a weight, white men have for black men a reality which is far from being reciprocal; and hence all black men have toward all white men an attitude which is designed, really, either to rob the white man of the jewel of his naïveté, or else to make it cost him dear.

The black man insists, by whatever means he finds at his disposal, that the white man cease to regard him as an exotic rarity and recognize him as a human being. This is a very charged and difficult moment, for there is a great deal of will power involved in the white man's naïveté. Most people are not naturally reflective any more than they are naturally malicious, and the white man prefers to keep the black man at a certain human remove because it is easier for him thus to preserve his simplicity and avoid being called to account for crimes committed by his forefathers, or his neighbors. He is inescapably aware, nevertheless, that he is in a better position in the world than black men are, nor can he quite put to death the suspicion that he is hated by black men therefore. He does not wish to be hated, neither does he wish to change places, and at this point in his uneasiness he can scarcely avoid having recourse to those legends which white men have created about black men, the most usual effect of which is that the white man finds himself enmeshed, so to speak, in his own language which describes hell, as well as the attributes which lead one to hell, as being as black as night.

Every legend, moreover, contains its residuum of truth, and the root function of language is to control the universe by describing it. It is of quite considerable significance that black men remain, in the imagination, and in overwhelming numbers in fact, beyond the disciplines of salvation; and this despite the fact that the West has been "buying" African natives for centuries. There is, I should hazard, an instantaneous necessity to be divorced from this so visibly unsaved stranger, in whose heart, moreover, one cannot guess what dreams of vengeance are being nourished; and, at the same time, there are few things on earth more attractive than the idea of the unspeakable liberty which is allowed the unredeemed. When, beneath the black mask, a human being begins to make himself felt one cannot escape a certain awful wonder as to what kind of human being it is. What one's imagination makes of other people is dictated, of course, by the laws of one's own personality and it is one of the ironies of black-white relations that, by means of what the white man imagines the black man to be, the black man is enabled to know who the white man is.

I have said, for example, that I am as much a stranger in this village today as I was the first summer I arrived, but this is not quite true. The villagers wonder less about the texture of my hair than they did then, and wonder rather more about me. And the fact that their wonder now exists on another level is reflected in their attitudes and in their eyes. There are the children who make those delightful, hilarious, sometimes astonishingly grave overtures of friendship in the unpredictable fashion of children; other children, having been taught that the devil is a black man, scream in genuine anguish as I approach. Some of the older women never pass without a friendly greeting, never pass, indeed, if it seems that they will be able to engage me in conversation; other women look down or look away or rather contemptuously smirk. Some of the men drink with me and suggest that I learn how to ski—partly, I gather, because they cannot imagine what I would look like on skis—and want to know if I am married, and ask questions about my *métier*. But some of the men have accused *le sale nègre*—behind my back—of stealing wood and there is already in the eyes of some of them that peculiar, intent, paranoiac malevolence which one sometimes surprises in the eyes of American white men when, out walking with their Sunday girl, they see a Negro male approach.

There is a dreadful abyss between the streets of this village and the streets of the city in which I was born, between the children who shout *Neger!* today and those who shouted *Nigger!* yesterday—the abyss is experience, the American experience. The syllable hurled behind me today expresses, above all, wonder: I am a stranger here. But I am not a stranger in America and the same syllable riding on the American air expresses the war my presence has occasioned in the American soul.

For this village brings home to me this fact: that there was a day, and not really a very distant day, when Americans were scarcely Americans at all but discontented Europeans, facing a great unconquered continent and strolling, say, into a marketplace and seeing black men for the first time. The shock this spectacle afforded is suggested, surely, by the promptness with which they decided that these black men were not really men but cattle. It is true that the necessity on the part of the settlers of the New World of reconciling their moral assumptions with the fact—and the necessity—of slavery enhanced immensely the charm of this idea, and it is also true that this idea expresses, with a truly American bluntness, the attitude which to varying extents all masters have had toward all slaves.

But between all former slaves and slave-owners and the drama which begins for Americans over three hundred years ago at Jamestown, there are at least two differences to be observed. The American Negro slave could not suppose, for one thing, as slaves in past epochs had supposed and often done, that he would ever be able to wrest the power from his master's hands. This was a supposition which the modern era, which was to bring about such vast changes in the aims and dimensions of power, put to death; it only begins, in unprecedented fashion, and with dreadful implications, to be resurrected today. But even had this supposition persisted with undiminished force, the American Negro slave could not have used it to lend his condition dignity, for the reason that this supposition rests on another: that the slave in exile yet remains related to his past, has some means—if only in memory—of revering and sustaining the forms of his former life, is able, in short, to maintain his identity.

This was not the case with the American Negro slave. He is unique among the black men of the world in that his past was taken from him, almost literally, at one blow. One wonders what on earth the first slave found to say to the first dark child he bore. I am told that there are Haitians able to trace their ancestry back to African kings, but any American

Negro wishing to go back so far will find his journey through time abruptly arrested by the signature on the bill of sale which served as the entrance paper for his ancestor. At the time—to say nothing of the circumstances—of the enslavement of the captive black man who was to become the American Negro, there was not the remotest possibility that he would ever take power from his master's hands. There was no reason to suppose that his situation would ever change, nor was there, shortly, anything to indicate that his situation had ever been different. It was his necessity, in the words of E. Franklin Frazier, to find a "motive for living under American culture or die." The identity of the American Negro comes out of this extreme situation, and the evolution of this identity was a source of the most intolerable anxiety in the minds and the lives of his masters.

For the history of the American Negro is unique also in this: that the question of his humanity, and of his rights therefore as a human being, became a burning one for several generations of Americans, so burning a question that it ultimately became one of those used to divide the nation. It is out of this argument that the venom of the epithet *Nigger!* is derived. It is an argument which Europe has never had, and hence Europe quite sincerely fails to understand how or why the argument arose in the first place, why its effects are frequently disastrous and always so unpredictable, why it refuses until today to be entirely settled. Europe's black possessions remained—and do remain—in Europe's colonies, at which remove they represented no threat whatever to European identity. If they posed any problem at all for the European conscience, it was a problem which remained comfortingly abstract: in effect, the black man, as a *man*, did not exist for Europe. But in America, even as a slave, he was an inescapable part of the general social fabric and no American could escape having an attitude toward him. Americans attempt until today to make an abstraction of the Negro, but the very nature of these abstractions reveals the tremendous effects the presence of the Negro has had on the American character.

When one considers the history of the Negro in America it is of the greatest importance to recognize that the moral beliefs of a person, or a people, are never really as tenuous as life—which is not moral—very often causes them to appear; these create for them a frame of reference and a necessary hope, the hope being that when life has done its worst they will be enabled to rise above themselves and to triumph over life. Life would scarcely be bearable if this hope did not exist. Again, even when the worst has been said, to betray a belief is not by any means to have put oneself beyond its power; the betrayal of a belief is not the same thing as ceasing to believe. If this were not so there would be no moral standards in the world at all. Yet one must also recognize that morality is based on ideas and that all ideas are dangerous—dangerous because ideas can only lead to action and where the action leads no man can say. And dangerous in this respect: that confronted with the impossibility of remaining faithful to one's beliefs, and the equal impossibility of becoming free of them, one can be driven to the most inhuman excesses. The ideas on which American beliefs are based are not, though Americans often seem to think so, ideas which originated in America. They came out of Europe. And the establishment of democracy on the American continent was scarcely as radical a break with the past as was the necessity, which Americans faced, of broadening this concept to include black men.

This was, literally, a hard necessity. It was impossible, for one thing, for Americans to abandon their beliefs, not only because these beliefs alone seemed able to justify the sacrifices they had endured and the blood that they had spilled, but also because these beliefs afforded them their only bulwark against a moral chaos as absolute as the physical chaos of the continent it was their destiny to conquer. But in the situation in which Americans found themselves, these beliefs threatened an idea which, whether or not one likes to think so, is the very warp and woof of the heritage of the West, the idea of white supremacy.

Americans have made themselves notorious by the shrillness and the brutality with which they have insisted on this idea, but they did not invent it; and it has escaped the world's notice that those very excesses of which Americans have been guilty imply a certain, unprecedented uneasiness over the idea's life and power, if not, indeed, the idea's validity. The idea of white supremacy rests simply on the fact that white men are the creators of civilization (the present civilization, which is the only one that matters; all previous civilizations are simply "contributions" to our own) and are therefore civilization's guardians and defenders. Thus it was impossible for Americans to accept the black man as one of themselves, for to do so was to jeopardize their status as white men. But not so to accept him was to deny his human reality, his human weight and complexity, and the strain of denying the overwhelmingly undeniable forced Americans into rationalizations so fantastic that they approached the pathological.

At the root of the American Negro problem is the necessity of the American white man to find a way of living with the Negro in order to be able to live with himself. And the history of this problem can be reduced to the means used by Americans—lynch law and law, segregation and legal acceptance, terrorization and concession—either to come to terms with this necessity, or to find a way around it, or (most usually) to find a way of doing both these things at once. The resulting spectacle, at once foolish and dreadful, led someone to make the quite accurate observation that "the Negro-in-America is a form of insanity which overtakes white men."

In this long battle, a battle by no means finished, the unforeseeable effects of which will be felt by many future generations, the white man's motive was the protection of his identity; the black man was motivated by the need to establish an identity. And despite the terrorization which the Negro in America endured and endures sporadically until today, despite the cruel and totally inescapable ambivalence of his status in this country, the battle for his identity has long ago been won. He is not a visitor to the West, but a citizen there, an American; as American as the Americans who despise him, the Americans who fear him, the Americans who love him—the Americans who became less than themselves, or rose to be greater than themselves by virtue of the fact that the challenge he represented was inescapable. He is perhaps the only black man in the world whose relationship to white men is more terrible, more subtle, and more meaningful than the relationship of bitter possessed to uncertain possessors. His survival depended, and his development depends, on his ability to turn his peculiar status in the Western world to his own advantage and, it may be, to the very great advantage of that world. It remains for him to fashion out of his experience that which will give him sustenance, and a voice.

The cathedral at Chartres, I have said, says something to the people of this village which it cannot say to me; but it is important to understand that this cathedral says something to me which it cannot say to them. Perhaps they are struck by the power of the spires, the glory of the windows; but they have known God, after all, longer than I have known him, and in a different way, and I am terrified by the slippery bottomless well to be found in the crypt, down which heretics were hurled to death, and by the obscene, inescapable gargoyles jutting out of the stone and seeming to say that God and the devil can never be divorced. I doubt that the villagers think of the devil when they face a cathedral because they have never been identified with the devil. But I must accept the status which myth, if nothing else, gives me in the West before I can hope to change the myth.

Yet, if the American Negro has arrived at his identity by virtue of the absoluteness of his estrangement from his past, American white men still nourish the illusion that there is some means of recovering the European innocence, of returning to a state in which black men do not exist. This is one of the greatest errors Americans can make. The identity they fought so hard to protect has, by virtue of that battle, undergone a change: Americans are as unlike any other white people in the world as it is possible to be. I do not think, for example, that it is too much to suggest that the American vision of the world—which allows so little reality, generally speaking, for any of the darker forces in human life, which tends until today to paint moral issues in glaring black and white—owes a great deal to the battle waged by Americans to maintain between themselves and black men a human separation which could not be bridged. It is only now beginning to be borne in on us—very faintly, it must be admitted, very slowly, and very much against our will—that this vision of the world is dangerously inaccurate, and perfectly useless. For it protects our moral high-mindedness at the terrible expense of weakening our grasp of reality. People who shut their eyes to reality simply invite their own destruction, and anyone who insists on remaining in a state of innocence long after that innocence is dead turns himself into a monster.

The time has come to realize that the interracial drama acted out on the American continent has not only created a new black man, it has created a new white man, too. No road whatever will lead Americans back to the simplicity of this European village where white men still have the luxury of looking on me as a stranger. I am not, really, a stranger any longer for any American alive. One of the things that distinguishes Americans from other people is that no other people has ever been so deeply involved in the lives of black men, and vice versa. This fact faced, with all its implications, it can be seen that the history of the American Negro problem is not merely shameful, it is also something of an achievement. For even when the worst has been said, it must also be added that the perpetual challenge posed by this problem was always, somehow, perpetually met. It is precisely this black-white experience which may prove of indispensable value to us in the world we face today. This world is white no longer, and it will never be white again.

How does Baldwin use his experience in the Swiss village as an example to discuss the subject of the Black's position in America?

Compare the reactions to the individual Black by the Swiss and by the Americans.

Baldwin writes that the Black's presence in America has occasioned a war in the American soul. What has been the White's response to this war? What has been the Black's response?

The Unknown Citizen

W. H. AUDEN

(To JS/07/M/378
This Marble Monument
Is Erected by the State

He was found by the Bureau of Statistics to be
One against whom there was no official complaint,
And all the reports on his conduct agree
That, in the modern sense of an old-fashioned word, he was a saint,
For in everything he did he served the Greater Community.
Except for the War till the day he retired
He worked in a factory and never got fired,
But satisfied his employers, Fudge Motors Inc.
Yet he wasn't a scab or odd in his views,
For his Union reports that he paid his dues,
(Our report on his Union shows it was sound)
And our Social Psychology workers found
That he was popular with his mates and liked a drink.
The Press are convinced that he bought a paper every day
And that his reactions to advertisements were normal in every way.
Policies taken out in his name prove that he was fully insured,
And his Health-card shows he was once in hospital but left it cured.
Both Producers Research and High-Grade Living declare
He was fully sensible to the advantages of the Installment Plan
And had everything necessary to the Modern Man,
A phonograph, a radio, a car and a frigidaire.
Our researchers into Public Opinion are content
That he held the proper opinions for the time of year;
When there was peace, he was for peace; when there was war, he went.

He was married and added five children to the population,
Which our Eugenist says was the right number for a parent of his
    generation,
And our teachers report that he never interfered with their education.
Was he free? Was he happy? The question is absurd:
Had anything been wrong, we should certainly have heard.

Was he free? Was he happy? What choices did the unknown citizen make?

Is it possible for the individual to serve both himself and the "Greater Community"? Is it possible for a person to hold "the proper opinions for the time of year" and still make his own choices?

Describe a person you know who is the opposite of the unknown citizen. Is he or she free? Happy?

still do I keep my look, my identity . . .

GWENDOLYN BROOKS

Each body has its art, its precious prescribed
Pose, that even in passion's droll contortions, waltzes,
Or push of pain—or when a grief has stabbed,
Or hatred hacked—is its, and nothing else's.
Each body has its pose. No other stock
That is irrevocable, perpetual
And its to keep. In castle or in shack.
With rags or robes. Through good, nothing, or ill.
And even in death a body, like no other
On any hill or plain or crawling cot
Or gentle for the lilyless hasty pall
(Having twisted, gagged, and then sweet-ceased to bother),
Shows the old personal art, the look. Shows what
It showed at baseball. What it showed in school.

In one sentence try summarizing the statement this poem makes.

Through what events does the body keep its identity?

Describe somebody's body, showing what is unique about it.

Why Don't You Look Where You're Going?

WALTER VAN TILBURG CLARK

White as a sainted leviathan, but too huge for even God to have imagined it, the liner played eastward easily. It swam at a much greater speed than appeared, for it was alone in open ocean, and there were only the waves to pass.

Everyone on board was comfortable, even satisfied. The sea was a light summer one, still blue, although the sun was far gone toward the mountain range of fog on the horizon astern. Its swelling, and the rippling of the swells, could not give the slightest motion to the vessel, whose long hulk glanced through it as through warm and even air. The sense of well-being in the passengers was made firm by the knowledge that their fate was somebody else's responsibility for the next three days. There was nothing an ordinary mortal could do about a ship like this; it was as far out of his realm as the mechanics of heaven. He could talk about it, as he might about one of the farther galaxies, in order to experience the almost extinct pleasure of awe, but he could not do anything about it, and what was even more comfortable, he could not be expected to do anything about it.

Even the crew shared this un-Olympian calm, for the liner was a self-sufficient creature who, once put upon her course, pursued it independently, with gently rhythmic joy. The wheel took care of itself, the fuel sped upon quick wires, the warm and supple steel joints rose and fell, self-oiled to perfect limberness. More like a white Utopian city than any the earth will ever bear, she parted the subservient waters and proceeded.

A school of flying fish, which looked like dragonflies from the upper deck, broke water for an instant and fled back, no more than a brief proof of the pace of the liner.

The tall man in the gray topcoat stopped his circumambulation and peered toward the smoke of dusk rising out of the ocean. The woman in white flannel paused impatiently beyond him.

"What's that?" he asked.

"What?"

"There, ahead. No, a little more to the right. Like a log or something. See?"

"No."

"Well, look. There." He leaned over the rail and pointed.

"No. Oh, yes. Seaweed, I suppose."

"No, that wouldn't show; not so far. It sticks up."

The man's gesture drew other passengers to the rail. A boy in a white jacket was moving through them, clinking a musical triangle, and intoning, "First call to dinner; first call to dinner," but they were impressed by the pointing finger, and remained at the rail.

"What is it?" asked the stout, moustached man in linen knickers.

"I don't know," said the tall man, not looking around because his discovery was so small on the darkening sea.

"There's something, though," he added, and pointed again.

The other passengers also leaned over and peered hopefully. Those too far along to have heard the tall man's explanation looked at the sea vaguely, then at the people who were nearer the tall man, then at the sea again.

"He says there's something," the fat man informed them.

Then, "Oh, yes, I see it now." He pointed also. "There. See it? Still too far away to tell what it is, though." He appeared to think for a moment, and produced an original idea.

"We ought to pass it pretty close," he said, protruding his lower lip and puckering his mouth as a sign that he was considering carefully. "Pretty close, I should say, as we're going now."

The passengers exclaimed gratefully, and were able to look intelligent when they returned to peering. They felt better. Anybody could see by their backs that they felt better; much more decisive. As landsmen they were grateful for the discovery. Other walkers, coming to the side of the vessel, asked questions, and were almost told what the fat man had said. But there was never any citation of authority, or any admission of the pioneering of the tall man. The reputation for discovery was not easy to resign.

The latecomers remained until the entire rail was lined, and the number of the gathering excited each individual in it; the expected event attained mythological proportions.

This scene was re-enacted on the other three decks, although the watchers were fewer because the decks were closed and all the watching had to be done from port-holes. Children jumped up and down behind their parents, inquiring in exasperated crescendos. Occasionally a beleaguered father or mother offered an unsatisfactory explanation, or held a child up to see that there was only water. The entire starboard wall of the gliding city was crowded with curious people, and their curiosity was toughened by their desire to be first in stating the nature of the discovery. Since the discovery had already been made, it was now accounted common property, and recognition of the object seemed more important. The first idle speculation died, as meriting scorn; most of the watchers were quiet and intent.

The young man with the fine blond hair left the rail and returned almost at once with a victorious air and a pair of binoculars. These he fixed to his eyes, turned upon the focal point, and began to manipulate with nimble fingers. At once others whose cabins were close also got binoculars. They appeared determined, as if to say the original inspiration was not what mattered here, but the use made of it. Those who either had no binoculars or had to go too far to get them, divided their attention between the ocean off the starboard bow and the blond young man, who had taken on the shining aspect of the clairvoyant. They watched his face minutely for signs of recognition, and were affected by his slightest movement. He bore their worship grandly, almost with an air of not suspecting it.

"What is it?" they asked.

"I can't make it out yet." He continued to adjust the binoculars.

When he ceased fingering and held the glasses steadily, they asked again, "What is it?" and "Can you see it now?"

"Yes," he said, "I think I can." But he withheld the information, as one who will not be pressed into a hasty, and therefore possibly erroneous, conclusion. He fingered the binoculars just the perfect trifle more. Even the tall man in the gray coat abandoned his scrutiny and turned a tanned and bony face, drawn by staring, toward the blond young man.

The object was now close enough so that its location could be clearly marked by everyone at the moments when it appeared on the crest of a billow and balanced before beginning the long, gentle descent into the concealing trough. It might have been a great, triangular fin, if it had been much closer.

"Whatever it is, it had better look out. We're going right for it."

The fat man's suggestion that it might be a portion of the super-structure of a derelict caused a pleasant worry.

"I've heard," said a man with spectacles, and a checkered cap over a big nose, "I've heard they're often heavy enough below water to sink a good large boat." He spoke with quiet joy.

The tall man, who had been thinking about the fat man's suggestion, snorted.

"What part?" he challenged.

But, although the fat man was not insensible of the challenge, it was neglected because the blond young man had become signally rigid behind his binoculars.

He overplayed his pause, however, and a square, masculine, young woman said factually and loudly, "It's a boat," and held her glasses a moment longer before lowering them to accept adulation in person.

"Yes," admitted the young man. "I was just going to say it's a boat." He added, "That thing that sticks up is a sail, a kind of triangular sail," and felt that this remark justified his lowering his glasses also, and looking around.

By now the boat was near enough so that the pace of the liner made it appear to draw nearer very rapidly. Since it was known to be a boat, and everyone could see it lay directly in the path of the liner, the guesses about what a small boat could be doing in mid-ocean gave way to irritation because it was doing nothing to save itself.

"We'd make matchwood of it," stated the fat man angrily.

"It would go to the bottom," declared the young man violently, "to the bottom, like a plummet."

The masculine young lady disagreed. "Not to the bottom; it would reach a level of suspension much sooner. The water is over three thousand feet deep here."

The other passengers rebuked her heartlessness with silence.

"Well, I do wish he'd wake up. I wish he'd get out of the way," complained the matron whose twin six-year-olds were extending her by their attempts to see over and under the rail. The passengers warmed to her humanity, and understanding that the young woman was quelled, all leaned over the rail and stared anxiously ahead.

High overhead the whistle of the liner hissed and squealed abortively, and then settled into a long, mournful, gigantic moo.

Immediately a man appeared in the small boat. The liner was so close upon him that the passengers could see him look up startled. He became very active. He leaned over, stood up, disappeared behind the box-like cabin, and reappeared almost at once. He was working rapidly with his hands, glancing up frequently without stopping his work. The passengers knew he was frightened. Then the triangular sail swung slowly across the box-like cabin, slatted idly, two, three, four times, and slowly filled out like a breathing chest. The man, energetic as a jumping-jack, worked at the rail for an instant, then threw himself aft, slipped the noose from the tiller, and projected himself, chest and shoulders, against the bar. The sail flapped limp again, but only once, and suddenly drew a deep breath. The little boat heeled over until it was nearly awash, slithered along at a dog-walk during the ascent of one billow, then perfectly bit in and skittered off toward safety.

Four times the height of his sail above him, the bow of the liner passed over the tiny man in his cockpit, and left him valiantly awash, bobbing under four, three-hundred-foot tiers of fascinated eyes. They could see that he had no hat, that he wore a black beard, and that his pants were held up by a knotted rope. He braced the tiller with a knee, raised both fists over his head, and shook them at the liner. The passengers were immensely relieved. The women laughed, and the men leaned far over the rail to shout at him between cupped hands. They saw that he was shouting also; his mouth was wide open and his teeth showed in his beard. Everyone became silent and listened. But there was such a rush of white water back from the stem, and the wind wuthered so in the railing, that the man appeared to be trying to free his jaw from a cramp, making no sound. He addressed them continuously and energetically, but not until the liner had nearly drawn its whole length by did a wind flaw bring up his voice with an item of his lecture. The passengers aft repeated it with glee; indeed they wriggled with glee at it, their bodies and their faces.

"He said, 'Why don't you look where you're going?' "

Everyone was charmed.

They leaned over farther and farther to watch the little boat as it diminished. Why don't you look where you're going? That was good. That was conceit for you; a man who didn't count himself less than he was worth. "Everybody's out of step but Johnny," sang the young man with the blond hair. He sang it at the man in the little boat, who was obviously too far away to hear, but everybody else appreciated it; they leaned back and looked at the young man with many kinds of grins and smiles to appreciate it, and quickly leaned over the rail again to watch.

The stern of the little boat said to them, *"The Flying Dutchman—Rockport—Me."* They became silent, and watched the puppet of a bearded man sit to his tiller and labor earnestly to navigate the wake of the liner. A great many of them unconsciously went farther and farther aft, to keep the "Flying Dutchman" in sight. The stern of the liner was crowded, and all the faces were serious and fixed.

When the little man was far enough astern to feel secure, and had his boat properly angled into the heave of the wake, he underwent a change of heart. The watchers could just see him, yet everybody recognized that he was standing up again and waving. Every face brightened spontaneously, and the afterdeck blossomed windily with hands, handkerchiefs, hats and caps.

The fat man bellowed astoundingly through the trumpet of his hands, "Good luck, sailor!"

" 'Why don't you look where you're going?' " he repeated gruffly. " 'Why don't you look where you're going?' That's good."

The masculine young lady stood with her hands on the rail and peered wistfully under the Andes of the cloud bank, where the tiny, black triangle of sail was only now and then visible, getting less so.

Contrast the choices open to the people on the ocean liner and to the man in the sailboat.

Clark describes the liner as "a self-sufficient creature who, once put upon her course, pursued it independently." Compare the liner and its passengers with society and its citizens.

After the man in the sailboat yells to the ocean liner "Why don't you look where you're going?", the author says, "Everyone was charmed." Why is the crowd charmed?

How would you characterize the man in the boat: egocentric, self-willed, individualistic?

KNOWN

AND

UNKNOWN

UNIT 22

PREWRITING

Mătrăgună, mătrăgună
Mărită-mă peste-o lună
De nu 'n asta 'n cealălaltă,
Mărită-mă după olaltă.

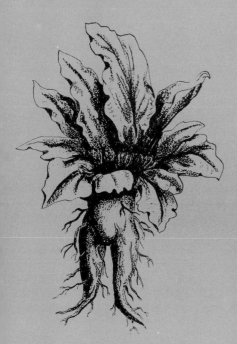

"Of all the plants that are sought out in Romania for their magical virtues . . . not one equals the mandragora, or mandrake. . . . The root of the mandragora can have a direct influence on the vital forces of man or Nature; it can arrange marriages for girls, bring luck in love and fertility in marriage; it can make cows give more milk; it has a beneficial effect on business affairs, it increases wealth, and, in general, brings prosperity, harmony, and so on. The magical properties of the mandragora can also be turned against another person, for example, against a girl, so that young men of the village will no longer ask her to dance, or against an enemy, to make him fall ill or even go mad."

MIRCEA ELIADE

Are there two "realities": one we know through our senses and reason; and another we don't know—at least not in the ways we usually know things? Is there an unknown world around us, or within us, a mysterious, enigmatic world here beyond our senses, beyond our reason, a world that we might contact through magic or intuition?

If there are two worlds, which is more real? Is the physical world an illusion, a shadowy imitation of an unseen real world beyond or behind it? Or is the supernatural world an illusion, empty imagination?

If the doors to the known world are sense perception and reason, what are the doors to the unknown, if it exists? People have claimed entrance to the unknown through mandrake root, mushrooms, Jimson weed, meditation, sorcery, prayer, magic, witches' brew, fasting, contemplation, and suffering.

In this chapter we ask you to write about one or both of these worlds. Have you at any time had an experience you believe was beyond sense and reason: a time when you felt a deep emotional-psychological awakening? Do you deny the possibility of such an experience? Do you have a reasonable explanation for what some people assume to be a mystical experience?

Use the discussion and writing exercises in this chapter to find material and a focus for your paper.

DISCUSSION

66 Hogen, a Chinese Zen teacher, lived alone in a small temple in the country. One day four traveling monks appeared and asked if they might make a fire in his yard to warm themselves.

While they were building the fire, Hogen heard them arguing about subjectivity and objectivity. He joined them and said: "There is a big stone. Do you consider it to be inside or outside your mind?"

One of the monks replied: "From the Buddhist viewpoint everything is an objectification of mind, so I would say that the stone is inside my mind."

"Your head must feel very heavy," observed Hogen, "if you are carrying around a stone like that in your mind." 99

A ZEN STORY

You see a rock. What is inside your mind and what is outside? Which is more real for you, what is inside your mind or what is outside?

❝The handiest of the marks by which I classify a state of mind as mystical is negative. The subject of it immediately says that it defies expression, that no adequate report of its contents can be given in words. It follows from that that its quality must be directly experienced; it cannot be imparted or transferred to others. . . . One must have musical ears to know the value of a symphony; one must have been in love oneself to understand a lover's state of mind. Lacking the heart or ear, we cannot interpret the musician or the lover justly, and are even likely to consider him weak-minded or absurd. The mystic finds that most of us accord to his experiences an equally incompetent treatment. ❞

WILLIAM JAMES

What is your reaction to people who say they have mystical experiences? Have you experienced an event or state of mind that some people would think impossible or absurd? Do you think your experience was mystical or supernatural or simply intuitive, simply beyond what is commonly thought sensible or reasonable?

❝An average man can "grab" the things of the world only with his hands, or his eyes, or his ears, but a sorcerer can grab them also with his nose, or his tongue, or his will, especially with his will. I cannot really describe how it is done, but you yourself, for instance, cannot describe to me how you hear. It happens that I am also capable of hearing, so we can talk about what we hear, but not about how we hear. A sorcerer uses his will to perceive the world. That perceiving, however, is not like hearing. When we look at the world or when we hear it, we have the impression that it is out there and that it is real. When we perceive the world with our will we know that it is not as "out there" or "as real" as we think. ❞

CARLOS CASTAÑEDA

What do you think this character in Castañeda's book *A Separate Reality* means when he speaks of perceiving the world with his will? Do you think this kind of perception is beyond anyone's comprehension except an accomplished "sorcerer's"?

> *Glendower:* I can call spirits from the vasty deep.
> *Hotspur:* Why, so can I, or so can any man; But will they come when you do call for them?
>
> SHAKESPEARE

What kind of powers (if any exist) do you think a man needs before spirits will come when he calls them?

> The representation of Nature as a friend . . . obscures the true position of man in the world, and diverts his energies from the pursuit of scientific power, which is the only fight that can bring long-continued well-being to the human race. . . . The search for happiness based upon untrue beliefs is neither very noble nor very glorious. There is a stark joy in the unflinching perception of our true place in the world, and a more vivid drama than any that is possible to those who hide behind the enclosing walls of myth. . . . No man is liberated from fear who dare not see his place in the world as it is.
>
> BERTRAND RUSSELL

Do you think that the pursuit of scientific knowledge is the one hope of the human race?

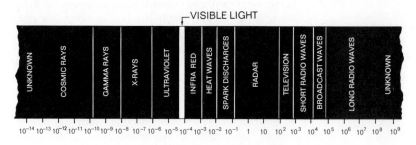

> The electromagnetic spectrum reveals the narrow range of radiation visible to man's eye. From the standpoint of physics, the only difference between radio waves, visible light, and such high-frequency forms of radiation as X-rays and gamma rays lies in their wave length. But out of this vast range of electromagnetic radiation, extending from cosmic rays with wave lengths of only one trillionth of a centimeter up to infinitely long radio waves, the human

eye selects only the narrow band indicated in white on the . . . chart. Man's perceptions of the universe in which he dwells are thus restricted by the limitations of his visual sense. "

LINCOLN BARNETT

We see a rainbow and know red, orange, yellow, green, blue, indigo, and violet. But other wave lengths, perhaps offering other colors, if we had eyes to see them, are invisible to us.

Do you think the unknown world is simply a physical reality that neither we nor scientific instruments can fully penetrate?

"The most beautiful and most profound emotion we can experience is the sensation of the mystical. It is the sower of all true science. He to whom this emotion is a stranger, who can no longer wonder and stand rapt in awe, is as good as dead. To know that what is impenetrable to us really exists, manifesting itself as the highest wisdom and the most radiant beauty which our dull faculties can comprehend only in their most primitive forms–this knowledge, this feeling is at the center of true religiousness. "

ALBERT EINSTEIN

Recall an experiment you performed in chemistry or biology, or a time you came to understand a mathematics problem, geological formation, the circulation of the blood, or some other piece of scientific knowledge. What was your emotional response? What do you see as the relation between the scientific, the mystical, and the religious? Are they all connected? Does one deny the other?

CONNECTING EXERCISES

▶ A. Investigate one apparently impossible scientific fact or do research on one seemingly untrue belief: that the moon has an influence on the tides, on sap in trees, on human emotions (It is said that murder is more frequent when the moon is full); that the human being emits impulses that affect the growth of plants; that a witch doctor sticks pins into a doll and a person miles away feels pain; that certain women, in trances, foresee the future; that the homing pigeon finds its way through its response to the earth's magnetic field; that the position of the stars in the heavens controls human events; that your astrological sign determines your character. . . .

▶ B. Recall the strangest experience you have had. Take notes: Where were you? What events preceded the experience? What events followed? How did you feel? Why? What do you think of the experience now? How do you understand it?

▶ C. Discuss some aspect of known/unknown as you have seen it in a recent TV show, advertisement, movie, book, or newspaper article.

UNIT 23
WRITING NARRATIVE

Tell your reader a story with meaning and he will listen. Give him one event, then another and he will want to know what happens next. But don't tell him a story that unravels like a ball of yarn, one that has an end but no meaning, one like the bear went over the mountain and what do you think he saw? he saw another mountain and what do you think he did? . . . In a story like this, the bear is the only one who gets anywhere. Try to have two essentials in any story you tell:

(1) *action*   Have things happen; show someone doing something; let one event follow another in a discernible pattern.

(2) *idea*   Let an idea emerge from the happenings; know the meaning the action has for you and in some way communicate this meaning to your reader.

Following is a factual narrative by George Gurdjieff, who taught a system of knowledge based on mysticism:

We sat, ate the halva, smoked and chatted. Soon after, Piotr Karpenko arrived with his eyes bandaged, accompanied by two other Russian boys, not members of the club. He came up to me demanding an explanation for my having insulted him the day before. Being one of those youths who read a good deal of poetry and love to express themselves in high-faluting language, he delivered a lengthy harangue which he brought to an abrupt close with the following categorical declaration: 'The earth is too small for both of us; hence one of us must die.'

On hearing his bombastic tirade I wanted to knock this nonsense right out of his head. But when my friends began to reason with me, saying that only people who have not yet been touched at all by contemporary culture, as, for instance, Kurds, square accounts in this manner, and that respectable people have recourse to more civilized methods, my pride began to assert itself; and in order not to be called uneducated or cowardly, I entered into a serious discussion of this incident.

After a lengthy dispute, called by us a debate, during which it turned out that several of the boys present were on my side and several on the side of my rival—and which debate at times developed into a deafening din and brought us perilously near to throwing each other down from the top of the bell-tower—it was decided that we must fight a duel.

Then the question arose, where to obtain weapons? Neither pistols nor swords were to be had anywhere and the situation became very perplexing. All our emotions, which a moment before had reached the limits of excitement, were suddenly concentrated on how to find a way out of the difficulty which had arisen.

Among the company was a friend of mine, a boy named Tourchaninov, who had a very squeaky voice and whom we all considered a very comical fellow. While we were sitting pondering on what was to be done, he suddenly chirped up and exclaimed: 'If it's difficult to get pistols, it's easy to get cannon.'

Everybody laughed, as they always did at everything he said.

'What are you laughing at, you silly devils!' he retorted. 'It's quite possible to use cannon for your purpose. There's only one drawback. You've decided that one of you must die, but in a duel with cannon both of you might die. If you consent to take such a risk, then to carry out my proposal is the easiest thing in the world.'

What he proposed was that we should both go to the artillery range where firing practice was held, lie down and hide somewhere between the guns and the targets and await our doom. Whichever of us should be hit by a random shell would be the one fated to die.

We all knew the artillery range very well. It was not far away in the mountains encircling the town. It was a fairly large tract of land, from six to nine miles square, which it was absolutely forbidden to enter at certain times of the year, during firing practice, and which was strictly guarded on all sides. . . .

As a result of the fresh debate held on Tourchaninov's proposal, it was categorically decided by all present to carry out this project the very next day.

According to the stipulations of the 'seconds', who were Kerensky and Korkhanidi on my side, and on the side of my rival the two strange boys whom he had brought along with him, we were to go to the artillery range early in the morning before the firing began, and at approximately one hundred yards from the target, lie down at a certain distance from each other in some large shell-hole where no one could see us, and remain there until dusk; whichever one was still alive by then could leave and go where he wished.

The seconds also decided to remain all day near the range, by the banks of the river Kars Chai, and in the evening to look for us in our holes to find out the result of the duel. If it should turn out that one or both of us were merely wounded, then they would do the necessary; and if it should turn out that we had been killed, they would then spread the tale that we had gone to collect copper and lead, not knowing that there would be firing that day, and so had been 'wiped out'.

The next morning at break of day the whole party of us, supplied with provisions, made our way to the Kars Chai. Arriving there, we two rivals were given our share of the provisions and were conducted by two of the seconds to the range, where we lay down in separate hollows. The seconds returned to the others at the river and passed the time fishing.

So far everything had seemed rather a joke, but when the firing began it was anything but a joke. I do not know either the form or the sequence in which the subjective experiencings and mental associations of my rival flowed, but I do know what proceeded in me as soon as the firing started. What I experienced and felt when the shells began to fly and burst over my head, I remember now as if it were only yesterday.

At the beginning I was completely stupefied, but soon the intensity of feeling which flooded through me, and the force of logical confrontation of my thought increased to such an extent that, at each moment, I thought and experienced more than during an entire twelvemonth.

Simultaneously, there arose in me for the first time the 'whole sensation of myself', which grew stronger and stronger, and a clear realization that through my thoughtlessness I had put myself in a situation of almost certain annihilation, because at that moment my death seemed inevitable.

Instinctive fear in face of this inevitability so took possession of my entire being that surrounding realities seemed to disappear, leaving only an unconquerable living terror.

I remember I tried to make myself as small as possible and to take shelter behind a ridge in the ground, so as to hear nothing and think about nothing.

The trembling which began in the whole of my body reached such a frightful intensity that it was as if each tissue vibrated independently, and, in spite of the roaring of the guns, I very distinctly heard the beating of my heart, and my teeth chattered so hard that it seemed as if at any moment they would break. . . .

I do not remember how long I lay there in this state; I can only say that in this case, as always and in everything, our most supreme, inexorable Sovereign, Time, did not fail to assert his rights, and I began to grow accustomed to my ordeal as well as to the roar of the cannon and the bursting of the shells round me. . . .

There was nothing to be done but to keep lying there quietly. After eating some lunch I even, without knowing it, fell asleep. Evidently the nervous system, after such intensive activity, urgently demanded rest. I do not know how long I slept, but when I woke up it was already evening and everything was quiet.

When I was fully awake and realized clearly the reasons for my being in that place, I first assured myself with great joy that I was safe and sound, and it was only when this egoistic gladness of mine had subsided that I suddenly remembered and began to feel concerned about my comrade in misfortune. So creeping quietly out of my hole and taking a good look round, I went over to the place where he should have been.

Seeing him lying there motionless, I was very frightened, though I thought and was even quite sure that he was asleep; but when I suddenly noticed blood on his leg, I completely lost my head, and all the hatred of the day before turned into pity. With a fear as great as I had experienced only a few hours earlier for my own life, I crouched down as though still instinctively trying not to be seen.

I was still in this position when the seconds crawled up to me on all fours. Seeing me looking so strangely at the outstretched Karpenko and then noticing the blood on his leg, they felt that something terrible had happened, and crouching there, glued to the spot, they also began to stare at him. As they later told me, they too were quite certain that he was dead. . . .

As soon as Karpenko came to, he looked round at everyone present; and when, resting his gaze on me longer than on the others, he smiled, something moved within me and I was overcome with remorse and pity. From that moment I began to feel towards him as towards a brother.

Gurdjieff indicates that the incident has two meanings for him: after the shells begin to fly, he experiences a previously unknown sensation of himself; and after Karpenko comes to and smiles, he experiences remorse accompanied by a feeling of brotherhood for a person who only a few hours earlier he had considered an enemy. Gurdjieff states these two meanings within the space of three sentences. All the other sentences of the narrative, with the exception of one or two short explanations, are devoted to showing the action.

When you tell a story, it is usually a good idea to let the action occupy nearly all the space. Limit any direct statements of meaning to a few sentences and allow your meaning to emerge from the action.

WRITING EXERCISE

▶ • Recall an experience that had special significance for you—one that revealed to you that there is only one world, the physical world we see and touch; or one which gave you an insight into another world, a world beyond sense and reason.

• Show things happening, give events, have people talk.

• Indicate in no more than four or five sentences the meaning the experience had for you.

WRITING HINT: GIVE SHAPE TO YOUR WRITING.

> **"**As the thought takes shape in the mind, it takes *a* shape. It has always been recognized that clear thinking precedes good writing. There is about good writing a visual actuality. It exactly reproduces what we should metaphorically call the contour of our thought.**"**
>
> HERBERT READ

When you write, your writing takes a shape. And this shape reflects the way your mind worked as you wrote.

Your mind is unique and works in a unique way. But, at the same time, it works in somewhat the same way as all human minds. Human thought takes a number of recognizable patterns. The following three most common kinds of writing organization are based on these patterns. They are not, of course, rigid categories, but overlap and usually mingle within any single piece of writing.

(1) You may let time determine the order of the parts of your composition—that is, you can give the events of your story as they occurred in time. A *chronological arrangement* is often used in narration, as it was in the Gurdjieff passage quoted above:

Soon after, Piotr Karpenko arrived. . . . He came up to me. . . . "The earth is too small for both of us"

After a lengthy dispute . . . it was decided that we must fight a duel.

Then the question arose, where to obtain weapons? . . .

The next morning at break of day. . .

when the shells began to fly and burst over my head . . .

Simultaneously, . . . a 'sensation of myself' . . .

The narrator has presented the happenings in straightforward chronological order. Event follows event as they actually happened. The student theme at the end of this unit also takes this form.

To achieve a special effect you may decide not to give the happenings in the order in which they occurred. Depending on your purpose, you may want to begin with the last event and proceed to the first, or begin in the middle and then go on from there to the end, giving intermittent flashbacks to inform your reader of actions that preceded the beginning of your narrative. However you do it, you will need to know your purpose and the effect you want to achieve.

(2) *Spatial organization* is most common in descriptive writing. Let your reader see a landscape, a house, a painting, a face by starting from the left of the object and moving detail by detail to the right, or by moving from top to bottom, or by proceeding from the most distinctive element to less distinctive.

Before you write a paper that is to be governed by spatial organization, decide on the parts of the object you are describing and know in what order or direction you are going to give them to your reader. For the sake of clarity and simplicity, try letting each paragraph of your composition deal with one part of the object. For example, if you are describing a face, you may decide that the eyes are the most distinctive feature and you may devote a paragraph to them. And then moving outward you may give a paragraph to the brow and cheekbones, and so on, indicating how each reinforces the dominant impression made by the eyes.

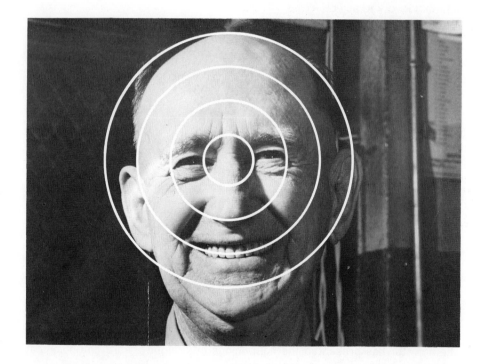

CLASS EXERCISES

▶ A. As a class select one of the illustrations in this book as a subject for description.

• Individually, consider the picture chosen, discriminating the parts that compose it.

▶B. Or describe this picture of Carlos Castañeda. (A chapter from one of Castañeda's novels follows in Unit 24.)

• Write a short description of the subject of the picture. Let each paragraph of your paper deal with one part of it. Help your reader see it as you have seen it.

• Read your paper aloud or exchange papers to see how the same subject may be looked at in different ways and may produce different and yet similar patterns of organization.

(3) In some of the writing you do, you may want to leave gaps and let your reader fill them. *Nonlinear writing* does not proceed step by step in a straight line. If you are writing reverie or doing a piece of free writing you may want to use nonlinear techniques. The reverie paper in Unit 14 brings together such apparently disconnected thoughts as "Marsha! . . . days of french toast and milk . . . freezing in the Colorado winter . . . that godawful space between her two front teeth . . . I'm torn apart." The writer does not lead us step by step as he would have had he organized his material according to chronological order or spatial order. He has presented his material so that readers are called on to make many of the connections and some of their own associations. (Look at Klee's *Outburst of Fear* on page 61.)

If you use this method, remember it contains the same pitfall as other patterns of organization: if you do not control the arrangement of your material, your writing may fail to communicate. You have to know what you want to do and be aware of how you are doing it.

Whether you use a nonlinear arrangement, spatial organization, chronological order, or any other technique to shape a piece of your writing, it will probably grow out of thesis-and-support thinking. Thought commonly moves in two distinct ways—from the particular to the general and from the general to the particular: You see details; you develop ideas about them; you search about to see if other details support or deny your idea. This thought process—

the habit of developing an idea with examples or reasons—will usually influence the shape of your composition.

Biologist Charles Darwin looked at the details: scotch firs, navel-frequenting flys, Galapagos finches, medicinal leeches, cats, donkeys, peacocks, geese. And from them he generalized the existence of an unseen mechanism in Nature that selects those individuals who are fittest for survival and that in this way produces change and the evolution of new species. An intimate combination of general and particular gives shape to Darwin's *Origin of Species,* to paragraphs, chapters, and to the whole structure of this book. On a lesser scale you do the same sort of thing when you write a paper.

One way to use thesis and support is to state your major idea—your thesis—in the first sentence of a paragraph (or in the first sentence of your composition) and then let all that follows support this one idea. Often, however, your material will elicit a more complex interweaving of general and particular. Read the following class paper and discuss its author's use of general statement and concrete detail.

REAL MAKE-BELIEVE

I was once near death for a few minutes. The experience of it put me in contact with a force I never knew existed. Today I can still taste the emotion of those few minutes.

When I was eleven, my father often took me trout fishing with him. I was not an avid fisherman, and I always grew bored after two or three hours of baiting and casting. But I always put on a show for my father and played at angling until I couldn't stand it any longer. Then I would dismantle my pole and go off into the meadows.

I was an enthusiastic rock climber and always sought out steep hills and small cliffs to scramble over. Usually I made up a game to accompany my movements. Generally the game consisted of my being pursued by a posse, or an enemy patrol forcing me to scale high passes and treacherous cliffs.

One day we fished along the Truckee River where it cuts through the mountains of the Nevada-California border. I tired of fishing and ate my lunch. Out in the river, up to the waist of his waders, my father worked his way upstream, patiently casting. Every ten or twenty minutes he moved further upstream and finally out of my sight.

I climbed a steep slide, dislodging loose rocks on

the way up. This was just the effect I wanted to add some authenticity to my game of make-believe. I followed the crest of the slide downstream, dodging bullets, crawling on my belly, making a run for it.

I ran and leapt from rock to rock and came upon a concrete wall higher than myself. Somewhere near me was the sound of rushing water. This was a wonderful discovery: a man-made structure, high up overlooking a river, with the sounds of turbulent water in the air, kindling my sense of adventure.

The wall ran parallel to the slope. At the end of it was a mass of broken timbers, deposited there when the river flooded over. I peered around the corner of the wall. There was a concrete slab sloping downwards very steeply with smooth vertical walls of concrete on either side. The sound of water was louder, almost a roar, issuing from somewhere at the other end of the slide. The walls took a turn about twenty feet down, leaving the other end invisible.

I placed a tennis shoe onto the smooth slope and tested the traction. It held, but in order to descend I would have to scoot down on my backside. My excitement mounted. Here was a real adventure—small in scale, perhaps, but infinitely more satisfying than a made-up one.

I wanted to support myself by pressing my hands against both walls, but the span between was longer than my arms. So I used my hands, feet, and buttocks to inch my way down. It was easy and I descended rapidly full of confidence. But the turbulence grew deafening inside the walls and as I approached the turn in the slide I wondered anxiously if there was a way out.

When I rounded the curve my stomach turned over. I had descended a steep spillway which dropped abruptly into a pit of churning water, enclosed by smooth walls streaked with slick moss. The water swirled violently. At one side of the pit was a gate of metal bars through which I saw the river rushing by. A torrent of mountain water conveyed by a flume was emptied into the river. At this point of intersection the two streams of water collided, producing a small maelstrom. The motion of the water was menacing. Anything dropped into it would be sucked under.

All this was taken in with a start. I looked for some place to stand or something to hold on to. There was nothing. I suddenly realized I was in danger of my life. The spillway slope increased toward the end and was smooth as glass. I wanted to grab for the walls, but if I let go or adjusted my position, I would slip and plunge in. I clung there frozen. This wasn't make-believe. This was real.

Time seemed to affect only the waters, which still churned and thundered. But I sensed a continuous, unmoving present instant as if time had stopped. With this came a kind of intelligence, a strong instinct that seemed to fill my body. I was aware of every muscle and contortion of my body. The texture of the concrete seemed to change. Now its surface was porous and I knew, or my hands knew, that if they pressed as much surface area as possible against the slab, one hand could be lifted and moved back without losing grip. Bodily intelligence had taken over, and I worked my way back up the slope. It seemed impossibly steep to me as I ascended, and if this mysterious state of calm-in-the-midst-of-terror were to cease or diminish, the natural law of gravity would wrench me loose.

I made my way up. My whole body, skin and bone, knew what to do at every instant, where to shift the weight, how to feel out each grip. I was in a curious state of calm. I sensed the possibility of death. But the fear of it simply remained there while another state of intelligence had appeared from nowhere and taken me over entirely.

When I reached the summit of the spillway and my rump felt the edge, I scrambled out. A wave of the shakes shot through me. My legs trembled so badly I could not stand.

That state of calm, the stark reality of the present instant, and the mobilization of unknown instincts had all disappeared. I was now safe. But now I trembled.

Yet that short period of time has retained a quality that has distinguished it from any other. After years I can recall it better than I can anything I did this morning. It was as if I'd been pulled out of my every-day make-believe world and been thrust into another world. This other world was not merely another world. It was the real world for me.

Allen Roth

SELECTIONS

Van Gogh, *The Starry Night.* (1889) Collection, Museum of Modern Art, New York.

Fire Walking in Ceylon

LEONARD FEINBERG

Although we had seen men walking barefoot on burning embers twice before, we were not prepared for the mass fire walk at Kataragama. The first time, on a pleasant summer afternoon, surrounded by playing children and laughing family groups, we watched four men walk quickly through a twelve-foot fire pit. The occasion was a Hindu festival, and the atmosphere was similar to that of a state fair in the United States. The second time we had been among the guests of a Ceylonese planter who included in the evening's entertainment a fire-walking exhibition by six men.

But at the temple of Kataragama everything was different. There, on the night of the full moon in August, fire walking climaxes a week's ceremonies in honor of the Hindu god Kataragama. From all over the island, worshipers and spectators (Buddhist as well as Hindu, although theoretically Buddhists do not believe in gods) had been converging on the little settlement in the jungle of southeastern Ceylon. During the early part of the week, devotees had paid tribute to Kataragama by hanging colored papers on trees near the temple or by breaking sacrificial coconuts on a rock provided for that purpose. Toward the week's end, the nature of the sacrifices was intensified, and zealous worshipers perforated their cheeks with pins, or walked on nails, or imbedded into their naked shoulders meathooks with which they pulled heavy carts along a pitted dirt road.

By midnight the crowd was feverishly tense. Since the logs in the twenty-by-six-foot pit had been burning for four hours, the fire walking would presumably take place about 4 A.M. But the tradition against making any sort of prediction about the immediate future is so strong at Kataragama that the local priest, asked by an American tourist when the fire walking would begin, replied that there probably would not be any walking at all. The crowd surged away from the pit slowly and steadily—slowly because every inch of the temple grounds had been packed for hours, and steadily because the heat from the pit was becoming unbearable. The men and women nearest the pit had held their places for days, eating and sleeping in one spot. The Ceylonese are ordinarily very clean, but the activity at Kataragama is more important than sanitation, and as the hours passed everything intensified: the heat, the tension, the odors of sweat and urine and incense. A wave of malevolent expectation permeated the air, a powerful undercurrent of suppressed sadism that made intruders like ourselves feel dilettantish, uncomfortable, and slightly ashamed. Fire walking is far more than just a spectacle to most of these people; it is a concrete symbol of intimate identification with a supernatural power. From time to time men would shout, "Hora Hora," an Oriental form of "Amen" in honor of the god whose power transcends the science of the West.

About 2 A.M. people near us suddenly scurried to make room for a young woman carrying in her bare hands a clay pot full of burning coconut husks. She did not seem to be feeling any pain, but she was abnormally excited as she staggered to the outer sanctum of the temple. There she threw the pot down, exultantly showed the crowd her hands—they were gray, but not burned—and began knocking on the temple door. She apparently wanted to demonstrate to the priest, or the god, what she had accomplished, but no one was being admitted that night, and she was still pounding frantically at the massive door when the attention of the crowd shifted to another woman. This one too had a red-hot pot full of burning husks, but she carried it in the conventional Ceylonese fashion—on top of her head. And when she removed the pot, neither her hair nor her hands showed any sign of scorching.

Shortly before four o'clock an ominous grumbling swept through the crowd. Then angry shouts, threatening arms, protests. By climbing a stone wall I was able to see what the trouble was. A row of chairs had been reserved for several wealthy Ceylonese from Colombo and their European guests. But when they arrived they found that a group of Buddhist monks had occupied the seats and refused to move. (For more than a year, as a calculated technique of growing nationalism, monks had been usurping reserved seats at public gatherings.) The police officer tried to persuade the monks to give up the seats, but the yellow-robed figures leaned placidly on their umbrellas and pretended that he did not exist. There was no question where the sympathy of the mob lay, and when their protests became loud the police officer shrugged his shoulders and motioned to the legal holders of the seats. They dispersed to the edges of the standing mob, far away from the pit.

At four in the morning wailing flutes and pounding drums announced the arrival of the walkers. The long procession was led by white-robed priests, their faces streaked with red and yellow and white ash. By this time the flames had stopped spurting and the pit consisted of a red-hot mass of burning wood, which attendants were leveling with long branches. The heat of the fire was still intense; within ten feet of the pit it was difficult to breathe. Then the priests muttered incantations, the drums built up to a crescendo, and the fire walking began.

Among the eighty persons who walked the fire that night there were ten women. But in the mad excitement of the crowd's cheers, the drumbeats, the odors, the tension, it was difficult to identify individuals. Some men skipped lightly through the fire, as if doing a restrained version of the hop, skip, and jump in three or four steps. Some raced through, determined, somber. Some ran through exultantly, waving spears. One man danced gaily into the center of the pit, turned, did a kind of wild jig for a few moments, then turned again and danced on through. Another man stumbled suddenly and the crowd gasped; he fell forward, hung for a ghastly moment on the coals, then straightened and stumbled on. The crowd sighed. Two women ran through, close together, holding hands, taking five or six steps. In the phantasmagoric blur of roars, screams, and incantations, the fire walkers looked less like human beings than grotesque puppets in a macabre shadow play. For a long moment one person stood out in the hectic cavalcade of charging, gyrating figures: a short, slim man in a white sarong strolled slowly and serenely through the fire, stepping on the solid earth at the end of the pit as gently as he had stepped on the embers.

After going through the fire, the walkers, some shuffling, some running, a few helped or led by attendants, proceeded to a spot beside the temple where the head priest placed a smear of a saffron ash on the forehead of each participant. The ash had been taken from the pit and blessed, and the fire walkers strode off proudly.

There are two types of fire walking, on stones (usually of volcanic origin) in Polynesia, and on embers in Asia and Africa. Theories which try to explain the secret of fire walking fall into three categories: physical, psychological, and religious. The most publicized attempts of scientists to find the solution took place in 1935 and 1936, when the London Council for Psychical Investigation arranged two series of fire walks at Surrey, England. The council took charge of building the pit and burning the logs, it provided a number of physicians, chemists, physicists, and Oxford professors to examine every stage of the proceedings, and it published an official report of its conclusions. Some of the scientists published individual reports, in general agreeing that fire walking can be explained in terms of certain physical facts, but they did not agree on precisely what those physical facts were.

At the first series of Surrey tests, an Indian named Kuda Bux walked uninjured through a fire pit the surface temperature of which was 430° C., the interior temperature 1400° C. In the 1936 test, for Ahmed Hussain, the surface temperature was over 500° C. Both Bux and Hussain insisted that the secret was "faith," and Hussain claimed that he could convey immunity to anyone who would walk the fire with him. A half-dozen English amateurs, who had answered the council's advertisement for volunteers, did walk the fire behind Hussain and were "slightly burned." One of these amateurs managed, a few days later, to walk through the fire pit alone, in three steps, without suffering the slightest injury.

In brief, the official report of the council stated that fire walking is a gymnastic feat operating on this principle: a limited number of quick and even steps on a poor conductor of heat does not result in burning of the flesh. "The secret of fire-walking," the report said, "lies in the low thermal conductivity of the burning wood. . . . The quantity of heat transferred may remain small, if . . . the time of contact is very short. . . . The time of contact is not above half a second in normal quick walking." To put it another way, it is safe to take three even steps, limiting each contact to half a second, on wood embers ("The thermal conductivity of copper . . . is about 1,000 times greater than that of wood"). The report conceded that "successive contacts . . . cause an accumulation of heat sufficient to cause injury, and . . . with fires whose temperature is 500° Centigrade or more, only two contacts can be made with each foot without erythema or blistering."

The weight of the walker makes a difference, the report suggested, each of the Indians weighing less than 126 pounds and sinking into the embers to a lesser degree, and for a shorter time, than the heavier English amateurs. An expert also has the advantage of walking steadily and distributing his weight evenly, whereas the inexperience and undue haste of the beginner make it difficult for him to avoid resting a part of his foot more heavily than he should. When the amateur walker took an uneven number of steps, the foot which had taken more steps suffered more burns.

Other observers of fire walking have offered various explanations, the most popular being that Orientals have very tough soles. They walk barefoot all their lives, often on hot surfaces. Sometimes they put out cigarette butts with their toes and, when marching in parades, step on burning husks which have fallen out of torchbearers' fires. This is true. But the English physicians who examined Bux and Hussain described their feet as very soft, not at all callused.

Another familiar conjecture is that fire walkers use chemical preparations to protect their feet. An American magician believes that a paste of alum and salt is applied, and other experts have speculated that soda, or soap, or juice of mysterious plants, or an anesthetic of some sort is used. But the physician and the chemist who examined Bux and Hussain at Surrey were positive that nothing had been applied to the feet; for control purposes, they washed one of Bux's feet and dried it carefully before he walked.

The "water-vapor protection" theory has a number of supporters. An American chemist recently wrote, in a popular magazine, that he could walk comfortably on burning coals and apply his tongue painlessly to a red-hot iron bar by utilizing this principle: at a certain range of high temperature, a thin film of water acts as absolute protection against heat. The trouble with this theory, as the Surrey tests showed, is (1) the fire walkers' feet were dry, (2) it would be difficult, under any conditions, to supply a uniform amount of water to the soles during a fire walk, and (3) moisture is not advisable, because embers are likely to stick to wet soles and cause blisters.

Still another explanation was offered by Joseph Dunninger. He asserts that the trick used by fire-walking Shinto priests in Japan consisted of making the fuel in the trench shallow in the center and deep on the sides, and starting the fire in the center. By the time the walking begins, the fire has burned out in the center, is still blazing at the edges, and the priests step on the cool ashes of the center. That may be the secret of the Shinto priests, but the pit at Surrey was filled evenly under the supervision of scientists. And an English planter in the Marquesas Islands, who was once teased by a local chief into fire walking, reported that the fire was hottest in the center.

These are the physical explanations. The psychological theories are more difficult to test. Having watched fire walking in Japan some years ago, Percival Lowell of Harvard concluded that the feat was made possible by the less sensitive nervous organism of the Oriental and the ecstasy of the walker (as well as the extremely tough calluses on his soles). A variation on the "ecstasy" theory is the suggestion of one psychologist that hypnosis is the secret. The fire walker, he says, has been hypnotized and provided with the same immunity to pain that can be observed even in a classroom demonstration of hypnosis. The fire walker may not know that he is hypnotized, but hypnosis is what the priest is actually practicing when he gives the walker his last-minute instructions. After the performance, while ostensibly putting a mark of holy ash on the fire walker's forehead, the priest breaks the hypnosis. Most psychologists, however, reject this explanation on the grounds that hypnosis may lessen the subjective feeling of pain but cannot prevent skin from burning.

It is well known in the East that yogis and fakirs can attain so profound a state of concentration on a single object that nothing else distracts them. In this state, the practitioner may lie on a bed of nails, keep a hand outstretched for days, remain motionless for a week, or perform other feats whose practical value is limited but which do demonstrate a control over the body that most human beings are unable to achieve. According to some yogis, he who masters concentration can separate the soul from the body, so that the vacant shell does not feel pain. But since a dead body will burn, this explanation is not satisfactory.

As far as the devout Ceylonese believer is concerned, the secret is simple: complete faith in Kataragama. Kataragama is a very powerful god. If, in desperation—at a time of serious illness, near-bankruptcy, dangerous competition from a hated rival—a man or woman vows to walk the fire in exchange for Kataragama's help, Kataragama may give that help. The amateur walker, then, is either a petitioner for supernatural assistance or a grateful recipient of it. His preparation may begin as early as May, when he arrives at Kataragama and puts himself under the direction of the chief priest. For three months he lives ascetically, abstaining from all sensual pleasures, eating only vegetables, drinking only water, bathing in the holy river near the temple, and going through religious rituals conducted by the priest. If he does all this, and if he has *absolute, unquestioning, complete* faith in Kataragama's power, he walks the fire unafraid and unharmed.

On the night we watched the fire walking at Kataragama, twelve people were burned badly enough to go to the hospital, and one of them died. These people, the devout believer will tell you, lacked either faith or preparation. Another man who lacked at least one of these ingredients was a young English clergyman who visited Ceylon a few years ago. This Protestant minister reasoned that the faith of a Christian was at least as strong as that of a Hindu, and he volunteered tó walk the fire with the others. He did, and spent the next six months in a hospital, where doctors barely managed to save his life.

It is believed by the Ceylonese that Kataragama exercises absolute and somewhat whimsical control of the area within a fourteen-mile radius of his temple. His portrait, presumably life-size, shows a handsome, seven-foot-tall, six-headed and twelve-armed god, with two women and a blue peacock for companionship and transportation. Although he is technically a Hindu god, many Buddhists also worship him, or at least ask for his help when they are in trouble. Officially the god of war and revenge, he is probably more fervently worshiped and more genuinely feared than any other god in Ceylon. He has an A-1 reputation for protecting his congregation and, according to numerous legends, exhibits a genial playfulness in devising disconcerting mishaps for those who violate his minor taboos.

Most Ceylonese try to make at least one visit a year to his temple, not necessarily during the August ceremonies, but at some other time of the year when the settlement in the jungle is sparse, quiet, and suitable for meditation. Everyone manages to get to Kataragama sooner or later, it seems. My Hindu friend in the police department went one week, my wife's Muslim jeweler another, my Buddhist tailor a third. It is considered especially commendable to walk all the way to Kataragama, and many Ceylonese do walk there, sometimes carrying a large, colorful paper-and-wood contraption in the form of an arch, which indicates that they are fulfilling a vow.

Our driver on the trip to Kataragama was a young Singhalese who told us that his name was Elvis. (He told Englishmen that his name was Winston.) His driving got a little erratic as the day wore on, and he finally admitted that, though a Buddhist, he was taking no chances with Kataragama and had been fasting all day. While we were eating, he warned our friends and us about certain taboos that visitors to the Kataragama territory were supposed to observe. One local rule forbade announcing an expected arrival time; that, said Elvis, was an infallible way of being delayed. Another dangerous thing to do was to speak disrespectfully of Kataragama. A Buddhist in a Renault immediately remarked that, the weather being ideal, we ought to arrive at Kataragama by six o'clock. And a Christian woman in a Vauxhall said that all this fear of Kataragama was nonsense; she had been there the previous year and had ridiculed the entire procedure, but nothing had happened.

When we finished eating we got into our Volkswagen and followed the other two cars. Suddenly it began to rain. It rained only for five minutes and, we learned later, only within a few hundred yards. As we carefully rounded a curve on the slick road we saw that the two other cars were now facing us. The Renault's hood was stuck halfway into a rock fence, and the Vauxhall was resting its side on the same fence. It turned out that the Renault had skidded and started turning in the road, and to avoid hitting it the driver of the Vauxhall put on her brakes. By the time the cars stopped skidding they had smashed into the fence. No one was injured except the scoffing woman, who had a painful but not serious bruise on the spot where an irritated parent might have been expected to spank his child. It took a long time to improvise pulling cables, disengage the cars, and tow them to a garage. We eventually reached the temple, just before midnight, and although all of these coincidences and superstitions can be logically accounted for, no one in our party made any more jeering remarks about Kataragama.

How does the author's view of fire walking differ from the Ceylonese's understanding of it?

Do you agree with any of the explanations of the secret of fire walking? Into which of the three categories (physical, psychological, religious) does your explanation fall?

How is this essay organized? Trace it through paragraph by paragraph.

Once More, the Round

THEODORE ROETHKE

What's greater, Pebble or Pond?
What can be known? The unknown.
My true self runs toward a hill
More! O more! Visible.

Now I adore my life
With the bird, the abiding leaf,
With the fish, the questing snail,
And the eye altering all;
And I dance with William Blake
For love, for Love's sake;

And everything comes to One,
As we dance on, dance on, dance on.

How do you interpret lines 8 and 11?

Describe the experience this poem expresses.

Is Roethke describing an experience similar to the one Carlos Castañeda describes in the passage from *The Teachings of Don Juan*? (pages 289–94) Point out similarities and differences between the two accounts.

EMILY DICKINSON

One need not be a Chamber—to be Haunted—
One need not be a House—

The Brain has Corridors—surpassing
Material Place—

Far safer, of a Midnight Meeting
External Ghost
Than its interior Confronting—
That Cooler Host.

Far safer, through an Abbey gallop,
The Stones a'chase—
Than Unarmed, one's a'self encounter—
In lonesome Place—

Ourself behind ourself, concealed—
Should startle most—
Assassin hid in our Apartment
Be Horror's least.

The Body—borrows a Revolver—
He bolts the Door—
O'erlooking a superior spectre—
Or More—

How do you understand the lines "The Brain has Corridors—surpassing/Material Place"?

Discuss the meaning of "superior spectre" in the next-to-last line.

The poet implies that there are two kinds of haunted places: one less concealed, more known, more exterior; and one more concealed, less known, more interior. Does this agree with your own findings in your own life?

from **The Teachings of Don Juan**

CARLOS CASTAÑEDA

My notes on my first session with don Juan are dated June 23, 1961. That was the occasion when the teachings began. I had seen him several times previously in the capacity of an observer only. At every opportunity I had asked him to teach me about peyote. He ignored my request every time, but he never completely dismissed the subject, and I interpreted his hesitancy as a possibility that he might be inclined to talk about his knowledge with more coaxing.

In this particular session he made it obvious to me that he might consider my request provided I possessed clarity of mind and purpose in reference to what I had asked him. It was impossible for me to fulfill such a condition, for I had asked him to teach me about peyote only as a means of establishing a link of communication with him. I thought his familiarity with the subject might predispose him to be more open and willing to talk, thus allowing me an entrance into his knowledge on the properties of plants. He had interpreted my request literally, however, and was concerned about my purpose in wishing to learn about peyote.

Friday, June 23, 1961

"Would you teach me about peyote, don Juan?"
"Why would you like to undertake such learning?"

"I really would like to know about it. Is not just to want to know a good reason?"

"No! You must search in your heart and find out why a young man like you wants to undertake such a task of learning."

"Why did you learn about it yourself, don Juan?"

"Why do you ask that?"

"Maybe we both have the same reasons."

"I doubt that. I am an Indian. We don't have the same paths."

"The only reason I have is that I *want* to learn about it, just to know. But I assure you, don Juan, my intentions are not bad."

"I believe you. I've smoked you."

"I beg your pardon!"

"It doesn't matter now. I know your intentions."

"Do you mean you saw through me?"

"You could put it that way."

"Will you teach me, then?"

"No!"

"Is it because I'm not an Indian?"

"No. It is because you don't know your heart. What is important is that you know exactly why you want to involve yourself. Learning about 'Mescalito' is a most serious act. If you were an Indian your desire alone would be sufficient. Very few Indians have such a desire."

Sunday, June 25, 1961

I stayed with don Juan all afternoon on Friday. I was going to leave about 7 P.M. We were sitting on the porch in front of his house and I decided to ask him once more about the teaching. It was almost a routine question and I expected him to refuse again. I asked him if there was a way in which he could accept just my desire to learn, as if I were an Indian. He took a long time to answer. I was compelled to stay because he seemed to be trying to decide something.

Finally he told me that there was a way, and proceeded to delineate a problem. He pointed out that I was very tired sitting on the floor, and that the proper thing to do was to find a "spot" *(sitio)* on the floor where I could sit without fatigue. I had been sitting with my knees up against my chest and my arms locked around my calves. When he said I was tired, I realized that my back ached and that I was quite exhausted.

I waited for him to explain what he meant by a "spot," but he made no overt attempt to elucidate the point. I thought that perhaps he meant that I should change positions, so I got up and sat closer to him. He protested my movement and clearly emphasized that a spot meant a place where a man could feel naturally happy and strong. He patted the place where he sat and said it was his own spot, adding that he had posed a riddle I had to solve by myself without any further deliberation.

What he had posed as a problem to be solved was certainly a riddle. I had no idea how to begin or even what he had in mind. Several times I asked for a clue, or at least a hint, as to how to proceed in locating a point where I felt happy and strong. I insisted and argued that I had no idea what he really meant because I couldn't conceive the problem. He suggested I walk around the porch until I found the spot.

I got up and began to pace the floor. I felt silly and sat down in front of him.

He became very annoyed with me and accused me of not listening, saying that perhaps I did not want to learn. After a while he calmed down and explained to me that not every place was good to sit or be on, and that within the confines of the porch there was one spot that was unique, a spot where I could be at my very best. It was my task to distinguish it from all the other places. The general pattern was that I had to "feel" all the possible spots that were accessible until I could determine without a doubt which was the right one.

I argued that although the porch was not too large (12 × 8 feet), the number of possible spots was overwhelming, and it would take me a very long time to check all of them, and that since he had not specified the size of the spot, the possibilities might be infinite. My arguments were futile. He got up and very sternly warned me that it might take me days to figure it out, but that if I did not solve the problem, I might as well leave because he would have nothing to say to me. He emphasized that he knew where my spot was, and that therefore I could not lie to him; he said this was the only way he could accept my desire to learn about Mescalito as a valid reason. He added that nothing in his world was a gift, that whatever there was to learn had to be learned the hard way.

He went around the house to the chaparral to urinate. He returned directly into his house through the back.

I thought the assignment to find the alleged spot of happiness was his own way of dismissing me, but I got up and started to pace back and forth. The sky was clear. I could see everything on and near the porch. I must have paced for an hour or more, but nothing happened to reveal the location of the spot. I got tired of walking and sat down; after a few minutes I sat somewhere else, and then at another place, until I had covered the whole floor in a semisystematic fashion. I deliberately tried to "feel" differences between places, but I lacked the criteria for differentiation. I felt I was wasting my time, but I stayed. My rationalization was that I had come a long way just to see don Juan, and I really had nothing else to do.

I lay down on my back and put my hands under my head like a pillow. Then I rolled over and lay on my stomach for a while. I repeated this rolling process over the entire floor. For the first time I thought I had stumbled upon a vague criterion. I felt warmer when I lay on my back.

I rolled again, this time in the opposite direction, and again covered the length of the floor, lying face down on all the places where I had lain face up during my first rolling tour. I experienced the same warm and cold sensations, depending on my position, but there was no difference between spots.

Then an idea occurred to me which I thought to be brilliant: don Juan's spot! I sat there, and then lay, face down at first, and later on my back, but the place was just like all the others. I stood up. I had had enough. I wanted to say good-bye to don Juan, but I was embarrassed to wake him up. I looked at my watch. It was two o'clock in the morning! I had been rolling for six hours.

At that moment don Juan came out and went around the house to the chaparral. He came back and stood at the door. I felt utterly rejected, and I wanted to say something nasty to him and leave. But I realized that it was not his fault; that it was my own choice to go through all that nonsense. I told him I had failed; I had been rolling on his floor like an idiot all night and still couldn't make any sense of his riddle.

He laughed and said that it did not surprise him because I had not proceeded correctly. I had not been using my eyes. That was true, yet I was very sure he had said to feel the difference. I brought that point up, but he argued that one can feel with the eyes, when the eyes are not looking right into things. As far as I was concerned, he said, I had no other means to solve this problem but to use all I had—my eyes.

He went inside. I was certain that he had been watching me. I thought there was no other way for him to know that I had not been using my eyes.

I began to roll again, because that was the most comfortable procedure. This time, however, I rested my chin on my hands and looked at every detail.

After an interval the darkness around me changed. When I focused on the point directly in front of me, the whole peripheral area of my field of vision became brilliantly colored with a homogeneous greenish yellow. The effect was startling. I kept my eyes fixed on the point in front of me and began to crawl sideways on my stomach, one foot at a time.

Suddenly, at a point near the middle of the floor, I became aware of another change in hue. At a place to my right, still in the periphery of my field of vision, the greenish yellow became intensely purple. I concentrated my attention on it. The purple faded into a pale, but still brilliant, color which remained steady for the time I kept my attention on it.

I marked the place with my jacket, and called don Juan. He came out to the porch. I was truly excited; I had actually seen the change in hues. He seemed unimpressed, but told me to sit on the spot and report to him what kind of feeling I had.

I sat down and then lay on my back. He stood by me and asked me repeatedly how I felt; but I did not feel anything different. For about fifteen minutes I tried to feel or to see a difference, while don Juan stood by me patiently. I felt disgusted. I had a metallic taste in my mouth. Suddenly I had developed a headache. I was about to get sick. The thought of my nonsensical endeavors irritated me to a point of fury. I got up.

Don Juan must have noticed my profound frustration. He did not laugh, but very seriously stated that I had to be inflexible with myself if I wanted to learn. Only two choices were open to me, he said: either to quit and go home, in which case I would never learn, or to solve the riddle.

He went inside again. I wanted to leave immediately, but I was too tired to drive; besides, perceiving the hues had been so startling that I was sure it was a criterion of some sort, and perhaps there were other changes to be detected. Anyway, it was too late to leave. So I sat down, stretched my legs back, and began all over again.

During this round I moved rapidly through each place, passing don Juan's spot, to the end of the floor, and then turned around to cover the outer edge. When I reached the center, I realized that another change in coloration was taking place, again on the edge of my field of vision. The uniform chartreuse I was seeing all over the area turned, at one spot to my right, into a sharp verdigris. It remained for a moment and then abruptly metamorphosed into another steady hue, different from the other one I had detected earlier. I took off one of my shoes and marked the point, and kept on rolling until I had covered the floor in all possible directions. No other change of coloration took place.

I came back to the point marked with my shoe, and examined it. It was located five to six feet away from the spot marked by my jacket, in a southeasterly direction. There was a large rock next to it. I lay down there for quite some time trying to find clues, looking at every detail, but I did not feel anything different.

I decided to try the other spot. I quickly pivoted on my knees and was about to lie down on my jacket when I felt an unusual apprehension. It was more like a physical sensation of something actually pushing on my stomach. I jumped up and retreated in one movement. The hair on my neck pricked up. My legs had arched slightly, my trunk was bent forward, and my arms stuck out in front of me rigidly with my fingers contracted like a claw. I took notice of my strange posture and my fright increased.

I walked back involuntarily and sat down on the rock next to my shoe. From the rock, I slumped to the floor. I tried to figure out what had happened to cause me such a fright. I thought it must have been the fatigue I was experiencing. It was nearly daytime. I felt silly and embarrassed. Yet I had no way to explain what had frightened me, nor had I figured out what don Juan wanted.

I decided to give it one last try. I got up and slowly approached the place marked by my jacket, and again I felt the same apprehension. This time I made a strong effort to control myself. I sat down, and then knelt in order to lie face down, but I could not lie in spite of my will. I put my hands on the floor in front of me. My breathing accelerated; my stomach was upset. I had a clear sensation of panic, and fought not to run away. I thought don Juan was perhaps watching me. Slowly I crawled back to the other spot and propped my back against the rock. I wanted to rest for a while to organize my thoughts, but I fell asleep.

I heard don Juan talking and laughing above my head. I woke up.

"You have found the spot," he said.

I did not understand him at first, but he assured me again that the place where I had fallen asleep was the spot in question. He again asked me how I felt lying there. I told him I really did not notice any difference.

He asked me to compare my feelings at that moment with what I had felt while lying on the other spot. For the first time it occurred to me that I could not possibly explain my apprehension of the preceding night. He urged me in a kind of challenging way to sit on the other spot. For some inexplicable reason I was actually afraid of the other place, and did not sit on it. He asserted that only a fool could fail to see the difference.

I asked him if each of the two spots had a special name. He said that the good one was called the *sitio* and the bad one the enemy; he said these two places were the key to a man's well-being, especially for a man who was pursuing knowledge. The sheer act of sitting on one's spot created superior strength; on the other hand, the enemy weakened a man and could even cause his death. He said I had replenished my energy, which I had spent lavishly the night before, by taking a nap on my spot.

He also said that the colors I had seen in association with each specific spot had the same overall effect either of giving strength or of curtailing it.

I asked him if there were other spots for me like the two I had found, and how I should go about finding them. He said that many places in the world would be comparable to those two, and that the best way to find them was by detecting their respective colors.

It was not clear to me whether or not I had solved the problem, and in fact I was not even convinced that there had been a problem; I could not avoid feeling that the whole experience was forced and arbitrary. I was certain that don Juan had watched me all night and then proceeded to humor me by saying that wherever I had fallen asleep *was* the place I was looking for. Yet I failed to see a logical reason for such an act, and when he challenged me to sit on the other spot I could not do it. There was a strange cleavage between my pragmatic experience of fearing the "other spot" and my rational deliberations about the total event.

Don Juan, on the other hand, was very sure I had succeeded, and, acting in accordance with my success, let me know he was going to teach me about peyote.

"You asked me to teach you about Mescalito," he said. "I wanted to find out if you had enough backbone to meet him face to face. Mescalito is not something to make fun of. You must have command over your resources. Now I know I can take your desire alone as a good reason to learn."

"You really are going to teach me about peyote?"

"I prefer to call him Mescalito. Do the same."

"When are you going to start?"

"It is not so simple as that. You must be ready first."

"I think I am ready."

"This is not a joke. You must wait until there is no doubt, and then you will meet him."

"Do I have to prepare myself?"

"No. You simply have to wait. You may give up the whole idea after a while. You get tired easily. Last night you were ready to quit as soon as it got difficult. Mescalito requires a very serious intent."

Give your interpretation of the events the narrator describes. Do you believe there are good spots and bad spots to sit on? Do Carlos's desire to learn and Don Juan's remarks about this desire make any sense to you?

Describe Carlos's method for trying to solve the riddle Don Juan has posed for him. What works and what doesn't work?

Don Juan says he wanted to find out if Carlos had "enough backbone" to meet Mescalito face to face. What do you think Don Juan means by "backbone"? Why would backbone be more necessary than desire, knowledge, or physical strength?

Recall a situation in your life in which you felt you had to quit or "to solve the riddle." What did you do? Describe the problem and your method for solving it.

UNIT 25

WRITING ABOUT A LITERARY WORK

There are many ways to write a paper about a literary work. The first step, of course, is to read the work carefully:

Bliss

KATHERINE MANSFIELD

Although Bertha Young was thirty she still had moments like this when she wanted to run instead of walk, to take dancing steps on and off the pavement, to bowl a hoop, to throw something up in the air and catch it again, or to stand still and laugh at—nothing—at nothing, simply.

What can you do if you are thirty and, turning the corner of your own street, you are overcome, suddenly, by a feeling of bliss—absolute bliss!—as though you'd suddenly swallowed a bright piece of that late afternoon sun and it burned in your bosom, sending out a little shower of sparks into every particle, into every finger and toe? . . .

Oh, is there no way you can express it without being "drunk and disorderly"? How idiotic civilization is! Why be given a body if you have to keep it shut up in a case like a rare, rare fiddle?

"No, that about the fiddle is not quite what I mean," she thought, running up the steps and feeling in her bag for the key—she'd forgotten it, as usual—and rattling the letterbox. "It's not what I mean, because—Thank you, Mary"—she went into the hall. "Is Nurse back?"

"Yes, M'm."

"And has the fruit come?"

"Yes, M'm. Everything's come."

"Bring the fruit up to the dining-room, will you? I'll arrange it before I go upstairs."

It was dusky in the dining-room and quite chilly. But all the same Bertha threw off her coat; she could not bear the tight clasp of it another moment, and the cold air fell on her arms.

But in her bosom there was still that bright glowing place—that shower of little sparks coming from it. It was almost unbearable. She hardly dared to breathe for fear of fanning it higher, and yet she breathed deeply, deeply. She hardly dared to look into the cold mirror—but she did look, and it gave her back a woman, radiant, with smiling, trembling lips, with big, dark eyes and an air of listening, waiting for something . . . divine to happen . . . that she knew must happen . . . infallibly.

Mary brought in the fruit on a tray and with it a glass bowl, and a blue dish, very lovely, with a strange sheen on it as though it had been dipped in milk.

"Shall I turn on the light, M'm?"

"No, thank you. I can see quite well."

There were tangerines and apples stained with strawberry pink. Some yellow pears, smooth as silk, some white grapes covered with a silver bloom and a big cluster of purple ones. These last she had bought to tone in with the new diningroom carpet. Yes, that did sound rather far-fetched and absurd, but it was really why she had bought them. She had thought in the shop: "I must have some purple ones to bring the carpet up to the table." And it had seemed quite sensible at the time.

When she had finished with them and had made two pyramids of these bright round shapes, she stood away from the table to get the effect— and it really was most curious. For the dark table seemed to melt into the dusky light and the glass dish and the blue bowl to float in the air. This, of course in her present mood, was so incredibly beautiful. . . . She began to laugh.

"No, no. I'm getting hysterical." And she seized her bag and coat and ran upstairs to the nursery.

Nurse sat at a low table giving Little B her supper after her bath. The baby had on a white flannel gown and a blue woollen jacket, and her dark, fine hair was brushed up into a funny little peak. She looked up when she saw her mother and began to jump.

"Now, my lovey, eat it up like a good girl," said Nurse, setting her lips in a way that Bertha knew, and that meant she had come into the nursery at another wrong moment.

"Has she been good, Nanny?"

"She's been a little sweet all the afternoon," whispered Nanny. "We went to the park and I sat down on a chair and took her out of the pram and a big dog came along and put its head on my knee and she clutched its ear, tugged it. Oh, you should have seen her."

Bertha wanted to ask if it wasn't rather dangerous to let her clutch at a strange dog's ear. But she did not dare to. She stood watching them, her hands by her sides, like the poor little girl in front of the rich little girl with the doll.

The baby looked up at her again, stared, and then smiled so charmingly that Bertha couldn't help crying:

"Oh, Nanny, do let me finish giving her her supper while you put the bath things away."

"Well, M'm, she oughtn't to be changed hands while she's eating," said Nanny, still whispering. "It unsettles her; it's very likely to upset her."

How absurd it was. Why have a baby if it has to be kept—not in a case like a rare, rare fiddle—but in another woman's arms? "Oh, I must!" she said.

Very offended, Nanny handed her over.

"Now, don't excite her after her supper. You know you do, M'm. And I have such a time with her after!"

Thank heaven! Nanny went out of the room with the bath towels.

"Now I've got you to myself, my little precious," said Bertha, as the baby leaned against her.

She ate delightfully, holding up her lips for the spoon and then waving her hands. Sometimes she wouldn't let the spoon go; and sometimes, just as Bertha had filled it, she waved it away to the four winds.

When the soup was finished Bertha turned round to the fire.

"You're nice—you're very nice!" said she, kissing her warm baby. "I'm fond of you. I like you."

And, indeed, she loved Little B so much—her neck as she bent forward, her exquisite toes as they shone transparent in the firelight—that all her feeling of bliss came back again, and again she didn't know how to express it—what to do with it.

"You're wanted on the telephone," said Nanny, coming back in triumph and seizing *her* Little B.

Down she flew. It was Harry.

"Oh, is that you, Ber? Look here. I'll be late. I'll take a taxi and come along as quickly as I can, but get dinner put back ten minutes—will you? All right?"

"Yes, perfectly. Oh, Harry!"

"Yes?"

What had she to say? She'd nothing to say. She only wanted to get in touch with him for a moment. She couldn't absurdly cry: "Hasn't it been a divine day!"

"What is it?" rapped out the little voice.

"Nothing. *Entendu*," said Bertha, and hung up the receiver, thinking how more than idiotic civilization was.

They had people coming to dinner. The Norman Knights—a very sound couple—he was about to start a theatre, and she was awfully keen on interior decoration, a young man, Eddie Warren, who had just published a little book of poems and whom everybody was asking to dine, and a "find" of Bertha's called Pearl Fulton. What Miss Fulton did, Bertha didn't know. They had met at the club and Bertha had fallen in love with her, as she always did fall in love with beautiful women who had something strange about them.

The provoking thing was that, though they had been about together and met a number of times and really talked, Bertha couldn't yet make her out. Up to a certain point Miss Fulton was rarely, wonderfully frank, but the certain point was there, and beyond that she would not go.

Was there anything beyond it? Harry said, "No." Voted her dullish, and "cold like all blond women, with a touch, perhaps, of anaemia of the brain." But Bertha wouldn't agree with him; not yet, at any rate.

"No, the way she has of sitting with her head a little on one side, and smiling, has something behind it, Harry, and I must find out what that something is."

"Most likely it's a good stomach," answered Harry.

He made a point of catching Bertha's heels with replies of that kind . . . "liver frozen, my dear girl," or "pure flatulence," or "kidney disease," . . . and so on. For some strange reason Bertha liked this, and almost admired it in him very much.

She went into the drawing-room and lighted the fire; then, picking up the cushions, one by one, that Mary had disposed so carefully, she threw them back on to the chairs and the couches. That made all the difference; the room came alive at once. As she was about to throw the last one she surprised herself by suddenly hugging it to her, passionately, passionately. But it did not put out the fire in her bosom. Oh, on the contrary!

The windows of the drawing-room opened on to a balcony overlooking the garden. At the far end, against the wall, there was a tall, slender pear tree in fullest, richest bloom; it stood perfect, as though becalmed against the jade-green sky. Bertha couldn't help feeling, even from this distance, that it had not a single bud or a faded petal. Down below, in the garden beds, the red and yellow tulips, heavy with flowers, seemed to lean upon the dusk. A grey cat, dragging its belly, crept across the lawn, and a black one, its shadow, trailed after. The sight of them, so intent and so quick, gave Bertha a curious shiver.

"What creepy things cats are!" she stammered, and she turned away from the window and began walking up and down. . . .

How strong the jonquils smelled in the warm room. Too strong? Oh, no. And yet, as though overcome, she flung down on a couch and pressed her hands to her eyes.

"I'm too happy—too happy!" she murmured.

And she seemed to see on her eyelids the lovely pear tree with its wide open blossoms as a symbol of her own life.

Really—really—she had everything. She was young. Harry and she were as much in love as ever, and they got on together splendidly and were really good pals. She had an adorable baby. They didn't have to worry about money. They had this absolutely satisfactory house and garden. And friends—modern, thrilling friends, writers and painters and poets or people keen on social questions—just the kind of friends they wanted. And then there were books, and there was music, and she had found a wonderful little dressmaker, and they were going abroad in the summer, and their new cook made the most superb omelettes. . . .

"I'm absurd. Absurd!" She sat up; but she felt quite dizzy, quite drunk. It must have been the spring.

Yes, it was the spring. Now she was so tired she could not drag herself upstairs to dress.

A white dress, a string of jade beads, green shoes and stockings. It wasn't intentional. She had thought of this scheme hours before she stood at the drawing-room window.

Her petals rustled softly into the hall, and she kissed Mrs. Norman Knight, who was taking off the most amusing orange coat with a procession of black monkeys round the hem and up the fronts.

"... Why! Why! Why is the middle-class so stodgy—so utterly without a sense of humour! My dear, it's only by a fluke that I am here at all—Norman being the protective fluke. For my darling monkeys so upset the train that it rose to a man and simply ate me with its eyes. Didn't laugh—wasn't amused—that I should have loved. No, just stared—and bored me through and through."

"But the cream of it was," said Norman, pressing a large tortoise-shell-rimmed monocle into his eye, "you don't mind me telling this, Face, do you?" (In their home and among their friends they called each other Face and Mug.) "The cream of it was when she, being full red, turned to the woman beside her and said: 'Haven't you ever seen a monkey before?'"

"Oh, yes!" Mrs. Norman Knight joined in the laughter. "Wasn't that too absolutely creamy?"

And a funnier thing still was that now her coat was off she did look like a very intelligent monkey—who had even made that yellow silk dress out of scraped banana skins. And her amber ear-rings; they were like little dangling nuts.

"This is a sad, sad fall!" said Mug, pausing in front of Little B's perambulator. "When the perambulator comes into the hall—" and he waved the rest of the quotation away.

The bell rang. It was lean, pale Eddie Warren (as usual) in a state of acute distress.

"It *is* the right house, *isn't* it?" he pleaded.

"Oh, I think so—I hope so," said Bertha brightly.

"I have had such a *dreadful* experience with a taxi-man; he was *most* sinister. I couldn't get him to stop. The *more* I knocked and called the *faster* he went. And *in* the moonlight this *bizarre* figure with the *flattened* head *crouching* over the *lit-tle* wheel..."

He shuddered, taking off an immense white silk scarf. Bertha noticed that his socks were white, too—most charming.

"But how dreadful!" she cried.

"Yes, it really was," said Eddie, following her into the drawing-room. "I saw myself *driving* through Eternity in a *timeless* taxi."

He knew the Norman Knights. In fact, he was going to write a play for N.K. when the theatre scheme came off.

"Well, Warren, how's the play?" said Norman Knight, dropping his monocle and giving his eye a moment in which to rise to the surface before it was screwed down again.

And Mrs. Norman Knight: "Oh, Mr. Warren, what happy socks!"

"I *am* so glad you like them," said he, staring at his feet. "They seem to have got so *much* whiter since the moon rose." And he turned his lean sorrowful young face to Bertha. "There *is* a moon, you know."

She wanted to cry: "I am sure there is—often—often!"

He really was a most attractive person. But so was Face, crouched before the fire in her banana skins, and so was Mug, smoking a cigarette and saying as he flicked the ash: "Why doth the bridegroom tarry?"

"There he is, now."

Bang went the front door open and shut. Harry shouted: "Hullo, you people. Down in five minutes." And they heard him swarm up the stairs. Bertha couldn't help smiling; she knew how he loved doing things at high pressure. What, after all, did an extra five minutes matter? But he would pretend to himself that they mattered beyond measure. And then he would make a great point of coming into the drawing-room, extravagantly cool and collected.

Harry had such a zest for life. Oh, how she appreciated it in him. And his passion for fighting—for seeking in everything that came up against him another test of his power and of his courage—that, too, she understood. Even when it made him just occasionally to other people, who didn't know him well, a little ridiculous perhaps. . . . For there were moments when he rushed into battle where no battle was. . . . She talked and laughed and positively forgot until he had come in (just as she had imagined) that Pearl Fulton had not turned up.

"I wonder if Miss Fulton has forgotten?"

"I expect so," said Harry. "Is she on the 'phone?"

"Ah! There's a taxi, now." And Bertha smiled with that little air of proprietorship that she always assumed while her women finds were new and mysterious. "She lives in taxis."

"She'll run to fat if she does," said Harry coolly, ringing the bell for dinner. "Frightful danger for blond women."

"Harry—don't," warned Bertha, laughing up at him.

Came another tiny moment, while they waited, laughing and talking, just a trifle too much at their ease, a trifle too unaware. And then Miss Fulton, all in silver, with a silver fillet binding her pale blond hair, came in smiling, her head a little on one side. "Am I late?"

"No, not at all," said Bertha. "Come along." And she took her arm and they moved into the dining-room.

What was there in the touch of that cool arm that could fan—fan—start blazing—blazing—the fire of bliss that Bertha did not know what to do with?

Miss Fulton did not look at her; but then she seldom did look at people directly. Her heavy eyelids lay upon her eyes and the strange half smile came and went upon her lips as though she lived by listening rather than seeing. But Bertha knew, suddenly, as if the longest, most intimate look had passed between them—as if they had said to each other: "You, too?"—that Pearl Fulton, stirring the beautiful red soup in the grey plate, was feeling just what she was feeling.

And the others? Face and Mug, Eddie and Harry, their spoons rising and falling—dabbing their lips with their napkins, crumbling bread, fiddling with the forks and glasses and talking.

"I met her at the Alpha show—the weirdest little person. She'd not only cut off her hair, but she seemed to have taken a dreadfully good snip off her legs and arms and her neck and her poor little nose as well."

"Isn't she very *liée* with Michael Oat?"

"The man who wrote *Love in False Teeth?*"

"He wants to write a play for me. One act. One man. Decides to commit suicide. Gives all the reasons why he should and why he shouldn't.

And just as he has made up his mind either to do it or not to do it—curtain. Not half a bad idea."

"What's he going to call it—'Stomach Trouble'?"

"I *think* I've come across the *same* idea in a lit-tle French review, *quite* unknown in England."

No, they didn't share it. They were dears—dears—and she loved having them there, at her table, and giving them delicious food and wine. In fact, she longed to tell them how delightful they were, and what a decorative group they made, how they seemed to set one another off and how they re-minded her of a play by Chekhov!

Harry was enjoying his dinner. It was part of his—well, not his nature, exactly, and certainly not his pose—his—something or other—to talk about food and to glory in his "shameless passion for the white flesh of the lob-ster" and "the green of pistachio ices—green and cold like the eyelids of Egyptian dancers."

When he looked up at her and said: "Bertha, this is a very admirable *soufflée!*" she almost could have wept with childlike pleasure.

Oh, why did she feel so tender towards the whole world tonight? Everything was good—was right. All that happened seemed to fill again her brimming cup of bliss.

And still, in the back of her mind, there was the pear tree. It would be silver now, in the light of poor dear Eddie's moon, silver as Miss Fulton, who sat there turning a tangerine in her slender fingers that were so pale a light seemed to come from them.

What she simply couldn't make out—what was miraculous—was how she should have guessed Miss Fulton's mood so exactly and so instantly. For she never doubted for a moment that she was right, and yet what had she to go on? Less than nothing. "I believe this does happen very, very rarely between women. Never between men," thought Bertha. "But while I am making the coffee in the drawing-room perhaps she will 'give a sign.'"

What she meant by that she did not know, and what would happen af-ter that she could not imagine.

While she thought like this she saw herself talking and laughing. She had to talk because of her desire to laugh.

"I must laugh or die."

But when she noticed Face's funny little habit of tucking something down the front of her bodice—as if she kept a tiny, secret hoard of nuts there, too—Bertha had to dig her nails into her hands—so as not to laugh too much.

It was over at last. And: "Come and see my new coffee machine," said Bertha.

"We only have a new coffee machine once a fortnight," said Harry. Face took her arm this time; Miss Fulton bent her head and followed after.

The fire had died down in the drawing-room to a red, flickering "nest of baby phoenixes," said Face.

"Don't turn up the light for a moment. It is so lovely." And down she crouched by the fire again. She was always cold . . . "without her little red flannel jacket, of course," thought Bertha.

At that moment Miss Fulton "gave the sign."

"Have you a garden?" said the cool, sleepy voice.

This was so exquisite on her part that all Bertha could do was to obey. She crossed the room, pulled the curtains apart, and opened those long windows. "There!" she breathed.

And the two women stood side by side looking at the slender, flowering tree. Although it was so still it seemed, like the flame of a candle, to stretch up, to point, to quiver in the bright air, to grow taller and taller as they gazed—almost to touch the rim of the round, silver moon.

How long did they stand there? Both, as it were, caught in that circle of unearthly light, understanding each other perfectly, creatures of another world, and wondering what they were to do in this one with all this blissful treasure that burned in their bosoms and dropped, in silver flowers, from their hair and hands?

For ever—for a moment? And did Miss Fulton murmur: "Yes, just *that.*" Or did Bertha dream it?

Then the light was snapped on and Face made the coffee and Harry said: "My dear Mrs. Knight, don't ask me about my baby. I never see her. I shan't feel the slightest interest in her until she has a lover," and Mug took his eye out of the conservatory for a moment and then put it under glass again and Eddie Warren drank his coffee and set down the cup with a face of anguish as though he had drunk and seen the spider.

"What I want to do is to give the young men a show. I believe London is simply teeming with first-chop, unwritten plays. What I want to say to 'em is: 'Here's the theatre. Fire ahead.' "

"You know, my dear, I am going to decorate a room for the Jacob Nathans. Oh, I am so tempted to do a fried-fish scheme, with the backs of the chairs shaped like frying pans and lovely chip potatoes embroidered all over the curtains."

"The trouble with our young writing men is that they are still too romantic. You can't put out to sea without being seasick and wanting a basin. Well, why won't they have the courage of those basins?"

"A *dreadful* poem about a *girl* who was *violated* by a beggar *without* a nose in a lit-tle wood. . . ."

Miss Fulton sank into the lowest, deepest chair and Harry handed round the cigarettes.

From the way he stood in front of her shaking the silver box and saying abruptly: "Egyptian? Turkish? Virginian? They're all mixed up," Bertha realized that she not only bored him; he really disliked her. And she decided from the way Miss Fulton said "No, thank you, I won't smoke," that she felt it, too, and was hurt.

"Oh, Harry, don't dislike her. You are quite wrong about her. She's wonderful, wonderful. And, besides, how can you feel so differently about someone who means so much to me. I shall try to tell you when we are in bed to-night what has been happening. What she and I have shared."

At those last words something strange and almost terrifying darted into Bertha's mind. And this something blind and smiling whispered to her: "Soon these people will go. The house will be quiet—quiet. The lights will be out. And you and he will be alone together in the dark room—the warm bed. . . ."

She jumped up from her chair and ran over to the piano.

"What a pity someone does not play!" she cried. "What a pity somebody does not play."

For the first time in her life Bertha Young desired her husband.

Oh, she loved him—she'd been in love with him, of course, in every other way, but just not in that way. And, equally, of course, she'd understood that he was different. They'd discussed it so often. It had worried her dreadfully at first to find that she was so cold, but after a time it had not seemed to matter. They were so frank with each other—such good pals. That was the best of being modern.

But now—ardently! ardently! The word ached in her ardent body! Was this what that feeling of bliss had been leading up to? But then—

"My dear," said Mrs. Norman Knight, "you know our shame. We are the victims of time and train. We live in Hampstead. It's been so nice."

"I'll come with you into the hall," said Bertha. "I loved having you. But you must not miss the last train. That's so awful, isn't it?"

"Have a whisky, Knight, before you go?" called Harry.

"No, thanks, old chap."

Bertha squeezed his hand for that as she shook it.

"Good night, good-bye," she cried from the top step, feeling that this self of hers was taking leave of them for ever.

When she got back into the drawing-room the others were on the move.

". . . Then you can come part of the way in my taxi."

"I shall be *so* thankful *not* to have to face *another* drive *alone* after my *dreadful* experience."

"You can get a taxi at the rank just at the end of the street. You won't have to walk more than a few yards."

"That's a comfort. I'll go and put on my coat."

Miss Fulton moved towards the hall and Bertha was following when Harry almost pushed past.

"Let me help you."

Bertha knew that he was repenting his rudeness—she let him go. What a boy he was in some ways—so impulsive—so—simple. And Eddie and she were left by the fire.

"I *wonder* if you have seen Bilks' *new* poem called *Table d'Hôte*," said Eddie softly. "It's *so* wonderful. In the last Anthology. Have you got a copy? I'd *so* like to *show* it to you. It begins with an *incredibly* beautiful line: 'Why Must it Always be Tomato Soup?' "

"Yes," said Bertha. And she moved noiselessly to a table opposite the drawing-room door and Eddie glided noiselessly after her. She picked up the little book and gave it to him; they had not made a sound.

While he looked it up she turned her head towards the hall. And she saw . . . Harry with Miss Fulton's coat in his arms and Miss Fulton with her back turned to him and her head bent. He tossed the coat away, put his hands on her shoulders and turned her violently to him. His lips said: "I adore you," and Miss Fulton laid her moonbeam fingers on his cheeks and smiled her sleepy smile. Harry's nostrils quivered; his lips curled back in a hideous grin while he whispered: "To-morrow," and with her eyelids Miss Fulton said: "Yes."

"Here it is," said Eddie. " 'Why Must it Always be Tomato Soup?' It's so *deeply* true, don't you feel? Tomato soup is so *dreadfully* eternal."

"If you prefer," said Harry's voice, very loud, from the hall, "I can phone you a cab to come to the door."

"Oh, no. It's not necessary," said Miss Fulton, and she came up to Bertha and gave her the slender fingers to hold.

"Good-bye. Thank you so much."

"Good-bye," said Bertha.

Miss Fulton held her hand a moment longer.

"Your lovely pear tree!" she murmured.

And then she was gone, with Eddie following, like the black cat following the grey cat.

"I'll shut up shop," said Harry, extravagantly cool and collected.

"Your lovely pear tree—pear tree—pear tree!"

Bertha simply ran over to the long windows.

"Oh, what is going to happen now?" she cried.

But the pear tree was as lovely as ever and as full of flower and as still.

You might begin a criticism of "Bliss" by plunging directly into the writing of your paper, discovering your thoughts and your organization of them in the activity of writing. If you use this method, or lack of method, you may find you need to write several preliminary drafts of your paper before you know exactly what it is you want to say.

Another way of writing a critical paper is to stand back, decide where you want to go, organize yourself, and only after these preliminary steps, begin the actual writing of the first draft. The following is an example, in outline, of one way this method would be applied to writing a critical paper on "Bliss":

Topic
    "Bliss"—a study in self-delusion
Topic limited
    "Bliss"—a study not of bliss but of imagination, of a continuous and impenetrable self-delusion
Thesis statement
    In Katherine Mansfield's "Bliss" the main character, Bertha Young, believes she is joyously alive, radiantly happy, but, in reality, lives in a stringent, screaming prison of self-delusion.
Organized support for thesis statement
    Bertha's relation (I) to herself, to her own emotional state, (II) to the guests at her party, and (III) to her husband and Miss Fulton and their affair. Each of these relationships shows the gap between (A) what Bertha believes to be true, and (B) what is, in fact, true.

I. Bertha's relation to herself
    A. She believes she is filled with "absolute bliss."
        1. Bertha wants to dance and laugh . . . "at nothing" . . . feels the "fire of bliss . . . blazing—blazing."
        2. She feels as if she has swallowed a "bright piece of sun."
    B. Her "bliss" is more akin to hysteria than bliss.
        1. When Bertha looks into the "cold mirror" we see a woman . . . "with smiling, trembling lips."
        2. Bertha laughs—she is on the verge of becoming "hysterical": "Bertha had to dig her nails into her hands—so as not to laugh too much."

II. Bertha's relation to her guests
    A. She believes they are "modern, thrilling friends . . . dears—dears."
        1. She thinks the Norman Knights "a very sound couple."
        2. She adores Eddie Warren—"a most attractive person."
    B. Her friends are more ridiculous than they are "sound" and "attractive."
        1. The Knights call each other "Face" and "Mug" and speak of things as being "creamy."
        2. Eddie Warren says his white stockings have gotten "so much whiter since the moon rose."

III. Bertha's relation to her husband and to Pearl Fulton
    A. She believes she loves both of them.
        1. "Oh, she loved him" . . . Harry "had such a zest for life" . . . Bertha "understood."
        2. Bertha "always did fall in love with beautiful women" . . . Miss Fulton is "wonderful, wonderful" . . . Bertha thinks she understands Miss Fulton "perfectly."
    B. Her relation to Harry and Miss Fulton is imaginary.
        1. Bertha and Harry have often talked about how cold she, Bertha, is to him.
        2. In the hall Bertha sees Harry whispering "I adore you" to Miss Fulton and arranging a liaison for the next day. Bertha's reaction to the affair reflects her inability to see and to respond to reality: Bertha runs to the window, " 'Oh, what is going to happen now?' she cried."

Conclusion

Bertha does not distinguish her own stringent, hysterical emotions from "bliss."

Bertha does not see that her friends are not "modern," "thrilling," and "delightful" but false and ridiculous.

Bertha does not realize that her feelings for Harry and Miss Fulton are based on the imaginary pictures she has of these two people. Nor does she perceive Harry's and Miss Fulton's feelings for her or their feelings for each other.

From the beginning of the story Bertha believes that her whole world is "good," is "right": "All that happened seemed to fill again her brimming cup of bliss."

Her world is not the way she imagines it.

WRITING EXERCISES

▶ A. Do a piece of free writing (Unit 5) on your impression of "Bliss" or any other piece of literature in the preceding chapters. Write your response to the work as quickly as you can. Write until you discover what you want to say and until you think you see the best way of saying it. Then take a little more time and do a first draft of your paper.

▶ B. Take notes on "Bliss" or any other literary work in the preceding chapters. Decide on your topic, thesis statement, and support-of-thesis statement. Sketch a tentative outline for your paper. You need not follow any one way of doing this so long as the outline is one *you* can work from, something you can actually use as you write your paper. Then do a first draft of your paper.

Whatever means you use, your objective should be (1) to give the reader new insights into the work you are writing about; (2) to give support for an original and possibly controversial idea you have formulated about the work. To reach this objective you will need to read the work closely (paying special attention to concrete details) and you will need to develop an idea of your own about its meaning. As, or before you write, you must shuffle back and forth between the concrete details of the work and your idea about them, attempting to get evidence and idea to match.

Following is one student's critical paper on "Bliss" based on the "free writing" unit referred to above.

BERTHA YOUNG'S VIEW OF LIFE—"BLISS"

Bertha Young's view of herself, her relationship with Harry, her husband, and her friend, Miss Pearl Fulton, is unrealistic, romanticized and ironic. "Although Bertha Young was thirty, she still had moments like this when she wanted to run instead of walk, to take dancing steps. . . ." Throughout this short story Bertha thinks and feels she is exhuberant, lighthearted and filled with "absolute bliss." This is only a veneer for an empty and unfulfilled life.

The outward trappings of Bertha's life are perfect
in every detail. She receives great satisfaction
from her material surroundings and believes they bring
her "bliss." She buys a collection of artificial fruit,
planning that the purple grapes will combine with
the carpet "to create an effect." Bertha's life is out-
wardly an effort to create an effect which will compensate for the emptiness within.

Many of Bertha's actions are playacting. One questions the sincerity of her feelings even concerning
Little B, the baby girl. "You're nice—you're very
nice. I'm fond of you. I like you." Earlier she stood
in front of Nanny, who was holding the child, "like a
poor little girl in front of the rich little girl with
the doll." The tragedy is that Bertha doesn't realize
she only plays with her child for personal gratification
and doesn't assume the role of mother.

Much of what Bertha does is a deliberate attempt to
create an outward effect. The cushions are carefully
and intentionally thrown on the chairs and couches,
making the room appear alive to Bertha. Their friends
are supposedly creative people like writers and
architects who are to supply vitality. This is another
of Bertha's pathetic efforts to gather objects to fill
the aching void within herself. "And friends—modern,
thrilling friends, writers and painters and poets or
people keen on social questions—just the kind of
friends they wanted."

Bertha thinks of herself as "a tall, slender, pear
tree, in fullest, richest bloom; it stood perfect. . . .
Bertha couldn't help feeling that it had not a single
bud or faded petal." She is not perfect, nor is any
human, and the tragedy is that she even believes it
possible to be perfect. Neither is she mature or "in
fullest, richest bloom."

When Bertha looks into the "cold mirror" she sees a
radiant woman with an intense air of listening, "waiting
for something divine to happen . . . that she knew
must happen—infallibly." The irony is that the cold
mirror should have reflected a cold woman, one who considers her husband "a really good pal." "It had worried
her dreadfully to find she was so cold, but after a
time it had not seemed to matter." It apparently
ceased to matter to Harry too, who had "such a zest for
life," because he had found Miss Fulton. Bertha
rationalizes away her lack of passion and sex for her

husband and, therefore, can not fill this inner need to be a woman. She must first learn to give of herself emotionally.

Bertha expresses the desire to reach Harry—to really communicate with him on the phone, but she doesn't know what to say. She blames her inability to reveal her feelings on convention and civilization. "She only wanted to get in touch with him for a moment." Bertha really wants to tell Harry that she has begun to feel for him emotionally. Later Bertha is described: "For the first time in her life Bertha Young desired her husband."

Harry has a passion for life although Bertha acknowledges that he appears ridiculous to some people —occasionally—but only because they don't know him well. Poor Bertha doesn't know Harry at all, except in a rather impersonal, polite household relationship. She thinks he dislikes Miss Fulton and that she feels it and is hurt. "How can you feel so differently about someone who means so much to me?" The irony is that no one means a great deal to Bertha.

Later Bertha says of Harry, "What a boy he was in some ways—so impulsive—so—simple." And then Bertha learns the truth as Harry helps Miss Fulton with her coat. His relationship with Pearl Fulton is not one a boy would conduct. Bertha is mistaken about his being simple. Humans are not simple, although their outward appearance may indicate simplicity. They are complicated with conflicting ideas and emotions, and Bertha is unable to recognize this basic fact.

Bertha's feelings toward Pearl Fulton are the strangest of all. "They had met at the club and Bertha had fallen in love with her as she always did fall in love with beautiful women who had something strange about them." "The way she has of sitting with her head a little on one side, and smiling, has something behind it, and I must find out what that something is." Miss Fulton—poised, silver, blonde—is inwardly warm and responsive to Harry. Bertha has apparently been attracted to other women with qualities that she herself does not possess, an inner warmth and emotion for a man and a willingness to give of herself. She senses that Harry admires these women, although she is not conscious of it.

It is not true she and Miss Fulton are "understanding each other perfectly" but Bertha knows she and
Miss Fulton share some special secret and that "Pearl
Fulton . . . was feeling just what she was feeling."
Bertha is getting closer to the truth, but she does not
realize it. Her awakening love for Harry is the bond
which links these two quite different women.

The story concludes with Bertha running to look out
the window and crying, "Oh, what is going to happen
now?" The pear tree may appear "as lovely as ever and
as full of flower and as still," but Bertha's life
has been touched and changed and is not the same as before. Her life is no longer still or stagnant within,
because she has reached out for her husband and has
had the experience of being hurt by someone she really
cares for.

Sara Alice Steubs

HELEN THURBER   For "The Secret Life of Walter Mitty" from *My World—and Welcome to It,* published by Harcourt Brace Jovanovich, Inc. Copyright © 1942 James Thurber. Copyright © 1970 Helen Thurber. Reprinted by permission of Helen Thurber.

TIME   For "The Anatomy of Angst." Reprinted by permission from *Time,* The Weekly Newsmagazine; Copyright Time Inc.

UNIVERSITY OF CALIFORNIA PRESS   For an excerpt from *The Teachings of Don Juan: A Yaqui Way of Knowledge* by Carlos Castañeda. Originally published by the University of California Press; reprinted by permission of The Regents of the University of California.

THE VIKING PRESS, INC.   For an excerpt from *A Portrait of the Artist As a Young Man* by James Joyce. Copyright © 1964 by the Estate of James Joyce. All rights reserved; for "City Life" from *The Complete Poems of D. H. Lawrence,* edited by Vivian de Sola Pinto and F. Warren Roberts. Copyright © 1964, 1971 by Angelo Ravagli & C. M. Weekley, Executors of the Estate of Frieda Lawrence Ravagli; and for excerpts from *Leonardo da Vinci: The Tragic Pursuit of Perfection* by Antonina Vallentin, translated by E. W. Dickes. Translation Copyright 1938, © 1966 by The Viking Press, Inc. All reprinted by permission of The Viking Press, Inc.

WADSWORTH PUBLISHING COMPANY, INC.   For "Theme, Thesis, and the Writing of a Critical Paper" from *Techniques for Understanding Literature: A Handbook for Readers and Writers* by Edward L. Hancock. © 1972 by Wadsworth Publishing Company, Inc., Belmont, California. Reprinted by permission.

A. P. WATT & SON   For "The Lake Isle of Innisfree" from *The Collected Poems of W. B. Yeats;* and for an excerpt from *A Vision* by W. B. Yeats. Reprinted by permission of Mr. M. B. Yeats, the Macmillan Company of Canada Ltd., and A. P. Watt & Son.

Picture Credits
Page

5   Escher Foundation—Haags Gemeentemuseum—The Hague

7   American Numismatic Society

8   Zen Master Rinzai from A FLOWER DOES NOT TALK: ZEN ESSAYS, by Abbot Zenkai Shibayama. Charles E. Tuttle, Co., Inc.

9   Jean-Michel Folon

13   (left) Henri Cartier-Bresson, Magnum; (right) Copyright 1952 by Philippe Halsman

17   (top) Photo by Paul Porter; (bottom) Photo by Kay Bell Reynal

18   (top) Photo by George Platt Lynes; (bottom) Photo by Mottke Weissman

19   (top) NBC Project 20; (bottom) Chris Corpus

33   Escher Foundation—Haags Gemeentemuseum—The Hague

34   (top) E. T. Adams, Time Magazine 1973

35   The Cleveland Museum of Art, Gift of Hanna Fund, 1945. Permission S.P.A.D.E.M. 1973 by French Reproduction Rights.

44   (left) Ediciones Poligrafa; (right) © Arnold Newman

61   (left) Paul Klee Foundation, Kunstmuseum, Berne. Permission S.P.A.D.E.M. 1973 by French Reproduction Rights; (right) From THE SECRET OF THE GOLDEN FLOWER, translated from Chinese into German and explained by Richard Wilhelm. English translation by Cary F. Baynes. Reproduced by permission of Harcourt Brace Jovanovich, Inc.

63   Musée de L'Homme, Paris

70   McGraw-Hill Book Company

74   Nasjonalgalleriet, Oslo

75   Musée du Louvre, Paris

110   Bell Telephone Labs.; South African Information Service; Smithsonian Office of Anthropology, Bureau of American Ethnology Collection; Metropolitan Museum of Art, Gift of Mrs. Stephen D. Tucker, 1903; Courtesy of Museum of the American Indian, Heye Foundation; N. Y. State Urban Development Corp.; IBM Corp.; U.S. Air Force; DPI, Frances Laping

116   Courtesy of the American Museum of Natural History

118   Courtesy of the Museum of Primitive Art, New York

119   Escher Foundation—Haags Gemeentemuseum—The Hague

121 History Division, Natural History Museum of Los Angeles County

151 Cosmopress/© by SPADEM PARIS

152 George Braziller, Inc.

156 Andrew Wyeth. CHRISTINA'S WORLD (1948). Tempera on gesso panel, $32\frac{1}{4}'' \times 47\frac{3}{4}''$. Collection, The Museum of Modern Art, New York

162 Marc Chagall. I AND THE VILLAGE (1911). Oil on canvas, $75\frac{5}{8}'' \times 59\frac{5}{8}''$. Collection, The Museum of Modern Art, New York. Mrs. Simon Guggenheim Fund. Permission ADAGP 1973 by French Reproduction Rights.

177 *Daedalus,* Journal of the American Academy of Arts and Sciences

192 (left) Copyright 1974 by The Barnes Foundation; (right) Museo Nazionale, Rome

193 (left) Philadelphia Museum of Art: The Louis and Walter Arensberg Collection '50–134–4; (right) Mycerinus and Queen. Egyptian, 4th Dynasty. Slate. Museum of Fine Arts Expedition Fund.   11.1738.   Courtesy Museum of Fine Arts, Boston.

231 Henry Moore

235 Collection Stedelijk Museum, Amsterdam

246 Eleanor Antin. 100 BOOTS IN THE MARKET, Solana Beach, California, May 17, 1971, 9:30 A.M. Photo by Philip Steinmetz

247 Photograph by John Hedgecoe

265 The University of Chicago Magazine

269 Copyright 1949 by Philippe Halsman

276 Standard Oil Co., N.J. Photo by Corsini

277 E. T. Adams, Time Magazine 1973

281 Vincent Van Gogh. THE STARRY NIGHT (1889). Oil on canvas, $29'' \times 36\frac{1}{4}''$. Collection, The Museum of Modern Art, New York. Acquired through the Lillie P. Bliss Bequest.